Cryptography and Network Security

ITL Education Solutions Limited
Research and Development Wing
New Delhi

ISBN 978-81-317-6452-7

First Impression

Published by Dorling Kindersley (India) Pvt. Ltd, licensees of Pearson Education in South Asia.

Head Office: 7th Floor, Knowledge Boulevard, A-8(A), Sector 62, Noida 201 309, UP, India.
Registered Office: 11 Community Centre, Panchsheel Park, New Delhi 110 017, India.

Compositor: Cameo Corporate Services Ltd., Chennai.
Printed in India at Sai Print-o-Pack Pvt. Ltd.

Contents

Preface

Today, the Internet has undoubtedly become the largest public data network that facilitates personal and business communications worldwide. The amount of traffic moving through the Internet as well as corporate networks is growing day by day. More and more people are communicating via e-mails, branch offices are using the Internet to remotely connect to their corporate networks and most commercial transactions such as shopping, bill payments and banking are also being done through the networks. Due to growing dependency of users, businesses and organizations on computer networks, it has become important to protect the information being exchanged from various security attacks. In addition, the confidentiality, authenticity and integrity of the messages moving across the networks must be ensured. This is where network security is important.

Network security is a set of protocols that facilitates the use of networks without any fear of security attacks. The most common and traditional technique used for providing network security is cryptography, which is a process of transforming messages into an unintelligible form before transmitting and converting them back to the original when received by the receiver. However, with the evolution of cryptography and network security disciplines, more practical and readily available applications such as Kerberos, Pretty Good Privacy (PGP), IPSec, Secure Socket Layer (SSL), Transport Layer Security (TLS) and firewalls have developed to implement the network security. Keeping in mind the importance of network security, almost all universities have integrated the study of cryptography and network security in B.Tech. (CSE and IT), MCA and MBA courses. The book in your hands, *Cryptography and Network Security*, in its unique easy-to-understand question-and-answer format directly addresses the need of students enrolled in these courses.

The book comprises questions and their corresponding answers on the basic issues to be addressed by cryptography and network security capability as well as practical applications that are being used for providing network security. The text has been designed to make it particularly easy for students to understand the principles and practice of cryptography and network security. An attempt has been made to make the book self-contained so that students can learn the subject by themselves. The organized and accessible format allows students to quickly find questions on specific topics.

The book *Cryptography and Network Security* is a part of series named *Express Learning Series*, which has a number of books designed as quick reference guides.

Unique Features

1. Designed as a student friendly self-learning guide, the book is written in a clear, concise and lucid manner.
2. Easy-to-understand question-and-answer format.
3. Includes previously asked as well as new questions organized in chapters.
4. All types of questions including multiple-choice questions, short and long questions are covered.

5. Solutions to numerical questions asked at examinations are provided.
6. All ideas and concepts are presented with clear examples.
7. Text is well structured and well supported with suitable diagrams.
8. Inter-chapter dependencies are kept to a minimum.
9. A comprehensive index at the end of the book for quick access to desired topics.

Chapter Organization

All the questions–answers are organized into ten chapters. A brief description of these chapters is as follows:

- *Chapter 1* provides an overview of basic concepts of network security. It discusses the need, goals and principles of network security as well as different kinds of attacks on computer systems and network. It also gives a brief idea of security services and security mechanisms.
- *Chapter 2* introduces the concept of cryptography, which is the most common technique used for providing network security. It describes important mathematical principles that are central to the design of ciphers. The chapter further discusses modular arithmetic, which is the fundamental concept to understand the working of ciphers. It also discusses the concept of cryptanalysis and various cryptanalysis attacks.
- *Chapter 3* deals with symmetric-key ciphers. It starts with a discussion on traditional symmetric-key ciphers that include various substitution ciphers such as additive, shift, multiplicative, affine, autokey, Playfair, Vigenere and Hill cipher and transposition ciphers. Then, the discussion moves on to two important categories of ciphers, namely stream and block ciphers. The chapter also includes a brief discussion on Shannon's theory of diffusion and confusion. Finally, the chapter concludes with a discussion on product ciphers proposed by Shannon, and the two categories of product ciphers, namely Feistel and non-Feistel ciphers.
- *Chapter 4* concentrates on the symmetric-key algorithms, which include Data Encryption Standard (DES) and Advanced Encryption Standard (AES). The chapter presents a detailed study on the design and analysis of DES. It also explains the general structure and the key expansion algorithm of AES.
- *Chapter 5* is based on the number theory, which provides a mathematical background required to understand the asymmetric-key cryptography. It covers several important concepts related to prime numbers such as Fermat's theorem, Euler's totient function, Euler's theorem, Miller–Rabin algorithm and Chinese Remainder theorem.
- *Chapter 6* deals with asymmetric-key algorithms, which include RSA, Diffie–Hellman algorithm, ElGamal encryption system and Elliptic curve cryptography (ECC).
- *Chapter 7* focuses on message authentication mechanisms used to ensure that the integrity of the received message has been preserved. It explains various authentication functions and message authentication code (MAC). It also gives a detailed description of standard hash functions such as MD5, SHA-1 and Whirlpool. The chapter also spells out the concept of birthday attacks against hash functions.
- *Chapter 8* familiarizes the reader with the concept of digital signatures, and presents the essential properties and requirements of digital signatures, possible attacks on digital signatures and various digital signature schemes including RSA, ElGamal and DSS. The chapter then shifts its focus on authentication protocol and discusses its two categories, namely mutual authentication and one-way authentication.

- *Chapter 9* presents the working principle of Kerberos protocol, X.509 authentication service and its certificates. The chapter also describes the security at the application layer covering PGP and S/MIME, security at the transport layer covering SSL and TSL, and security at the network layer describing IPSec.
- *Chapter 10* provides a description on system security, covering the concepts of intrusion prevention and detection, Honeypots, malicious software, viruses, digital immune system, behaviour-blocking software, firewalls and trusted systems.

Acknowledgements

- Our publisher Pearson Education, their editorial team and panel reviewers for their valuable contributions toward content enrichment.
- Our technical and editorial consultants for devoting their precious time to improve the quality of the book.
- Our entire research and development team who have put in their sincere efforts to bring out a high-quality book.

Feedback

For any suggestions and comments about this book, please feel free to send an e-mail to itlesl@rediffmail.com.

Hope you enjoy reading this book as much as we have enjoyed writing it.

Rohit Khurana
Founder and CEO
ITL ESL

1

Overview of Network Security

1. What is the need for network security? Explain its goals.

Ans.: During the last two decades, computer networks have revolutionized the use of information. Information is now distributed over the network. Authorized users can use computer networks for sending and receiving information from a distance. People can also perform various tasks such as shopping, bill payments and banking over a computer network. This implies that the computer networks are nowadays used for carrying personal as well as financial data. Thus, it becomes important to secure the network, so that unauthorized people cannot access such sensitive information.

For secure communication, there are some basic goals of network security that should be achieved. These are as follows:

- *Confidentiality:* This refers to maintaining the secrecy of the message being transmitted over a network. Only the sender and the intended receiver should be able to understand and read the message, and eavesdroppers should not be able to read or modify the contents of the message. To achieve confidentiality the message should be transmitted over the network in an encrypted form.
- *Integrity:* Any message sent over the network must reach the intended receiver without any modification made to it. If any changes are made, the receiver must be able to detect that some alteration has happened. Integrity can be achieved by attaching a checksum to the message. This checksum ensures that an attacker cannot alter the message and, hence, that integrity is preserved.
- *Availability:* Information created and stored by an organization should be available all the time to authorized users, failing which the information ceases to be useful. Availability is also equally important for organizations, because unavailability of information can adversely affect an organization's day-to-day operations. For example, imagine the status/service of a bank if its customers are unable to make transactions using their accounts.

2. What are the principles of network security?

Ans.: The principles of network security include *confidentiality, integrity, availability, nonrepudiation, access control* and *authentication.*

- *Confidentiality:* Refer previous question.
- *Integrity:* Refer previous question.

- *Availability:* Refer previous question.
- *Nonrepudiation:* After a message has been sent and received, the sender and receiver should not be able to deny about the sending and receiving of the message, respectively. The receiver should be able to prove that the message has come from the intended sender and not from anyone else. In addition, the receiver should be able to prove that the received message's contents are the same as sent by the sender.
- *Access control:* The term 'access' involves writing, reading, executing and modifying. Thus, access control determines and controls *who* can access *what*. It regulates which user has access to a resource, under what circumstances the access is possible and which operations the user can perform on that resource. For example, we can specify that user A is allowed to only view the records in a database but not to modify them. However, user B is allowed to read as well as update the records.
- *Authentication:* Authentication is concerned with determining whom you are communicating with. Authentication is necessary to ensure that the receiver has received the message from the actual sender, and not from an attacker. That is, the receiver should be able to authenticate the sender, which can be achieved by sharing a common secret code word, by sending digital signatures or by the use of digital certificates.

3. Define a network security attack?

Ans.: A *network security attack* refers to an act of breaching the security or authentication routines of a network. Such an act is a threat to the basic goals of secure communication, such as confidentiality, integrity and authentication.

4. Explain passive attacks and active attacks.

Ans.: Network security attacks can be classified into two categories—*passive attacks* and *active attacks*.

Passive Attacks

In a passive attack, the attacker indulges in eavesdropping, that is, listening to a communication channel and monitoring the contents of a message. The term 'passive' indicates that the main goal of the intruder is just to gather information and not to do any alteration to the message or harm the system resources. A passive attack is hard to recognize, as the message is not tampered with or altered; therefore, the sender and receiver remains unaware that the message contents have been read by another party. However, some measures such as encryption are available to prevent such attacks.

Two types of passive attacks are:

- *Release of message contents:* This type of passive attack involves (1) capturing the sensitive information that is sent via email or (2) tapping a conversation that is conducted over a telephone line.
- *Traffic analysis:* In this type of attack, an intruder observes the frequency and length of messages being exchanged between communicating nodes. A passive attacker can then use this information for guessing the nature of the communication that was taking place.

Active Attacks

In an active attack, an intruder either alters the original message or creates a fake message. This attack tries to affect the operation of system resources. When compared to passive attacks, it is easier to recognize an active attack, but harder to prevent it. Active attacks can be classified into four categories, as follows:

- *Masquerade:* In computer terms, 'masquerading' is said to happen when an entity impersonates another. In such an attack, an unauthorized entity tries to gain more privileges than it is authorized for. Masquerading is generally done by using stolen IDs and passwords, or through bypassing authentication mechanisms.
- *Replay:* This active attack involves capturing a copy of the message sent by the original sender and retransmitting it later to bring about an unauthorized result.
- *Modification of messages:* This attack involves making certain modifications to the captured message, or delaying or reordering the messages to cause an unauthorized effect.
- *Denial of service* (DoS): This attack prevents the normal functioning or proper management of communication facilities. For example, a network server can be overloaded by unwanted packets, thus resulting in performance degradation. DoS attacks can interrupt and slow down the services of a network, or even completely jam a network.

5. Explain various network security services.

Ans.: The International Telecommunication Union-Telecommunication Standardization Sector (ITU-T), also known as *X.800*, defines security service as 'a service provided by a protocol layer of communicating open system, which ensures adequate security of the systems or of data transfers'. Another definition of security service is found in RFC 2828, which defines it as 'a processing or communication service that is provided by a system to give a specific kind of protection to system resources; security services implement security policies and are implemented by security mechanisms'. According to X.800, security services are divided into five categories and 14 specific services (see Figure 1.1).

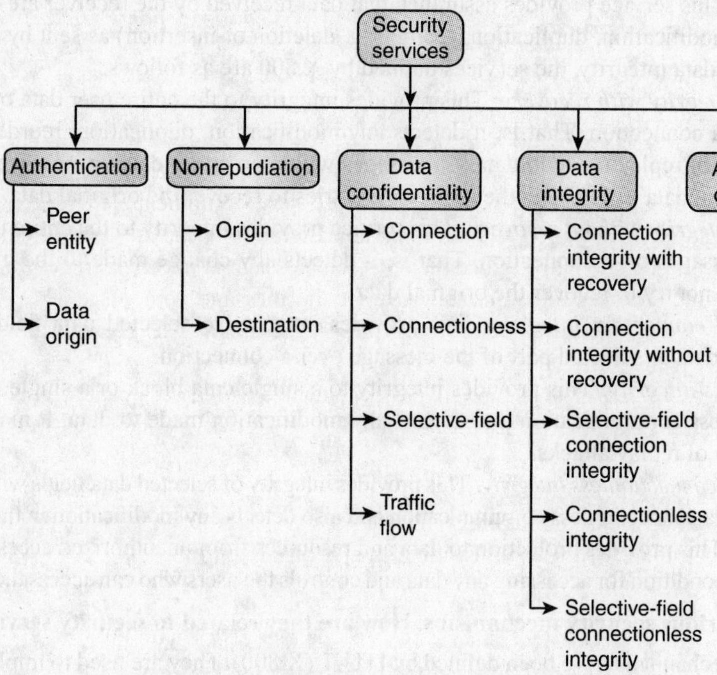

Figure 1.1 Security Services

- *Authentication:* This service provides the assurance that the communicating party at the other end of the line is the correct party. Two types of authentication services defined by X.800 are:
  - *Peer entity authentication:* This provides authentication of the receiver or sender during the connection establishment phase in connection-oriented communication.
  - *Data origin authentication:* This service provides authentication of the data source in a connectionless communication.
- *Nonrepudiation:* This service provides the assurance that the sender and receiver are not able to deny about the sending and receiving of the message, respectively. X.800 defines two types of services for nonrepudiation:
  - *Origin nonrepudiation:* This helps the receiver prove that the message was sent by the intended sender.
  - *Destination nonrepudiation:* This helps the sender prove that the message was delivered to the intended receiver.
- *Data confidentiality:* This service provides protection against the disclosure of data to unauthorized parties. For data confidentiality, X.800 defines four types of services:
  - *Connection confidentiality:* This provides confidentiality for all the messages transmitted between two users on a connection-oriented transmission, such as over a TCP connection.
  - *Connectionless confidentiality:* This service provides confidentiality for all user data in a single data block.
  - *Selective-field confidentiality:* This provides confidentiality for a single message or some selected data fields of a message in a single data block or on a connection.
  - *Traffic flow confidentiality:* This provides confidentiality for the data derived from the traffic flow analysis.
- *Data integrity:* This service provides assurance that data received by the receiver are exactly the same (with no modification, duplication, reordering, deletion or insertion) as sent by the authorized sender. For data integrity, the services defined by X.800 are as follows:
  - *Connection integrity with recovery:* This provides integrity to the entire user data or stream of messages on a connection. That is, it detects any modification, duplication, reordering, deletion, insertion or replay made to data or messages within an entire data or message sequence. If any change in data is detected, then this service tries to recover the original data.
  - *Connection integrity without recovery:* This service provides integrity to the entire user data or stream of messages on a connection. That is, it detects any change made to the messages or data, but does not try to recover the original data.
  - *Selective-field connection integrity:* This provides integrity to selected data fields within a block of user data or selected part of the message over a connection.
  - *Connectionless integrity:* This provides integrity to a single data block or a single message in a connectionless communication and detects any modification made to data. It may also provide detection of replay attacks.
  - *Selective-field connectionless integrity:* This provides integrity of selected data fields within a block of user data in a connectionless communication and also detects any modification in these fields.
- *Access control:* This provides protection to data and resources from unauthorized access. This service defines the condition for accessing any data and controls the users who can access the resources.

6. Explain various security mechanisms. How are they related to security services?

Ans.: Security mechanisms have been defined by ITU-T (X.800). They are used to implement OSI security services and are incorporated into the suitable protocol layer. Some of the security mechanisms recommended by ITU-T (X.800) are shown in Figure 1.2.

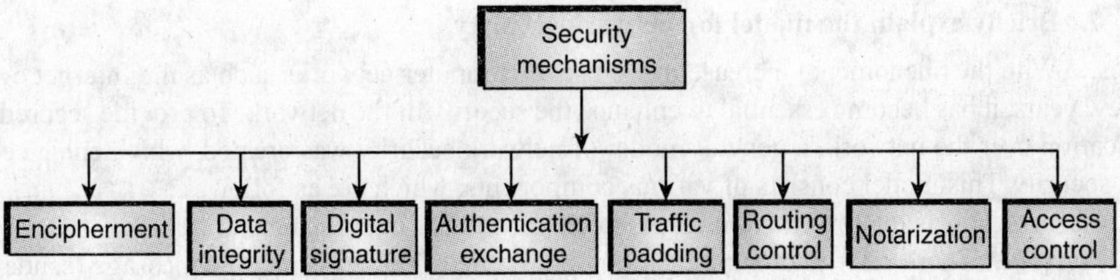

Figure 1.2 Security Mechanisms

- *Encipherment:* This refers to the transformation of the message or data with the help of mathematical algorithms. The main aim of this mechanism is to provide confidentiality. The two techniques that are used for encipherment are *cryptography* and *steganography*.
- *Data integrity:* This refers to the method of ensuring the integrity of data. For this, the sender computes a check value by applying some process over the data being sent, and then appends this value to the data. On receiving the data, the receiver again computes the check value by applying the same process over the received data. If the newly computed check value is same as the received one, then it means that the integrity of data is preserved.
- *Digital signature:* This refers to the method of electronic signing of data by the sender and electronic verification of the signature by the receiver. It provides information about the author, date and time of the signature, so that the receiver can prove the sender's identity.
- *Authentication exchange:* This refers to the exchange of some information between two communicating parties to prove their identity to each other.
- *Traffic padding:* This refers to the insertion of extra bits into the stream of data traffic to prevent traffic analysis attempts by attackers.
- *Routing control:* This refers to the selection of a physically secured route for data transfer. It also allows changing of route if there is any possibility of eavesdropping on a certain route.
- *Notarization:* This refers to the selection of a trusted third party for ensuring secure communication between two communicating parties.
- *Access control:* It refers to the methods used to ensure that a user has the right to access the data or resource.

Security services and mechanisms share a close relationship with each other. One or more security mechanisms are used together to provide a security service. In addition, the same mechanism can also be used in many security services. Table 1.1 lists the security services along with the mechanisms that are used in these services.

Table 1.1 Relationship between Security Services and Mechanisms

Security services	Security mechanisms
Authentication	Encipherment, digital signature and authentication exchange
Nonrepudiation	Data integrity, digital signature and notarization
Data confidentiality	Encipherment and routing control
Data integrity	Encipherment, data integrity, and digital signature
Access control	Access control mechanism

7. Briefly explain the model for network security.

Ans.: With the phenomenal increase in the use of computer networks such as the Internet over the last few years, it has become essential to enhance the security of the network. To provide secured communication over the network, a general model of network security was created, which enhanced network security. This model consists of various components, which are as follows:

- *Message:* This is the information that is to be transmitted over the network.
- *Principals:* These refer to communication nodes, one which transmits the message (sender) and the other receives it (receiver).
- *Security-related transformation:* This refers to the transformations made to the information to be sent, so that it is unreadable to an intruder. An example for such transformation includes either encryption of the message or inserting a message to verify the identity of the sender.
- *Secret information:* This refers to the information that is shared between the two principals and used while applying the transformation at both the sender's and receiver's ends. For example, in case of encryption, the secret information can be a key used for encrypting and decrypting the message.
- *Secure message:* This refers to the message obtained after applying a transformation. It contains the secret code that helps the receiver retrieve the original message.
- *Logical information channel:* This refers to the transmission route from a source to a destination, connected via a network. The route is established by the supportive use of communicating protocols by both parties.
- *Trusted third party:* This is an entity that may either be responsible for transmitting the secret information to the two trusted parties while protecting it from an attacker, or may be responsible for settling disputes regarding the authenticity of a message transmission between two parties.

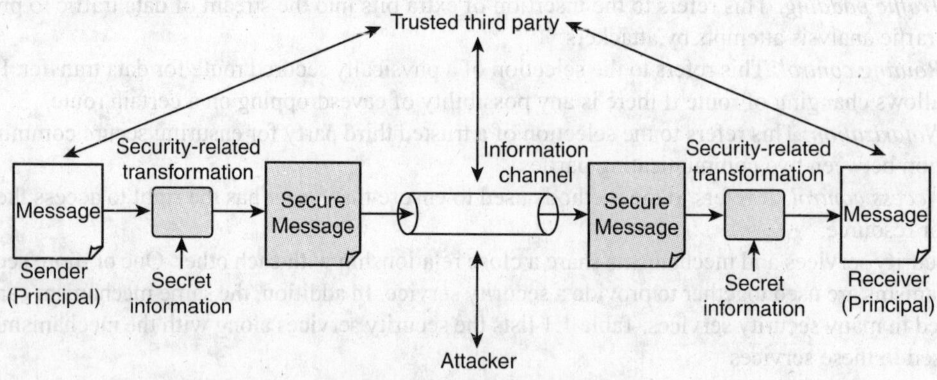

Figure 1.3 Model of Network Security

According to this model, there are four basic tasks that are required for designing any security service. These tasks are:

- Designing an algorithm to perform security-related transformation. The algorithm should be designed in such a way that an intruder cannot defeat its purpose.
- Generating the secret information to be used with the algorithm.
- Developing some techniques for the sharing and distribution of the secret information.

- Selecting a protocol to be used by the two parties. This protocol makes use of the secret information and security algorithm to achieve a specific security service.

This model secures the information in such a way that an intruder on the network cannot access it. However, within the organization, the information's security can still be threatened by unauthorized access, or by software attacks such as viruses and worms. To protect information from such threats, some security mechanisms should be implemented, as follows:

- *Password-based login:* This is used to deny access to all unauthorized users.
- *Screening login:* This is used to detect and remove viruses, worms and other similar attacks.

8. Categorize different types of network security attacks on the basis of security goals.

Ans.: As we know, for secured communication, some goals such as confidentiality, integrity and availability have been defined. However, these goals can be threatened by various security attacks. The categorization of attacks on the basis of security goals is shown in Figure 1.4.

- *Attacks to integrity:* The attacks that threaten the integrity of the data are *masquerading, modification, repudiation* and *replay*.
    - *Masquerading:* Refer Question 4 in this chapter.
    - *Modification:* Refer Question 4 in this chapter.
    - *Repudiation:* Repudiation occurs when the message sender denies that the message was sent by him/her, or when the message receiver denies that the message was received by him/her.
    - *Replay:* Refer Question 4 in this chapter.

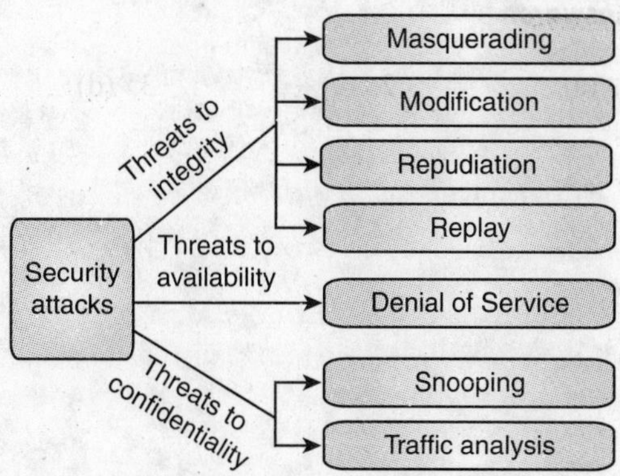

Figure 1.4 Categorization of Attacks in Relation to Security Goals

- *Attacks to confidentiality:* The attacks that threaten the confidentiality of data are *snooping* and *traffic analysis.*
    - *Snooping:* Snooping refers to interception or unauthorized access of data. For example, an unauthorized entity may access a file containing confidential information during its transmission over a network and use that information for its benefits. Snooping can be prevented with the help of various encryption techniques, by making the data non-understandable to the unauthorized entity.
    - *Traffic analysis:* Refer Question 4 in this chapter.
- *Attacks to availability:* The attack that threatens availability is called denial of service (DoS).
    - *Denial of service* (DoS): Refer Question 4 in this chapter.

Multiple-choice Questions

1. __________ ensures that a message was received by the receiver from the actual sender and not from an attacker.

   (a) Authentication (b) Authorization
   (c) Integration (d) None of these

2. Which of the following services is not an authentication service?
   (a) Peer entity authentication
   (b) Data origin authentication
   (c) Data destination authentication
   (d) None of these
3. Which of the following is a passive attack?
   (a) Masquerade
   (b) Replay
   (c) Denial of service (DoS)
   (d) Traffic analysis
4. Which of the following attacks is not a threat to the integrity of data?
   (a) Masquerade
   (b) Modification
   (c) Repudiation
   (d) Snooping
5. Which RFC document includes a definition of security service?
   (a) RFC 2828
   (b) RFC 2401
   (c) RFC 3310
   (d) RFC 6600

Answers

1. (a) 2. (c) 3. (d) 4. (d) 5. (a)

2

Cryptography and Finite Fields

1. Explain the term cryptography in brief.

Ans.: Cryptography is a means for implementing some security mechanisms. The term cryptography is derived from the Greek word *kryptos*, which means "secret writing". In simple terms, *cryptography* is the process of altering messages in a way that their meaning is hidden from adversaries who might intercept them. It allows the sender to disguise a message to prevent it from being read or altered by an intruder, and it also enables the receiver to recover the original message from the disguised one.

In data and telecommunications, cryptography is an essential technique required for communicating over any untrusted medium, which includes any network, such as the Internet. By using cryptographic techniques, the sender can first encrypt a message and then transmit it through the network. The receiver on the other hand can decrypt the message and recover its original contents.

Cryptography relies upon two basic components: an algorithm (or cryptographic methodology) and a key. *Algorithms* are the complex mathematical formulae and *keys* are the strings of bits. For two parties to communicate over a network (the Internet), they must use the same algorithm (or algorithms that are designed to work together). In some cases, they must also use the same key.

2. Define the following terms:

(a) Plaintext
(b) Ciphertext
(c) Encryption
(d) Decryption
(e) Cipher
(f) Key

Ans.: These terms can be defined as follows:

(a) *Plaintext:* It refers to the original unencrypted message that the sender wishes to send.
(b) *Ciphertext:* It refers to the encrypted message that is received by the receiver.

(c) *Encryption:* It is the process of encrypting the plaintext so that the ciphertext can be produced. Plaintext is transformed into ciphertext using the encryption algorithm.

(d) *Decryption:* It is the reverse of the encryption process. In this process, the ciphertext is converted back to the plaintext using a decryption algorithm.

(e) *Ciphers:* The encryption and decryption algorithms are together known as ciphers. Ciphers need not necessarily be unique for each communicating pair; rather a single cipher can be used for communication between multiple pairs of senders and receivers.

(f) *Key:* A key is usually a number or a set of numbers on which the cipher operates. Encryption and decryption algorithms make use of a key to encrypt or decrypt messages, respectively. At the sender's end, the encryption algorithm and encryption key are required to convert the plaintext into ciphertext. At the receiver's end, a decryption algorithm uses the decryption key to convert ciphertext back into the plaintext. The longer the key is, the harder it is for an attacker to decrypt the message.

3. Explain symmetric-key and asymmetric-key encipherment.

Ans.: Traditionally, cryptography involves the use of the same key for encrypting or decrypting the messages (*symmetric-key encipherment*). However, modern cryptography involves the use of different keys for encryption and decryption (*asymmetric-key encipherment*).

Symmetric-key Encipherment

The *symmetric-key encipherment*, sometimes also called *secret-key encipherment* or *secret-key cryptography*, uses a single shared key (secret key) for both encryption and decryption of data. Thus, it is obvious that the key must be known to both the sender and the receiver. As shown in Figure 2.1, the sender uses the shared key and the encryption algorithm to transform the plaintext into ciphertext. The ciphertext is then sent to the receiver via a communication network. The receiver applies the same key and the decryption algorithm to decrypt the ciphertext and to recover the plaintext. Some examples of symmetric-key algorithms include Data Encryption Standard (DES), double DES, triple DES, and Advanced Encryption Standard (AES).

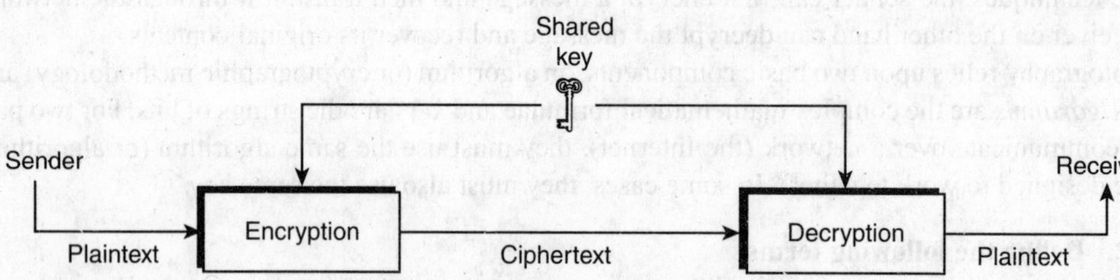

Figure 2.1 Message exchange using secret key

The main problem in secret-key cryptography is getting the sender and receiver to agree on the secret key without anyone else finding it out. If the key is compromised, the security offered by secret-key cryptography is severely reduced or eliminated. Secret-key cryptography assumes that the parties who share a key rely upon each other not to disclose the key and protect it against modification. If they are in separate physical locations, they must trust a medium such as the courier or a phone system to prevent the disclosure of the secret key. Anyone who overhears or intercepts the key in transit can later read, modify, and forge all messages encrypted or authenticated using that key.

Asymmetric-key Encipherment

The asymmetric-key encipherment, sometimes also called *public-key encipherment* or *public-key cryptography*, was introduced by *Diffie and Hellman* in 1976 to overcome the problem found in symmetric-key cryptography. It involves the use of two different keys for encryption and decryption. These two keys are referred to as the *public key* (used for encryption) and the *private key* (used for decryption). Each authorized user has a pair of public and private keys. The public key of each user is known to everyone, whereas the private key is known to its owner only.

Now, suppose that a user A wants to transfer some information to user B securely. The user A encrypts the data by using the public key of B and sends the encrypted message to B. On receiving the encrypted message, B decrypts it by using his/her private key. Since decryption process requires a private key of user B, which is only known to B, the information is transferred securely. Figure 2.2 illustrates the whole process. RSA is a well-known example of asymmetric-key algorithm.

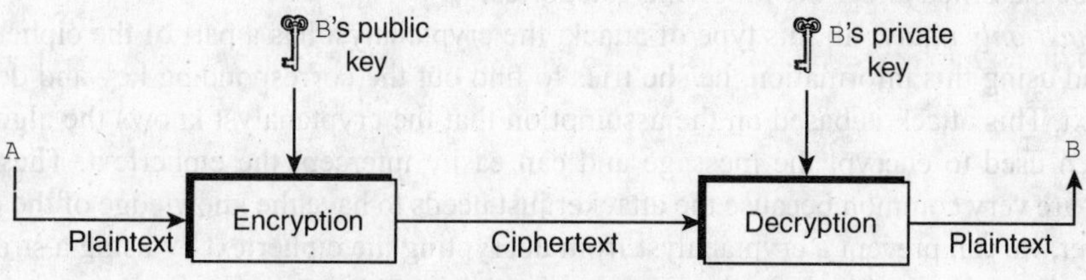

Figure 2.2 Message exchange using public key

The main advantage of public-key cryptography is that the need for the sender and the receiver to share the secret key is eliminated and all communication involves only public keys. Thus, the private key is never transmitted or shared. Anyone can send a confidential message using a public key, but the message can only be decrypted with a private key, which is in the sole possession of the intended recipient.

4. Differentiate between symmetric-key and asymmetric-key cryptography.

Ans.: Some differences between symmetric-key and asymmetric-key cryptography are listed in Table 2.1.

Table 2.1 Differences Between Symmetric-key and Asymmetric-key Cryptography

Symmetric-key cryptography	Asymmetric-key cryptography
1. It uses a single key for both encryption and decryption of data.	1. It uses two different keys—public key for encryption and private key for decryption.
2. Both the communicating parties share the same algorithm and the key.	2. Both the communicating parties should have at least one of the matched pair of keys.
3. The processes of encryption and decryption are very fast.	3. The encryption and decryption processes are slower as compared to symmetric-key cryptography.
4. Key distribution is a big problem.	4. Key distribution is not a problem.
5. The size of encrypted text is usually same or less than the original text.	5. The size of encrypted text is usually more than the size of the original text.

(Continued...)

Table 2.1 (...Continued)

Symmetric-key cryptography	Asymmetric-key cryptography
6. It can only be used for confidentiality, that is, only for encryption and decryption of data.	6. It can be used for confidentiality of data as well as for integrity and non-repudiation checks (that is, for digital signatures).
7. DES and AES are the commonly used symmetric-key algorithms.	7. The most commonly used asymmetric-key algorithm is RSA.

5. What is cryptanalysis? Also, discuss different cryptanalysis attacks.

Ans.: *Cryptanalysis* is the art and science of breaking the encrypted codes that are created by applying some cryptographic algorithms. The person who performs cryptanalysis is known as a *cryptanalyst*. A cryptanalysis attack is made by a cryptanalyst to obtain the plaintext or the key that was used to encrypt a message. Depending on the information that the cryptanalyst has, cryptanalysis attacks can be classified under the following categories:

- *Ciphertext-only attack:* In this type of attack, the cryptanalyst has a part of the ciphertext available and using this information, he/she tries to find out the corresponding key and decipher the plaintext. This attack is based on the assumption that the cryptanalyst knows the algorithm that has been used to encrypt the message and can easily intercept the ciphertext. These types of attacks are very common because the attacker just needs to have the knowledge of the ciphertext. However, we can prevent a cryptanalyst from decrypting the ciphertext by using a strong cipher, which makes it very difficult for the cryptanalyst to decrypt the message. Some common methods that can be used to determine the key or break the ciphers in ciphertext-only attacks include brute-force, statistical, and pattern attacks. Figure 2.3 depicts the process of ciphertext-only attack where `A` and `B` are the communicating parties and `C` is the cryptanalyst (attacker).

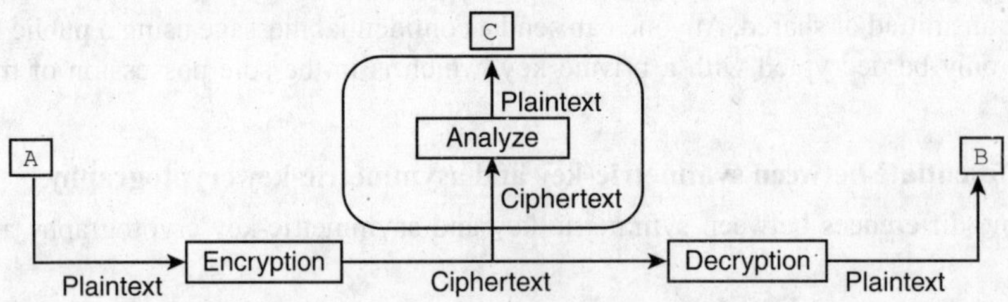

Figure 2.3 Ciphertext-only attack

- *Known-plaintext attack:* In this type of attack, the attacker already has some plaintext–ciphertext pairs in addition to the ciphertext that he/she wishes to break. Figure 2.4 depicts the process of known-plaintext attack by `C` during communication between `A` and `B`. Suppose that `A` sent a secret message to `B`; however, later, `A` made the contents of that message public. Further, assume that the attacker `C` has kept both ciphertext and plaintext (which is now public). Thus, `C` tries to obtain a relationship between these pairs to find the key used to encrypt the plaintext so that he/she can break the next block of ciphertext from `A` to `B`; provided that `A` uses the same key to encrypt the message as that for the previous message. This type of attack is easy to implement because the attacker has more information to analyze the ciphertext. However, this attack happens rarely because it is more likely that the sender changes the key for every transmission of message, or that the message contents are not made public.

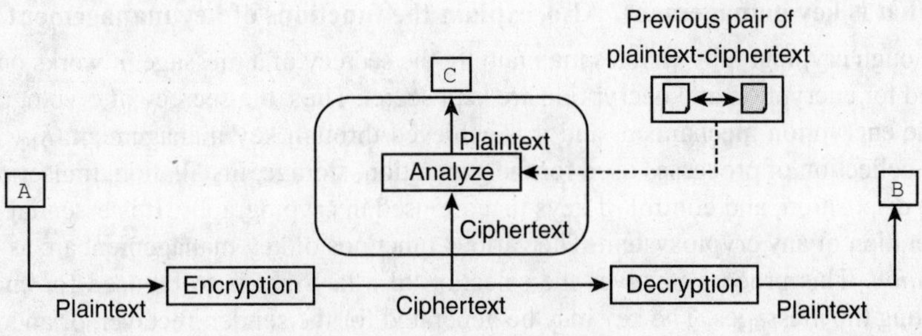

Figure 2.4 Known-plaintext attack

- *Chosen-plaintext attack:* This attack is similar to the known-plaintext attack with the only difference being that in this attack, the attacker C himself/herself chooses the plaintext–ciphertext pairs. However, it is possible only if C gets access to A's computer by some means. The attacker C can then select some plaintext from A's computer that helps him/her to intercept the created ciphertext. This process is shown in Figure 2.5.

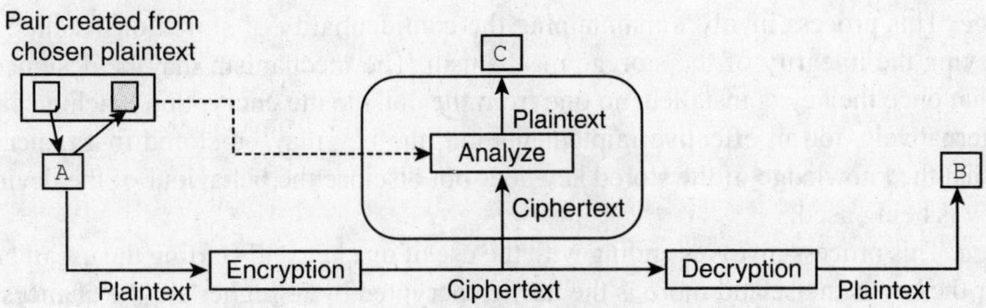

Figure 2.5 Chosen-plaintext attack

- *Chosen-ciphertext attack:* A chosen-ciphertext attack is similar to a chosen-plaintext attack. The only difference between the two being that in chosen-ciphertext attack, the attacker C chooses some ciphertext and then decrypts it to make a ciphertext–plaintext pair. This is possible if C gets access to B's computer. This process is shown in Figure 2.6.

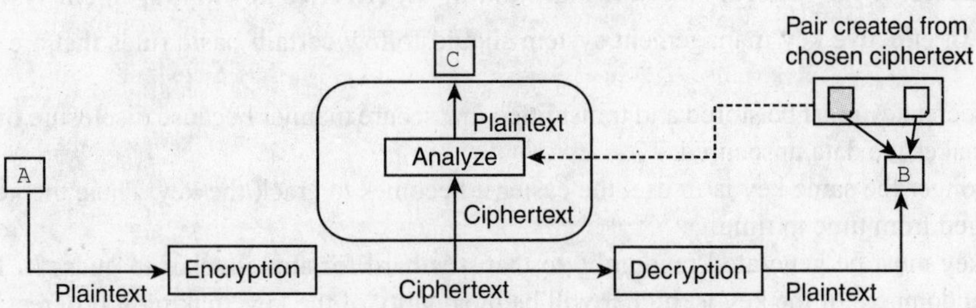

Figure 2.6 Chosen-ciphertext attack

- *Chosen-text attack:* A chosen-text attack is a combination of chosen-plaintext and chosen-ciphertext attack.

6. What is key management? Also, explain the functions of key management.

Ans.: Though cryptography enables maintaining the secrecy of a message, it works only as long as the keys used for encryption and decryption are kept secret. Thus, the secrecy of cryptographic keys is central to the encryption mechanism, and it is achieved through key management. *Key management* refers to the collection of processes used for the generation, storage, installation, transcription, recording, change, disposition, and control of keys that are used in cryptography. It is essential to the secure ongoing operation of any cryptosystem. The various functions of key management are as follows:

- *Generation:* This process involves the selection of a key that is to be used for encrypting and decrypting the messages. The key may be generated for the sender, receiver, or an application. It must be long enough to be predicted by a cryptanalyst. Moreover, it must be chosen randomly and its information must not be leaked during the whole process.
- *Distribution:* This process involves all the efforts made in carrying the key from the point where it is generated to the point where it is to be used. Distribution is more difficult in symmetric-key cryptography where the key has to be transmitted via a secure channel.
- *Installation:* This process involves getting the key into the storage of the device or the process that needs to use this key. Note that if this process involves manual operations, then it might result in leakage of key information.
- *Storage:* This process involves maintaining the confidentiality of stored or installed keys while preserving the integrity of the storage mechanism. The mechanism may be designed in such a way that once the key is installed, no one from the outside the encryption machine can intercept it. Alternatively, for an effective implementation, the key may be stored in an encrypted form such that the knowledge of the stored key does not disclose the behaviour of the device in which the key is being used.
- *Change:* This process involves ending with the use of one key and starting the use of another. The longer the key is in use and more is the traffic encrypted by it, higher are the chances that it will be intercepted. Therefore, the key must be changed after some time. It may noted that the information about the key is prone to leakage during the key change time.
- *Control:* This process refers to the ability to implement a directing or restraining influence over the content and use of the key. For example, the decision of selecting a key from a set of keys for a specific application comes under key control. This process is crucial for maintaining an effective key management system.

7. Describe the general rules for maintaining an effective key management system?

Ans.: An effective key management system should follow certain basic rules that are defined as follows:

- The secret key must be stored and transmitted in a secure manner because disclosure of the secret key makes the data unsecured.
- The longer the same key is in use, the easier it becomes to crack the key. Thus, the key must be changed from time to time.
- The key must be generated randomly, so that it is hard for any attacker to guess it. The higher the randomness of the key is, higher will be the quality of the key, making it progressively more difficult to guess it.
- If the length of the key is short, its lifetime must also be short. That is, a short key must not be used for a longer period of time.
- The key must be destroyed properly after its use.

8. Briefly discuss the concept of steganography.

Ans.: Steganography, like cryptography, is a technique to implement security mechanisms. The term steganography comes from the Greek word *steganos*, which means "concealed writing". *Steganography* is the technique of writing a message in such a way that apart from the sender and the receiver, no one will suspect the existence of the message. It enables the sender to hide a message inside another message. Although both steganography and cryptography are security mechanisms intended to protect the messages from attackers, but still they differ from each other. Where cryptography conceals the contents of a message by enciphering, steganography conceals the message itself by covering it with something.

Some of the traditional techniques of steganography include:

- Marking selected letters of a printed document with a pencil such that the marks are visible only when the document is exposed at a specific angle to bright light.
- Use of some invisible ink (such as onion juice, lemon juice, or some ammonia salt) to write a secret message such that the contents of a message are not visible until heated or some other chemical is applied.
- Use of microdots or pin punchers on selected letters such that these dots are not visible until the paper is exposed in front of a light.

Some modern techniques of steganography include hiding of a secret message within an image, audio or video file by inserting secret binary message information during the digitization process. Although the digitization process may result in an extra overhead to hide a relatively small message, it is more effective when used along with cryptography.

9. Explain Euclidean algorithm for finding the greatest common divisor.

Ans.: The *Euclidean algorithm* (also called *Euclid's algorithm*) is an efficient algorithm for finding the *greatest common divisor* (*GCD*) of two positive integers. This algorithm was invented by the Greek mathematician Euclid and is hence named after him. Given two positive integers `x` and `y`, then another positive number (say, `a`) is called the GCD of `x` and `y` if and only if the following conditions are satisfied:

(i) `a` divides both `x` and `y`.
(ii) Any other common divisor of `x` and `y` also divides `a`.

In other words, `gcd(x,y)=a` if `a` is the largest integer that divides both `x` and `y`.

Euclidean's algorithm computes the gcd of two positive integers, `x` and `y`, based on the following facts:

(i) `gcd(x,0)=x`, that is, if the second integer is zero, then the gcd is the first integer.
(ii) `gcd(x,y)=gcd(y,r)`, where `r` is the remainder obtained on dividing `x` by `y`.

Algorithm

The following are the steps to find the gcd of two positive integers `x` and `y`, where `x>y>0` using Euclidean's algorithm, are as follows:

```
1. a:=x
2. b:=y
3. while (b>0)
   {
     q:=a/b
```

```
    r:=a-q*b
    a:=b
    b:=r
  }
```
4. `gcd(x,y):=a`

In this algorithm, we have used two variables a and b to hold the remainders produced during the reduction process. To start with, a and b are initialized with x and y, respectively. During each step in the reduction process, we calculate the remainder of a divided by b and then store it into the variable r. Then, a and b are replaced with b and r, respectively. This process is continued until the value of b becomes zero. Eventually, we get the gcd(x, y) as a.

10. Write a short note on modular arithmetic.

Ans.: In mathematics, to perform a division operation, we need two inputs, a divisor (say, m) and a dividend (say, x). After performing the operation we get two outputs, a quotient (say, q) and a remainder (say, r). That is, the division relationship can be expressed as follows:

$$x = m*q+r$$

However, in modular arithmetic, we are interested in only one output, that is, the remainder, while the other output (that is, the quotient) is not considered. Thus, in this case, the division operation can be expressed as a binary operator having two inputs, the integers x and m and only one output r. This binary operator is referred to as the *modulo operator* (written as mod). The input m (divisor) to the modulo operator is referred to as the *modulus*, while the output r is referred to as the *residue*. Thus, we can say that:

$$x \bmod m = r$$

where x is an integer from the set of integers Z = {...,-3,-2,-1,0,1,2,3,...} and the modulus (m) and residue (r) are the positive integers. In case the value of x is negative, the value of r also comes out negative. Thus, to make it non-negative, the modulus m is added to r.

11. Explain the following with reference to modular arithmetic:

(a) Set of residues

(b) Congruence

(c) Additive and multiplicative inverse

Ans.: (a) *Set of residues:* Consider a modulo operation x mod m = r, where x is an integer from a set of integers Z while m and r are positive integers. The result of this operation is always an integer less than m. That is, the value of r lies between 0 and m−1. Thus, it can be said that the modulo operation results in a set containing elements from 0 to m−1. In modular arithmetic, this set is called the *set of least residues modulo* m (denoted as Z_m) or simply the *set of residues*. There can be infinite possible instances of Z_m, one for each value of m. For example, Z_{11} can have 11 values {0, 1, 2, 3, 4, 5, 6, 7, 8, 9, 10}, Z_4 can have four values {0, 1, 2, 3}, and so on.

Modular arithmetic allows three binary operations: addition, subtraction, and multiplication to be applied on the elements of Z_m. After applying each operation, the result obtained may need to be mapped to Z_m with the help of the modulo operator. To understand, consider three elements x, y, and z such that both x and y belong to Z (or Z_m) and z belongs to Z_m. Then the binary operations in Z_m can be expressed as (also see Figure 2.7):

$$(x+y) \bmod m = z$$
$$(x-y) \bmod m = z$$
$$(x*y) \bmod m = z$$

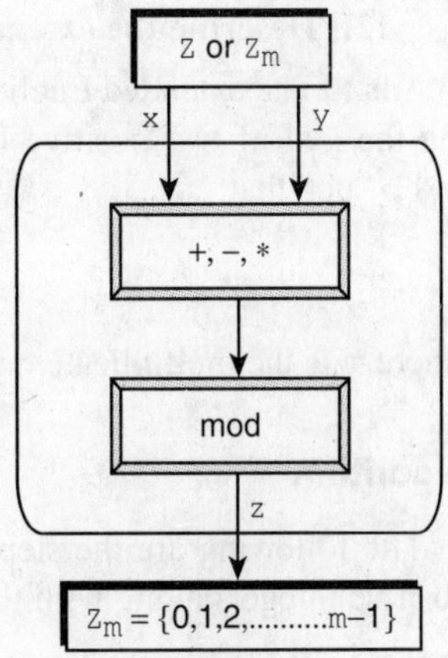

Figure 2.7 Binary operations in Z_m

(b) *Congruence:* There is always a many-to-one relationship between Z and Z_m. That is, many elements of the set Z can map to a single element of Z_m. For example, modulo operations 3 mod 10, 13 mod 10, and 23 mod 10 result in the same value (equal to 3). Thus, these numbers (3, 13, and 23) are referred to as congruent mod 10 in modular arithmetic. To represent the congruence relationship between two integers, the *congruence operator* represented by the '≡' symbol is used. For example, we can write that $3 \equiv 13 \pmod{10}$, $13 \equiv 23 \pmod{10}$, and $3 \equiv 23 \pmod{10}$.

(c) *Additive and multiplicative inverse:* While working with modular arithmetic, we often need to determine the inverse of an element with respect to some operation. Two commonly required inverses are additive and multiplicative inverses. The former is the inverse with respect to the addition operation, while the latter is the inverse with respect to the multiplication operation.

Each element in modular arithmetic has only one additive inverse, which is always unique; sometimes, the additive inverse of an element is the element itself. Let x and y be two elements of the set Z_m. Now, x is said to be the *additive inverse* of y and vice versa if:

$$x+y \equiv 0 \pmod{m}$$

Simply put, the additive inverse of any element, say x in Z_m is equal to m−x. For example, the additive inverse of 11 in $Z_{15} = \{0,1,2,...,13,14\}$ is 4 (15−11).

On the other hand, an element may or may not have a multiplicative inverse. Let x and y be two elements of the set Z_m. Now, x is said to the multiplicative inverse of y and vice versa if:

$$x*y \equiv 1 \pmod{m}$$

For example, the multiplicative inverse of 7 in $Z_{15} = \{0,1,2,...,13,14\}$ is 13, as $7*13 \equiv 1 \pmod{15}$.

The simple method to determine whether or not a number (x) in Z_m has a multiplicative inverse is to compute the GCD of x and m. If gcd(x,m) comes out to be one, x has a multiplicative inverse; otherwise, the multiplicative inverse for x in Z_m does not exist. For example, there does not exist a multiplicative inverse for number 5 in Z_{15} because $\gcd(5,15) \neq 1$. Notice that if $\gcd(x,m) = 1$, x and m are said to be *relatively prime*.

12. Describe the extended Euclidean algorithm to find the multiplicative inverse.

Ans.: The extended Euclidean algorithm is an extension to the Euclidean algorithm. Besides finding the gcd of two positive integers `x` and `y`, it simultaneously finds the multiplicative inverses `a` and `b` such that:

`m*x + n*y = gcd(x,y)`

where `m` is the multiplicative inverse of `x mod y` and `n` is the multiplicative inverse of `y mod x`.

Algorithm

The following are the steps involved in the extended Euclidean algorithm to find the gcd of two positive integers along with the multiplicative inverses are as follows:

```
1. a:=x
2. b:=y
3. c:=1
4. d:=0
5. e:=0
6. f:=1
7. while (b>0)
   {
      q:=a/b
      r:=a-q*b
      a:=b
      b:=r

      m:=c-q*d
      c:=d
      d:=m

      n:=e-q*f
      e:=f
      f:=n
   }
8. gcd(x,y):=a
9. m:=c
10. n:=e
```

Similar to the Euclidean algorithm, the extended Euclidean algorithm also uses the reduction process to find the gcd and multiplicative inverses. It uses three sets of variables, (`a,b`), (`c,d`), and (`e,f`) and during each step of the reduction process, three sets of calculations are made, one per each set of variables. To start with, the variables `a, b, c, d, e,` and `f` are initialized with `x, y, 1, 0, 0,` and `1`, respectively. In the while loop, variables `q` and `r` are used to hold the quotient and the remainder of `a` divided by `b`, respectively. Then, variables `a` and `b` are updated in a similar manner as in the Euclidean algorithm. The set of variables (`c,d`) and (`e,f`) are also updated on the basis of `q`'s value. This process continues until the value of `b` becomes zero. Finally, we obtain the `gcd(x,y)` as `a` as well as the values of `m` and `n`.

13. What is an algebraic structure? Also, explain group, ring, and field.

Ans.: An *algebraic structure* refers to the combination of a set of integers and the operations that are defined on the elements of the set. The commonly used algebraic structures are as follows:

Group

A *group* (G), denoted as G=<{...}, •>, is a set of elements along with a binary operation "•" performed on each ordered pair (x, y) of elements of G such that x • y satisfies the following four properties:

(a) *Closure:* If both x and y belong to the same group G, then x • y also is in G. That is, if x and y are the elements of the same group, then the result of a binary operation on these elements is another element of that group.
(b) *Associativity:* If x, y, and z belong to the same group G, then (x • y) • z = x • (y • z). That is, the order of operation does not affect the result.
(c) *Existence of identity:* For each element x in G, there always exists an *identity element* e within the same group such that x • e = e • x = x.
(d) *Existence of inverse:* For each element x in G, there always exists an *inverse element* x′ within the same group such that x • x′ = x′ • x = e.

A group that satisfies all the four properties of a group and an additional property called *commutativity* is said to be an *abelian group*, also called *commutative group*. The commutative property states that for all x and y belonging to G, x • y = y • x.

A group that contains a finite number of elements is referred to as a *finite group*, whereas a group that is not finite is called an *infinite group*. For example, a group G_1 = <{1,3,5,7,9}, +> is a finite group while a group G_2 = <Z_n, +> where Z_n is a set of integers, is an infinite group. The number of elements in a group indicates the *order* of the group. For example, the order of group G_1 is five while the order of group G_2 is infinite.

Ring

A *ring* (R), denoted as R=<{...}, •, ■>, is a set of elements with two binary operations, "•" and "■" such that:

- R is an abelian group with respect to the first operation (•). In other words, R satisfies the closure, associativity, commutativity, existence of identity, and existence of inverse properties with respect to the "•" operation.
- R satisfies the closure and associativity properties with respect to the second operation (■). In addition, the second operation (■) must be distributed over the first operation (•). The **distributivity** of the second operation over the first means that if x, b, and c are the elements of ring R, then x ■ (y • z) = (x ■ y) • (x ■ z) and (x • y) ■ z = (x ■ z) • (y ■ z).

A ring is said to be a *commutative ring* if it satisfies all the properties of a ring plus if the second operation (■) also satisfies the commutative property, that is for all x and y belonging to the ring R, x ■ y = y ■ x.

Field

A *field* (F), denoted as F=<{...}, •, ■>, is a set of elements with two binary operations, "•" and "■", such that F is a commutative ring where the second operation (■) satisfies all the five properties defined for the first operation (•) except that there is no inverse for the identity element of the first operation with respect to the second operation.

14. Explain each finite field of the form GF (p^n).

Ans.: A field with a finite number of elements is called a *finite field*. The finite fields are the most important and most frequently used in cryptography for performing modular arithmetic operations. The concept and theory of finite fields was given by Galois, according to which if a field is finite, then it contains p^n number of elements, where p is a prime number and n is a positive integer. Thus, the finite fields are usually known as *Galois field* and is denoted by GF (p^n).

A finite field with n = 1 is called the GF (p) field. This field is in fact the set Z_p={0,1,...,p−1}, in which two arithmetic operations, addition and multiplication, can be applied. Each element of this set has an additive and multiplicative inverse except zero, which has no multiplicative inverse.

As we know, positive integers are stored in computers in the form of n-bit words, where the value of n can be 8, 16, 32, and so on. This implies that the range of integers that can be stored is 0 to 2^n-1 and the modulus is 2^n. Now, using the GF (p) finite field with the set Z_p, where p is the largest prime number less than 2^n-1, would be inefficient as the integers ranging from p to 2^n-1 will not be used. To overcome this inefficiency of the GF (p) field, the GF (2^n) field is used. This field uses a set of 2^n elements, and each element is an n-bit word.

15. Find out the result of the following operations:

(a) 140 mod 10

(b) −73 mod 13

(c) 0 mod 7

Ans.: (a) When 140 is divided by 10, we get the remainder r = 0. This means that 140 mod 10 = 0.

(b) When −73 is divided by 13, we get the remainder r = −8. To make r non-negative, we need to add modulus (13) to r. That is, r = −8+13 = 5. This means that −73 mod 13 = 5.

(c) When 0 is divided by 7, we get the remainder r = 7. This means that 0 mod 7 = 7.

16. Find the GCD of 2740 and 1760 using the Euclidean algorithm.

Ans.: Using the Euclidean algorithm as explained in Question 9, we have x = 2740 and y = 1760. Now, initializing a = x and b = y, we get a = 2740 and b = 1760. As b > 0, we move to the first iteration of the while loop.

Algorithm

First iteration

q=2740/1760=1
r=2740−1*1760=980
a=1760
b=980
As 980 > 0, we move to the next iteration.

Second iteration

q=1760/980=1
r=1760−1*980=780
a=980

b=780
As 780 > 0, we move to the next iteration.

Third iteration

q=980/780=1
r=980−1*780=200
a=780
b=200
As 200 > 0, we move to the next iteration.

Fourth iteration

q=780/200=3
r=780−3*200=180
a=200
b=180
As 180 > 0, we move to the next iteration.

Fifth iteration

q=200/180=1
r=200−1*180=20
a=180
b=20
As 20 > 0, we move to the next iteration.

Sixth iteration

q=180/20=9
r=180−9*20=0
a=20
b=0
As the value of b has become zero, the while loop terminates.

Thus, gcd(x, y)=a
⇒gcd(2740, 1760)=20

17. Find the greatest common divisor of 400 and 60 using the extended Euclidean algorithm. Also, find the values of *m* and *n*.

Ans.: Using the extended Euclidean algorithm as explained in Question 12, we have x = 400 and y = 60. Now, initializing a = x and b = y, we get a = 400 and b = 60. We also know that c = 1, d = 0, e = 0, and f = 1.

As b>0, we move to the first iteration of the while loop.

First iteration

q=400/60=6
r=400−6*60=40
a=60
b=40

m=1−6*0=1
c=0
d=1

n=0−6*1=−6
e=1
f=−6

As 40 > 0, we move to the next iteration.

Second iteration

q=60/40=1
r=60−1*40=20
a=40
b=20

m=0−1*1=−1
c=1
d=−1

n=1−1*(−6)=7
e=−6
f=7

As 20 > 0, we move to the next iteration.

Third iteration

q=40/20=2
r=40−2*20=0
a=20
b=0

m=1−2*(−1)=3
c=−1
d=3

n=(−6) −2*7=−20
e=7
f=−20

As the value of b has become zero, the while loop terminates.

Now, gcd(x, y)=a, m=c, and n=e. Thus, gcd(400, 60)=20, m=−1, and n=7.

Multiple-choice Questions

1. The conversion of ciphertext into plaintext is known as ___________.
   (a) Encryption (b) Decryption
   (c) Cryptography (d) Cryptanalyst
2. Which of the following is a component of cryptography?
   (a) Ciphertext (b) Ciphers
   (c) Key (d) All of these

3. Which of the following is needed to implement a chosen-plaintext attack?
   (a) The attacker must have knowledge of the ciphertext.
   (b) The attacker must have access to the receiver's computer.
   (c) The attacker must have access to the sender's computer.
   (d) Both (a) and (b)
4. Which of the following is needed to implement a chosen-ciphertext attack?
   (a) The attacker must have knowledge of the ciphertext.
   (b) The attacker must have access to the receiver's computer.
   (c) The attacker must have access to the sender's computer.
   (d) Both (a) and (b)
5. What is a chosen-text attack?
   (a) It is a combination of known-plaintext attack and chosen-ciphertext attack.
   (b) It is a combination of chosen-plaintext attack and known-ciphertext attack.
   (c) It is a combination of known-plaintext attack and known-ciphertext attack.
   (d) It is a combination of chosen-plaintext attack and chosen-ciphertext attack.
6. Which of the following are the functions of key management?
   (a) Key generation, distribution, and installation
   (b) Key storage, key change, and key control
   (c) Both (a) and (b)
   (d) None of these
7. Which of the following is true in the context of steganography?
   (a) It conceals the existence of the message.
   (b) It conceals the contents of the message.
   (c) It involves less overhead than cryptography.
   (d) Both (a) and (b)
8. In public-key cryptography, __________ key is used for encryption.
   (a) Public (b) Private
   (c) Both (a) and (b) (d) Shared
9. The multiplicative inverse of 13 in Z_{15} is __________.
   (a) Five (b) Seven
   (c) Nine (d) Eight
10. Which of the following properties designates a group as an abelian group?
   (a) Closure (b) Associativity
   (c) Distributivity (d) Commutativity

Answers

1. (b)	2. (d)	3. (c)	4. (d)	5. (d)	6. (c)
7. (a)	8. (a)	9. (b)	10. (d)		

3

Symmetric-key Ciphers

1. Define a symmetric-key cipher.

Ans.: A cipher (a combination of encryption and decryption algorithms) that uses the same key for both encryption and decryption is referred to as a *symmetric-key cipher*.

2. Explain the symmetric cipher model.
Or
Explain the conventional encryption model.

Ans.: A symmetric cipher model (also referred to as a *conventional encryption model*) consists of various components (see Figure 3.1), which are described as follows:

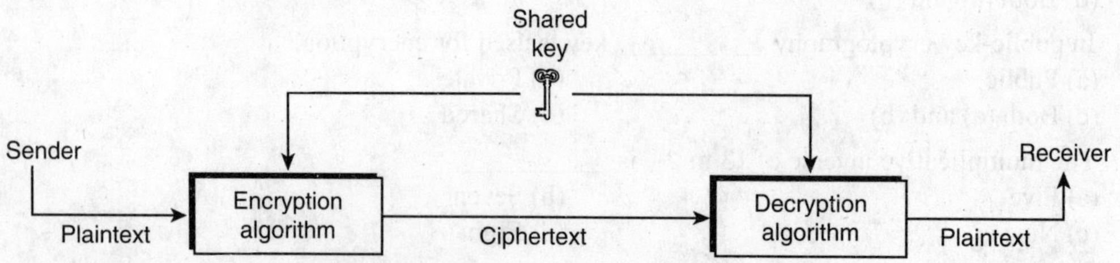

Figure 3.1 Symmetric Cipher Model

(a) *Plaintext:* This refers to the original message that the sender wishes to send securely. It is an input to the encryption algorithm.

(b) *Encryption algorithm:* This algorithm applies various substitutions and transpositions on the plaintext, with the help of a secret key, to transform it into an unintelligible form. The encryption algorithm is used at the sender's end.

(c) *Ciphertext:* This refers to the coded (scrambled) message that is produced by the encryption algorithm. The ciphertext is sent to the receiver through a communication channel.

(d) *Decryption algorithm:* This is the opposite of an encryption algorithm. It is used at the receiver's end to convert ciphertext back into plaintext (original message). The encryption and decryption algorithms are together known as *ciphers*.

(e) *Secret (shared) key:* This usually refers to a number or a set of numbers on which the cipher operates. Both encryption and decryption algorithms use the same key (shared between the sender and receiver) to encrypt or decrypt the messages, respectively.

3. What are the issues in a conventional encryption model?

Ans.: Though conventional encryption is fast, efficient and excellent for large data transmissions such as file transfers, it suffers from certain limitations, which are as follows:

- As the sender and receiver share a single key, the key must be sent via a secure channel. However, if such a secure channel already exists, the question then arises as to why encryption was required in the first place.
- Exchanging the secret key using unsecure channels such as telephone lines, which are prone to eavesdropping, may violate the confidentiality of the key.
- There are some organizations that deal with thousands or million's of clients on a daily basis. In such organizations, it is extremely difficult to assign a unique key to each client.

4. What are the different categories of classical encryption techniques?

Ans.: The classical encryption techniques, also referred to as *traditional symmetric-key ciphers*, are divided into two categories: *substitution ciphers* and *transposition ciphers*.

- *Substitution cipher:* This cipher replaces a symbol (a single letter or a group of letters) of the plaintext with another symbol. For example, the letter `A` can be replaced with letter `C`, and letter `P` with letter `Z`. If the symbols are digits, then the digit 2 can be replaced by digit 5, and digit 3 with digit 6. Substitution ciphers are further categorized into *monoalphabetic ciphers* and *polyalphabetic ciphers*.
- *Transposition cipher:* In this cipher, there is no substitution of characters; rather, the location of characters in plaintext is changed to form the ciphertext. In other words, a transposition cipher reorders (transposes) the symbols in the plaintext, thereby creating the ciphertext. Thus, the order of characters in the plaintext is no longer preserved in the ciphertext. For example, a symbol at the third position in the plaintext may be placed at the eighth position in the ciphertext, or a symbol at the fifth position in the plaintext may appear at the fifteenth position in the ciphertext. Transposition ciphers are further categorized into *keyless transposition ciphers* and *keyed transposition ciphers*.

5. What is a monoalphabetic cipher? Explain different techniques of monoalphabetic ciphers.

Ans.: A *monoalphabetic cipher* is a substitution cipher where a symbol in the plaintext has a one-to-one relationship with a symbol in the ciphertext. It means that a symbol in the plaintext is always replaced with the same symbol in the ciphertext, irrespective of its position in the plaintext. The different techniques based on monoalphabetic ciphers are as follows:

Additive cipher

This is the easiest and simplest monoalphabetic cipher, where each letter in plaintext is coded by shifting a certain number of spaces from it. For this, it uses a key that defines the number of spaces to be shifted. In this technique, each character in the plaintext is first assigned a numeric value according to its position in Z_{26}, the set of alphabets. For example, `a` (or `A`) will be assigned 0, `b` (or `B`) will be assigned 1, `c` (or `C`) will be assigned 2, and so on. The key (say, `K`) used for encrypting the plaintext is also an integer in Z_{26}.

At the sender's end, the key (K) is added to plaintext (say, P) and the result is mapped to Z_{26}, using the modular arithmetic to form the ciphertext (say, C), as shown here.

$$C = (P + K) \bmod 26$$

At the receiver's end, the reverse process is followed for converting the ciphertext back to plaintext. That is, the additive inverse of key K in Z_{26}, denoted as −K, is added to ciphertext (C) and the result is mapped to Z_{26} using the modular arithmetic to obtain plaintext (P), as shown here.

$$P = (C - K) \bmod 26$$

Figure 3.2 depicts the process of encryption and decryption in additive cipher. An example given in **Question 17** illustrates the encryption and decryption processes using additive cipher.

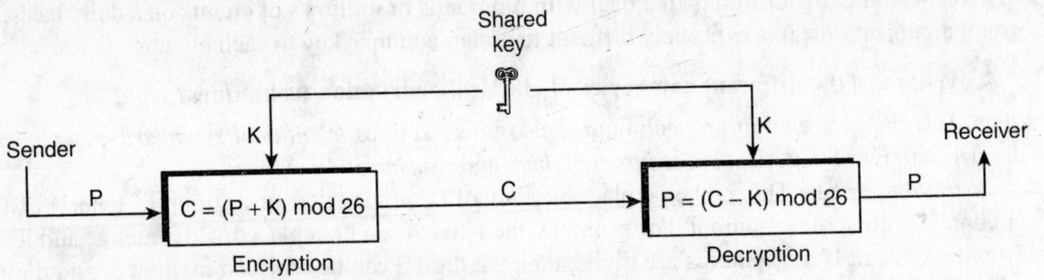

Figure 3.2 Additive Cipher

Shift cipher

In this cipher, an encryption algorithm can be interpreted as 'a shift by a key number of characters in the clockwise direction, that is, towards the end of the alphabet' while a decryption algorithm can be interpreted as 'a shift by a key number of characters in the anti-clockwise direction, that is, towards the beginning of the alphabet'. For example, for key = 5, the encryption algorithm moves five characters down in the set of alphabets (Z_{26}), while the decryption algorithm moves five characters up the alphabet in the set of alphabets. Notice that during encryption and decryption, as the end or the beginning of the alphabet is reached, we wrap round. For the same value of the key K, both shift and additive ciphers produce the same ciphertext; thus, traditionally, additive ciphers have also been referred to as *shift ciphers*.

Caesar cipher

This cipher has been named after its inventor, Julius Caesar. It is simply an additive cipher with key = 3. That is, during encryption, each plaintext character is replaced with a character obtained by moving three places down in the alphabet and the reverse happens during decryption. Like shift cipher, on reaching the end or beginning of the alphabet, we wrap around. The simplicity of Caesar cipher becomes its weakness as anyone can determine the plaintext by just replacing each ciphertext character with a character obtained by moving three characters up in the alphabet.

To overcome this limitation of Caesar cipher, its enhanced version, named *modified Caesar cipher*, was proposed. In this cipher, a character can be replaced with any other character. However, as we know, the English alphabet has only 26 characters; hence, a character can be replaced only with one of the other 25 characters. Thus, the cipher is vulnerable to the brute-force attack, as an attacker just needs to choose one out of 25 possible characters.

Multiplicative cipher

In this cipher, the plaintext is encrypted by multiplying it with the key, while the ciphertext is decrypted by performing division on it with the key (K). Since the operations are in Z_{26}, the result needs to mapped to Z_{26} using modular arithmetic. Moreover, division by key during decryption implies multiplication by the multiplicative inverse of the key in Z_{26} (denoted as K^{-1}). The following are the formulae used to encrypt the plaintext (P) and decrypt the ciphertext (C), respectively.

$$C = (P * K) \bmod 26$$
$$P = (C * K^{-1}) \bmod 26.$$

Figure 3.3 depicts the process of encryption and decryption in a multiplicative cipher. The example given in **Question 17** illustrates encryption and decryption using multiplicative cipher.

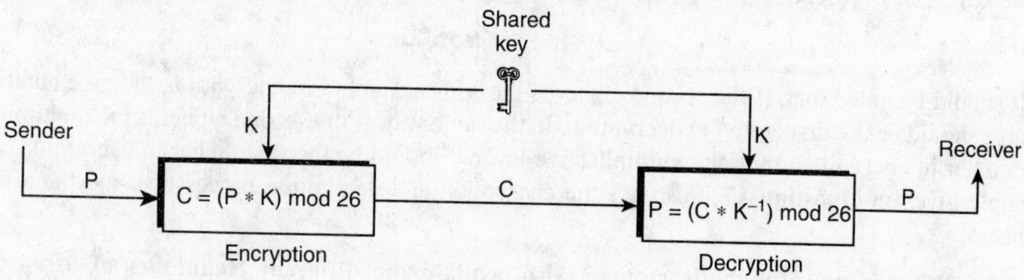

Figure 3.3 Multiplicative Cipher

Affine cipher

Affine cipher is the combination of additive and multiplicative ciphers with a pair of keys. Two ciphers are applied one after another, and a separate key is used for each. The first key of the key-pair is used for the first cipher (either additive or multiplicative), while the second key is used for the other. The process of encryption and decryption in affine cipher is shown in Figure 3.4.

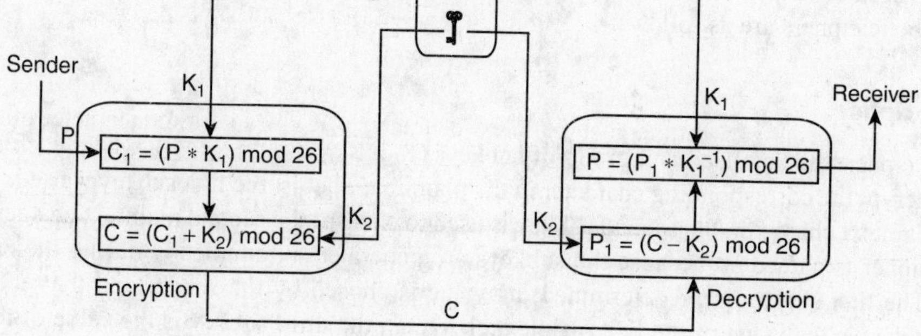

Figure 3.4 Affine Cipher

At the sender's side, the plaintext (P) is first encrypted using the multiplicative cipher and key K_1 to obtain the temporary ciphertext (C_1), as shown here:

$$C_1 = (P * K_1) \bmod 26$$

Then, the ciphertext C_1 is again encrypted using the additive cipher and key K_2 to obtain the final ciphertext (C), as shown here:

$$C = (C_1 + K_2) \bmod 26.$$

At the receiver's side, the algorithm first decrypts the received ciphertext (C) using the additive cipher and additive inverse of the key K_2 in Z_{26} (denoted as $-K_2$) to obtain a temporary plaintext (P_1), as shown here:

$$P_1 = (C - K_2) \bmod 26$$

Then, the plaintext P_1 is again decrypted using the multiplicative cipher and multiplicative inverse of the key K_1 in Z_{26} (denoted as K_1^{-1}) to obtain the original plaintext (P), as shown here:

$$P = (P_1 * K_1^{-1}) \bmod 26.$$

It should be noted that, if the second cipher is the additive cipher in encryption, then the additive inverse should be the first cipher in decryption. In the same way, if the second cipher is the multiplicative cipher in encryption, then the multiplicative inverse should be the first cipher in decryption. An example given in **Question 17** illustrates the encryption and decryption processes using the affine cipher.

6. What is polyalphabetic cipher? Also, explain the different techniques of using the polyalphabetic cipher.

Ans.: In *polyalphabetic cipher*, the characters in the plaintext may have a one-to-many relationship with the characters in the ciphertext. This means that the same character appearing in plaintext can be replaced with a different character in the ciphertext. For example, 'hello' can be encrypted to ARHIF using a polyalphabetic cipher. That is, the two occurrences of the letter 'l' in the plaintext are replaced with different characters. Due to the one-to-many relationship between the characters of plaintext and ciphertext, the key used must indicate which of the possible characters can be used for replacing a character in the plaintext. For this, the plaintext is divided into groups of characters, and a set of keys $K = (K_1, K_2, K_3, \ldots)$ is used for encrypting the groups of plaintext, such that the ith key (K_i) is used to encrypt the ith character of a plaintext group. The different techniques based on polyalphabetic ciphers are as follows:

Autokey cipher

In this cipher, the key used is a group of subkeys ($K_1, K_2, K_3, \ldots, K_n$), where each subkey is used to encrypt the corresponding character in the plaintext. That is, the first subkey is used to encrypt the first plaintext character, the second subkey is used to encrypt the second plaintext character and so on. The cipher is named so because the subkeys are generated automatically during the encryption process. The first subkey is predetermined; its value is chosen by the sender and the receiver. The second subkey is the value of the first plaintext character, the third subkey is the value of the second plaintext character and so on.

At the sender's end, a plaintext character (say, P_i) is added with the respective subkey (K_i), and the result is mapped to Z_{26}, using modular arithmetic to obtain the corresponding ciphertext character (C_i), as shown here:

$$C_i = (P_i + K_i) \bmod 26$$

At the receiver's end, the reverse process is followed to decrypt the ciphertext. That is, a ciphertext character (say, C_i) is added with the additive inverse of the respective subkey (denoted as, $-K_i$) and the result is mapped to Z_{26} using the modular arithmetic to obtain the corresponding plaintext character (P_i) as shown here:

$$P_i = (C_i - K_i) \bmod 26$$

An example given in **Question 18** illustrates the encryption and decryption processes using the autokey cipher.

Playfair cipher

The *Playfair cipher*, also known as *Playfair square*, was used by the British army during World War I, and then by Australians during World War II. Despite its invention by Wheatstone in 1854, it is popularly known after the name of Lord Playfair, who heavily promoted its use. Here, the secret key is formed of 25 alphabets organized into a 5 × 5 matrix. (I and J are considered as same and inserted in the same cell in the matrix.) Different keys can be obtained from different possible arrangements of alphabets in the matrix.

The first step in the Playfair encryption technique is to create and populate the matrix. Initially, a keyword (or phrase) is chosen by the sender and receiver that may not necessarily contain all the 25 alphabets. To organize this keyword in the matrix, it is entered starting from the top left position to right (that is, row-wise), and from top to bottom. While entering, the duplicate letters in the keyword are dropped; that is, each letter of the keyword is entered only once. The remaining empty positions of the keyword matrix are filled with the alphabets (in order) that are not included in the keyword. Moreover, if either I or J appears in the keyword, both are ignored while filling the empty positions of the matrix. However, if neither I nor J appears in the keyword, both are placed at the same position in the matrix. This organization of 25 alphabets in the matrix becomes the secret key for encryption and decryption.

The next step is to encrypt the plaintext. However, before encryption, the plaintext message is broken into diagraphs (group of two characters). If both characters in a pair are the same, then we insert a bogus letter (say, X) between them to distinguish. In case the plaintext consists of an odd number of characters, then also a bogus character is inserted at the end of the plaintext to make the number of characters even. For example, if the plaintext is GREETING, then we have four groups of two letters each as GR, EE, TI, and NG. As the second pair of the message contains repeated letter E, the bogus letter X is inserted between two E's. Now, the pairs of the message become GR, EX, ET, IN and G. To make the number of characters even, the bogus character X is inserted at the end, making the last pair as GX.

At the sender's end, each pair of alphabets in the plaintext is encrypted using the following rules:

- If the two letters in a pair appear in the same row of the keyword matrix, they must be replaced with the letters at their immediate right positions. We must wrap around to the beginning of the row if the any of the letters appears at the end of the row.

- If the two letters in a pair appear in the same column of the keyword matrix, they must be replaced with the letters at their immediate below positions. We must wrap around to the beginning of the column if any of the letters is the last letter in the column.
- If the two letters in a pair do not appear in the same row or column of the keyword matrix, each of them must be replaced with the letter placed at the intersecting position of its own row and the column of another.

At the receiver's end, the ciphertext is decrypted using the same rules as for encryption, with some differences. If the two letters of a pair in the ciphertext satisfy the condition of rule 1, they are replaced with the letters at their immediate left positions. If the two letters of a pair in the ciphertext satisfy the condition of rule 2, they are replaced with the letters at their immediate above positions. The rule 3 is same for decryption. During decryption, the bogus letters are also removed. An example given in **Question 19** illustrates the encryption and decryption processes using the Playfair cipher.

Vigenere cipher

The Vigenere cipher has been named after its designer Blaise de Vigenere. In this cipher, the group of subkeys used depends on the position of the characters in the plaintext, rather than the character itself. Thus, the group of subkeys can be created independent of the plaintext. The initial secret key of length n (where $1 \leq n \leq 26$) is chosen by the sender and receiver. Then, the chosen key is repeated till the end of the plaintext. That is, if the initial secret key chosen is $(K_1, K_2, ..., K_m)$, then the set of keys used for encryption and decryption will be $K=[(K_1, K_2, ..., K_m), (K_1, K_2, ..., K_m), ...]$. Thus, this cipher helps to encrypt plaintext of any size.

At the sender's end, each plaintext character (P_i) is added with the respective key character (K_i) and the result is mapped to Z_{26} using the modular arithmetic to obtain the corresponding ciphertext character (C_i) as shown here:

$$C_i = (P_i + K_i) \bmod 26$$

At the receiver's end, the reverse process is followed to decrypt the ciphertext. That is, a ciphertext character (say, C_i) is added with the additive inverse of the respective key character (denoted as, $-K_i$) and the result is mapped to Z_{26} using the modular arithmetic to obtain the corresponding plaintext character (P_i) as shown here:

$$P_i = (C_i - K_i) \bmod 26$$

An example given in **Question 20** illustrates the encryption and decryption processes using the Vigenere cipher.

Hill cipher

The Hill cipher was invented in 1929 by Lester S. Hill, and it is named after him. In the Hill cipher, the plaintext is first divided into equal-size blocks. Then, the blocks are encrypted in such a way that each block element (character) participates in the encryption of other block elements in the block. The key (K) used in the Hill cipher is in the form of an $n \times n$ square matrix, where n is the block size (see Figure 3.5). Each element of the key matrix is represented as K_{ij}, where $1 \leq i, j \leq n$.

$$K = \begin{pmatrix} K_{11} & K_{12} & \dots & K_{1n} \\ K_{21} & K_{22} & \dots & K_{2n} \\ . & . & & \\ . & . & & \\ K_{n1} & K_{n2} & \dots & K_{nn} \end{pmatrix}$$

Figure 3.5 Key Matrix

Consider a plaintext block (P) that contains n characters is to be encrypted. Let $P_1, P_2, \dots, P_n$ represent the plaintext characters in this block and their corresponding ciphertext characters are represented as $C_1, C_2, \dots, C_n$. Then, we get the ciphertext as shown here:

$$C_1 = (P_1K_{11} + P_2K_{21} + \dots + P_nK_n) \bmod 26$$
$$C_2 = (P_1K_{12} + P_2K_{22} + \dots + P_nK_{n2}) \bmod 26$$
$$\vdots$$
$$C_m = (P_1K_{1n} + P_2K_{2n} + \dots + P_nK_{nn}) \bmod 26$$

The preceding equations can be expressed as:

$$\begin{pmatrix} C_1 \\ C_2 \\ . \\ . \\ . \\ C_n \end{pmatrix} = \begin{pmatrix} K_{11} & K_{12} & \dots & K_{1n} \\ K_{21} & K_{22} & \dots & K_{2n} \\ . & . & & \\ . & . & & \\ . & . & & \\ K_{n1} & K_{n2} & \dots & K_{nn} \end{pmatrix} \begin{pmatrix} P_1 \\ P_2 \\ . \\ . \\ . \\ P_n \end{pmatrix} \pmod{26}$$

In general, the encryption in the Hill cipher can be expressed as shown here:

$$C = K\,P \bmod 26$$

To perform decryption at the receiver's end, the inverse of the key is first determined in Z_{26}, and then the ciphertext is decrypted, as shown here:

$$P = K^{-1}\,C \bmod 26$$

An example given in **Question 21** illustrates the encryption and decryption processes using the Hill cipher.

7. What are keyless and keyed transposition ciphers?

Ans.: Keyless and keyed ciphers are two categories of transposition ciphers that reorder (permute) the symbols of plaintext to form ciphertext. These are described as follows:

- *Keyless transposition ciphers:* These are the traditional ciphers, and are easy to use. They do not use any key to permute the characters in the plaintext and thus, are named as keyless ciphers. To permute the characters, the plaintext characters are written in a table either column-wise or row-wise. In the former case, ciphertext is formed by reading the characters from the table row-wise, while in the latter case, column-wise.

- *Keyed transposition ciphers:* These ciphers make use of a key to permute the characters in the plaintext and, thus, are named as keyed ciphers. These ciphers first divide the plaintext into blocks of predefined size, and then a key is used to permute the characters within each block individually.

8. Write a short note on columnar transposition ciphers.

Ans.: A *columnar transposition cipher* is the combination of keyless and keyed transposition ciphers. It performs encryption and decryption in three steps; the first and third steps are keyless, while the second step is performed on the basis of a key. The plaintext characters are first arranged in the table row-wise. Secondly, these characters are permuted by reordering the columns based on a key. And, finally, the characters are read from the new table column-wise.

To understand, consider the plaintext 'hellohowareyou', and the key 'BACKIN'. Initially, the plaintext characters are arranged in the table row-wise, as shown in the following. The rows are padded with extra characters to fill the table, if required.

h	e	l	l	o	h
o	w	a	r	e	y
o	u	a	b	c	d

After arranging the plaintext, the letters of the key BACKIN are numbered according to the alphabetical order. For example, A is assigned the number 1, B is 2, C is 3, I is 4, K is 5 and N is 6. Now, the columns of the table are reordered according to numbers assigned to the key letters. For example, the column 1 is interchanged with column 2, column 4 with column 5, while columns 3 and 6 remain intact. After reordering the columns, the new table is as shown in the following:

e	h	l	o	l	h
w	o	a	e	r	y
u	o	a	c	b	d

The characters are now read out column-wise from the new table to form the ciphertext. That is, the ciphertext is 'ewuhoolaaoeclrbhyd'.

9. What is the difference between stream cipher and block cipher?

Ans.: *Stream cipher* and *block cipher* are two categories of symmetric ciphers.

- *Stream cipher:* This cipher operates on one symbol (character) of plaintext at a time and produces a corresponding symbol of ciphertext. As the name of the cipher implies, we have a plaintext stream $P = (P_1, P_2, P_3, \ldots)$, a ciphertext stream $C = (C_1, C_2, C_3, \ldots)$, and a key stream $K = (K_1, K_2, K_3, \ldots)$. The plaintext characters are input into the encryption algorithm, one character at a time. The encryption algorithm uses the respective subkey to encrypt each plaintext character, which results in a corresponding ciphertext character. Each character is encrypted and decrypted using the same key, regardless of the fact that multiple keys are being used. For example, consider that the plaintext is 'user' and the key stream used is (K_1, K_2 and K_3). Now, the plaintext is encrypted such that the characters 'u' and 'r' are encrypted using the key K_1, the characters 's' is encrypted using the key K_2 and the character 'e' is encrypted using K_3. During decryption also, the same set of keys (K_1, K_2 and K_3) is used, such that the characters 'u' and 'r' are decrypted using the key K_1, the character 's' is decrypted using the key K_2 and the character 'e' is decrypted using the key K_3. The Additive cipher and Vigenere cipher can be categorized as stream ciphers.

- *Block cipher:* This cipher encrypts a group or block (with size > 1) of symbols in plaintext at one time, producing a block of ciphertext of the same size. Similarly, during decryption, a block of ciphertext symbols is converted back to a block of plaintext with one block at a time. A single key is used to encrypt or decrypt the entire block, even if the key contains multiple values. The Hill cipher and Playfair cipher can be categorized as block ciphers.

10. Explain the term *one time pad*.

Ans.: The *one-time pad* (also known as the *Vernam cipher*) was first implemented at AT&T using a device called the *Vernam machine*. It is actually a random set of non-repeating characters that is used as a key for generating the ciphertext message. As the name suggests, the set of characters can be used only once and, therefore, cannot be used for any other message. The algorithm used in generating a ciphertext message by the one-time pad scheme is as follows:

1. The alphabets in the plaintext are assigned numbers in an increasing order. For example, `A = 0`, `B = 1, . . .`, and `Z = 25`.
2. The one-time pad alphabets are randomly chosen, and numbers are assigned in the same manner as in the plaintext. For example, `C = 2`, `D = 3` and so on.
3. The numbers that correspond to the plaintext and the one-time pad input are added.
4. Then the mod 26 operation is done with each generated character of the sum.
5. The numbers obtained from the sum are translated back to the corresponding alphabet, which gives the output ciphertext.

The security of the one-time pad method is very high because of its randomness and one-time use. Thus, it can only be used for small plaintext messages. The ciphertext message generated using the one-time pad method is also random; that is, the same ciphertext message is not generated for two same plaintexts, thus making it less vulnerable to attacks. In spite of these benefits, it faces some difficulties in practical implementation. One problem is that it is difficult to generate a large set of random numbers each time for the same nodes to communicate with each other. Another problem is that of key distribution and protection, as a key of equal length is needed by both the sender and the receiver in every message exchange. An example illustrating the use of one-time pad is shown in **Question 22**.

11. What do you understand by bit-oriented ciphers? Why do we need them?

Ans.: The ciphers that perform encryption or decryption at the bit level rather than at the character level are referred to as *bit-oriented ciphers*. Earlier, most of the information to be encrypted was in textual form; thus, the use of character-oriented ciphers was justified. However, these days, the information to be encrypted is not just text, but may comprise graphics, audio and video. Thus, bit-oriented ciphers are needed, because such types of data can be conveniently transformed into streams of bits, which can then be encrypted and sent to the intended receiver. Moreover, as the text is treated at the bit level, each character of plaintext can be replaced with 8 bits or 16 bits. This increases the number of symbols in the plaintext by 8 or 16 times, thereby also increasing the security.

12. What do you mean by modern block cipher? What are its components?

Ans.: The *modern block cipher* is a bit-oriented symmetric-key cipher that encrypts an *m*-bit block of plaintext at a time to produce an *m*-bit block of ciphertext. Similarly, during decryption, an *m*-bit block of ciphertext is converted back to an *m*-bit block of plaintext, one block at a time. Each block of bits is encrypted or decrypted using the *k*-bit key (see Figure 3.6). The decryption algorithm used is the inverse of the encryption algorithm, and the same secret key is used for both encryption and decryption. Thus, the same block of plaintext is always encrypted to same block of ciphertext.

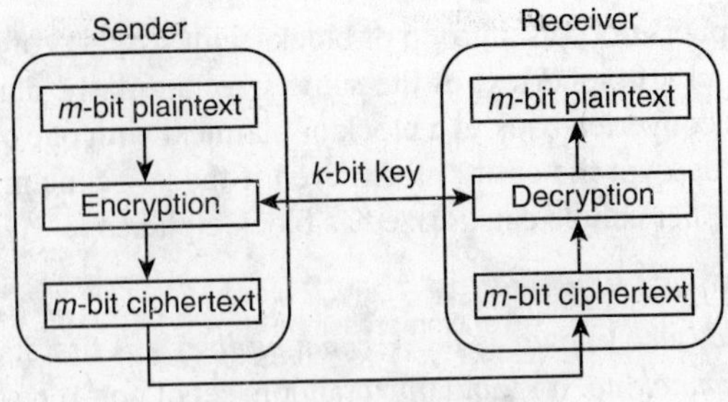

Figure 3.6 Modern Block Cipher

If the plaintext contains less than *m* bits, extra bits (padding) are added to make it an *m*-bit block. On the other hand, if the plaintext contains more than *m* bits, the plaintext is divided into blocks of *m* bits each and extra bits are added to the last block to make it an *m*-bit block if it contains less than *m* bits.

The modern block cipher consists of various components, described as follows:

- *S-box:* This is a substitution box having the same characteristics as that of the substitution cipher, except that the substitution of several bits is performed in parallel. It takes *n* bits of plaintext at a time as input and produces *m* bits of ciphertext as output, where the value of *n* and *m* may be the same or different. An S-box can be *keyed* or *keyless*. In a *keyed S-box*, the mapping of *n* inputs to *m* outputs is decided with the help of a key, whereas in a *keyless S-box*, the mapping from inputs to outputs is predetermined. Usually, keyless S-boxes are used in modern block ciphers.
- *P-box:* This is a permutation box having the same characteristics as that of the traditional transposition cipher, except that it performs transposition at the bit-level, and that transposition of several bits is performed at the same time. The input bits are permuted to produce the output bits. For example, the first input bit can be the second output bit, the second input bit can be the third output bit and so on. A P-box is sometimes also referred to as a *D-box* (*diffusion box*). It is normally a keyless cipher and can be classified into the following three types (see Figure 3.7), based on the length of input and output:
  - *Straight P-box:* This P-box takes *n* bits as input, permutes them and produces *n* bits as output. As the number of inputs and outputs is the same, there are a total of $n!$ ways to map *n* inputs to *n* outputs.
  - *Compression P-box:* This P-box takes *n* bits as input and permutes them in such a way that an output of *m* bits is produced, where $m < n$. This implies that some of the inputs are blocked and do not reach the output. Compression P-boxes are used in those situations where we need to permute the bits and at the same time need lesser number of bits at each successive stage.
  - *Expansion P-box:* This P-box takes *n* bits as input and permutes them in such a way that an output of *m* bits is produced, where $m > n$. This implies that a single input is mapped to more than one output. The expansion P-boxes are used in those situations where we want a higher number of bits at each successive stage.
- *Circular shift:* Another important component involved in modern block cipher is the circular shift operation, which tends to conceal the bit patterns in a transmitted word. The bits can be shifted either in the left or the right direction. In a *circular left shift* operation [see Figure 3.8 (a)], every bit of an *m*-bit word is shifted by a specific number of positions (say, *n*) in the left direction. In other words, the *n* leftmost bits of the word are removed and placed at the rightmost positions.

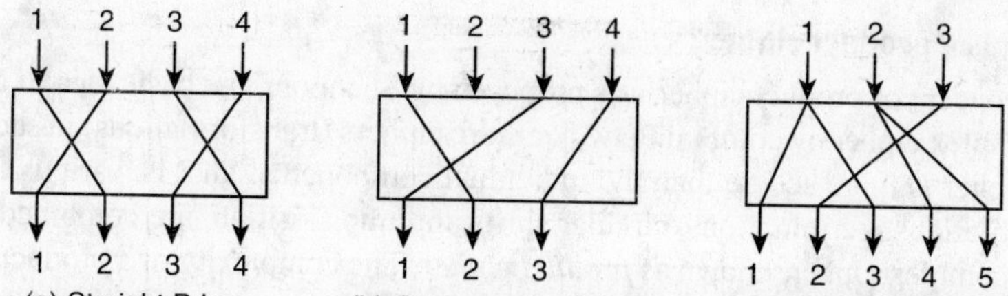

(a) Straight P-box (b) Compression P-box (c) Expansion P-box

Figure 3.7 Types of P-Boxes

The reverse happens in a *circular right-shift* operation [see Figure 3.8 (b)], where each bit of an *m*-bit word is shifted by *n* positions in the right direction. That is, the *n* rightmost bits of the word are removed and placed at the leftmost position. The circular shift operation can be either keyed or keyless. In the former case, the key defines the number of positions by which the bits are to be shifted. On the other hand, in the latter case, the number of positions to be shifted is usually fixed and predetermined. It is important to note that if a circular left shift operation is used in encryption, then a circular right shift operation is used in decryption, and vice-versa. Thus, both these operations are inverses of each other.

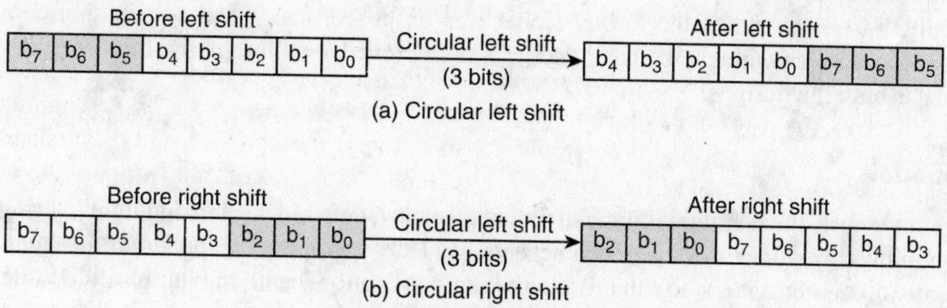

Figure 3.8 Circular Shift Operation

13. Explain Shannon's theory of diffusion and confusion.

Ans.: The theory of diffusion and confusion was proposed by Claude Shannon in attempt to thwart cryptanalysis based on statistical analysis. Both diffusion and confusion are the essential properties of block ciphers. *Diffusion* is based on the idea of hiding the relationship between the ciphertext and plaintext. This will frustrate a cryptanalyst who examines the ciphertext statistics in order to determine the plaintext. To achieve diffusion, a ciphertext symbol must depend on some or all symbols in the plaintext. That is, a change in a single symbol in the plaintext causes change in several or all symbols in the ciphertext.

On the other hand, *confusion* is based on the idea of hiding the relationship between the ciphertext and the key. This will frustrate a cryptanalyst who attempts to determine the key using the ciphertext. To prevent intruders from discovering the key, confusion attempts to make the relationship between the value of encryption key and the statistics of ciphertext as complex as possible. This can be achieved by making sure that a ciphertext symbol depends on some or all symbols of the key used. That is, a change in a single bit of the key causes changes in several or all symbols in the ciphertext.

14. What is a product cipher?

Ans.: The concept of product cipher was proposed by Shannon. The basic idea of a product cipher is to build a complex cipher by combining two or more ciphers (transformations) in such a manner that the resulting cipher is more secure than the individual components. That is, various transformations, including substitutions, permutations, circular shifts and transposition, are combined within a single unit to make a complex cipher, known as *product cipher*. The complexity of a product cipher makes it more secure and resistant to various attacks, thereby making it more difficult for a cryptanalyst to thwart the security. All modern ciphers are product ciphers, and are classified into two categories on the basis of the type of components used in them, namely, *Feistel* and *non-Feistel* ciphers.

15. Explain Feistel cipher and its structure.

Ans.: The *Feistel cipher*, proposed by Horst Fiestel, belongs to a class of product ciphers that permits the use of invertible as well as noninvertible components. The Feistel cipher uses three types of components (units), namely, *self-invertible*, *invertible* and *noninvertible* components. This cipher works by combining all noninvertible units into a single unit and then using the same unit in encryption and decryption algorithms. Now, the problem is that since both encryption and decryption algorithms use noninvertible units, how can they be the inverses of each other? To resolve this problem, we use the XOR operation, so that the effects of a noninvertible component in encryption can be cancelled out during decryption.

Initially, a basic model of the Fiestel cipher was proposed, which had certain shortcomings. To overcome these shortcomings, the basic model was improved, resulting in the final design. Here, we will discuss both the designs.

Basic model

In this structure, the plaintext is divided into two equal-length blocks: left and right. During encryption, a noninvertible function (`f`), which accepts key (`K`) as an input, is applied to the right block of the plaintext (denoted as R_p), and the resultant output is XOR-ed with the left block (denoted as L_p). The output of the XOR operation becomes the left block of the ciphertext (denoted as L_c), while the right block of ciphertext (denoted as R_c) is same as the right block of plaintext. The function `f` and the XOR operation together are referred to as the *mixer*, which is self-invertible in nature. During decryption, the reverse process is followed. However, the input to the function `f` remains the same in both the encryption and decryption processes, as shown in Figure 3.9.

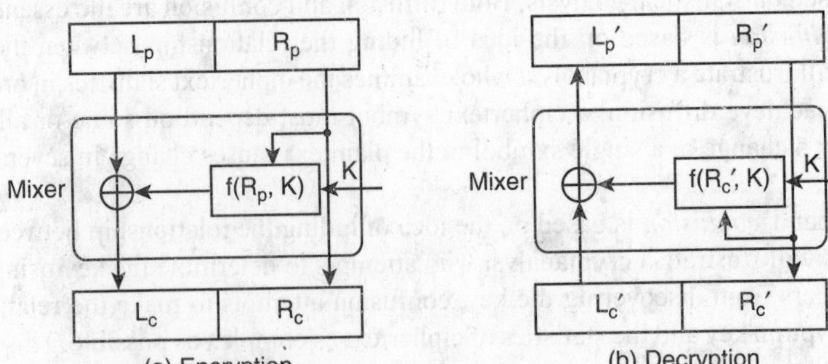

Figure 3.9 Basic Model of Fiestel Cipher

To verify the correctness of the design, we need to ensure that the encryption and decryption algorithms are inverses of each other. That is, it must be proved that $L_p = L'_p$ and $R_p = R'_p$. To prove this, let us assume that there is no change in the ciphertext during transmission, which means $L_c = L'_c$ and $R_c = R'_c$. As $R_c = R_p$ and $R'_c = R'_p$, we have $R'_p = R_p$.

Now, we can write that

$$L'_p = L'_c \oplus f(R'_c, K)$$
$$\Rightarrow L_c \oplus f(R_c, K) \quad (1)$$

As we know that $L_c = L_p \oplus f(R_p, K)$ and $R_c = R_p$, the equation (1) can be written as:

$$L'_p = L_p \oplus f(R_p, K) \oplus f(R_p, K)$$
$$\Rightarrow L_p \oplus (000.........0) \quad \text{(using the identity property of XOR, } X \oplus X = 0\text{)}$$
$$\Rightarrow L_p$$

Hence, the decryption algorithm produces the same plaintext as used by the encryption algorithm. In other words, the encryption and decryption algorithms are the inverses of each other.

Final design of the Feistel cipher

In the basic model of the Feistel cipher, the right block of the plaintext never changes and remains the same in the ciphertext also. Due to this, the generated ciphertext becomes vulnerable to attacks and is more prone to interception by a hacker. Thus, the design was improved by including the following enhancements:

- The number of rounds was increased in the final design.
- A new element called *swapper* was added to each round. The role of the swapper is to swap the left and right blocks in each round. In addition, the effect of the swapper during encryption is cancelled out with the effect of the swapper during decryption.
- Two round keys (K_1 and K_2) are used during encryption and decryption. The encryption and decryption algorithms use the keys in reverse order.

Figure 3.10 shows the final design of the Feistel cipher with two rounds.

The mixers and swappers used in encryption and decryption are inverses of each other, respectively. This implies that the encryption and the decryption algorithms are also inverses of each other. To prove this fact, we need to show that $L_p = L'_p$ and $R_p = R'_p$. To prove this, let us assume that there is no change in the ciphertext during transmission, which means $L_c = L'_c$ and $R_c = R'_c$. First, we will prove the equality between the middle texts (L and L', R and R'), and then between the final text. As $R' = L'_c$, $L'_c = L_c$ and $L_c = R$, we have $R' = R$.

We can write that:

$$L' = R'_c \oplus f(L'_c, K_2)$$
$$\Rightarrow R_c \oplus f(L_c, K_2) \quad (2)$$

As we know that $R_c = L \oplus f(R, K_2)$ and $L_c = R$, Equation (2) can be written as:

$$L' = L \oplus f(R, K_2) \oplus f(R, K_2)$$
$$\Rightarrow L \oplus (000.........0)$$
$$\Rightarrow L$$

Now, we have $R'_p = L'$, $L' = L$ and $L = R_p$. Thus, it is proved that $R'_p = R_p$.

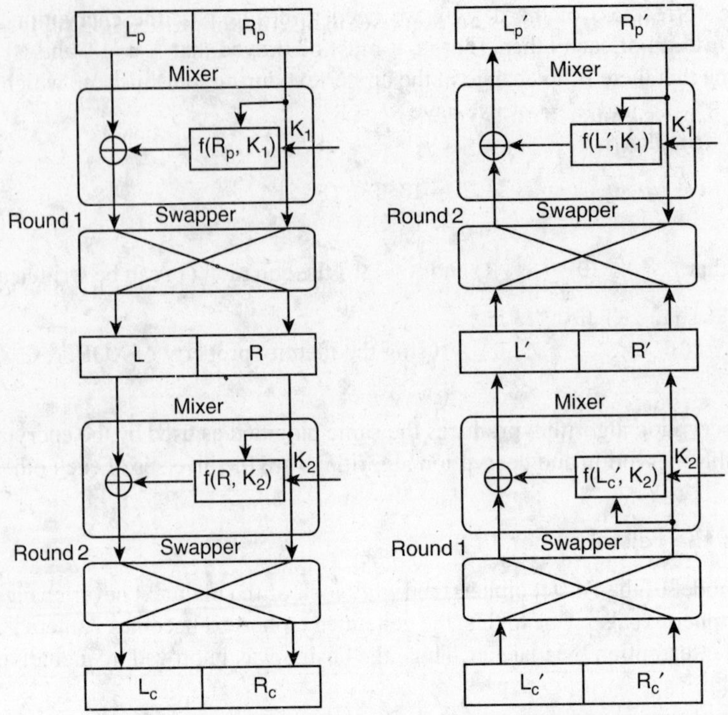

(a) Encryption (b) Decryption

Figure 3.10 Final Design of Fiestel Cipher with two Rounds

We can also write that:

$$L'_p = R' \oplus f(L', K_1) \tag{3}$$

As $R' = R$ and $L' = L$, Equation (3) can be written as:

$$L'_p = R \oplus f(L, K_1) \tag{4}$$

As we know that $L = R_p$ and $R = L_p \oplus f(R_p, K_1)$, Equation (4) can be written as:

$$L'_p = L_p \oplus f(R_p, K_1) \oplus f(R_p, K_1)$$
$$\Rightarrow L_p \oplus (000.........0)$$
$$\Rightarrow L_p$$

Hence, the decryption algorithm produces the same plaintext as used by the encryption algorithm. In other words, encryption and decryption algorithms are the inverses of each other.

16. What is a non-Feistel cipher?

Ans.: A *non-Feistel cipher* uses only invertible components. Each element in the plaintext has a respective element in the cipher. For example, if an S-box is used, then it must have the same number of inputs and outputs. In addition, only the straight P-boxes can be used, because the compression and expansion P-boxes are non-invertible in nature. Unlike the Fiestel cipher, it is not required to break the plaintext into two halves in a non-Fiestel cipher.

17. Encrypt the message 'this is an exercise' using the following ciphers. Ignore the spaces between the words while encrypting. Also, decrypt the message to get the original plaintext.

(a) Additive cipher with key = 20

(b) Multiplicative cipher with key = 15

(c) Affine cipher with key = (15, 20)

Ans.: (a) *Additive cipher with key = 20*

Plaintext (P) = 'this is an exercise'

Key (K) = 20

❑ *Encryption:* In additive cipher, the ciphertext (C) = (P + K) mod 26, which can be found as follows:

Plaintext	t	h	i	s	i	s	a	n	e	x	e	r	c	i	s	e
P's values	19	07	08	18	08	18	00	13	04	23	04	17	02	08	18	04
C's values	13	01	02	12	02	12	20	07	24	17	24	11	22	02	12	24
Ciphertext	n	b	c	m	c	m	u	h	y	r	y	l	w	c	m	y

Hence, the corresponding ciphertext is 'nbcmcmuhyrylwcmy'.

❑ *Decryption:* To decrypt the ciphertext (C), we first need to determine the additive inverse of 20 in Z_{26}, which is equal to 6 (26–20). Now, the ciphertext (C) can be decrypted to obtain the plaintext (P) using the formula (C+6) mod 26, as shown here:

Ciphertext	n	b	c	m	c	m	u	h	y	r	y	l	w	c	m	y
C's values	13	01	02	12	02	12	20	07	24	17	24	11	22	02	12	24
P's values	19	07	08	18	08	18	00	13	04	23	04	17	02	08	18	04
Plaintext	t	h	i	s	i	s	a	n	e	x	e	r	c	i	s	e

(b) *Multiplicative cipher with key = 15*

Plaintext (P) = 'this is an exercise'

Key (K) = 15

❑ *Encryption:* In multiplicative cipher, the ciphertext (C) = (P * K) mod 26, which can be found as follows:

Plaintext	t	h	i	s	i	s	a	n	e	x	e	r	c	i	s	e
P's values	19	07	08	18	08	18	00	13	04	23	04	17	02	08	18	04
C's values	25	01	16	10	16	10	00	13	08	07	08	21	04	16	10	08
Ciphertext	z	b	q	k	q	k	a	n	i	h	i	v	e	q	k	i

Hence, the corresponding ciphertext is 'zbqkqkanihiveqki'.

❑ *Decryption:* To decrypt the ciphertext, first we need to determine the multiplicative inverse of 15 in Z_{26}, which is equal to 7, as $15 * 7 \equiv 1 \pmod{26}$. Now, the ciphertext (C) can be decrypted to obtain the plaintext (P) using the formula (C * 7) mod 26, as shown here:

Ciphertext	z	b	q	k	q	k	a	n	i	h	i	v	e	q	k	i
C's values	25	01	16	10	16	10	00	13	08	07	08	21	04	16	10	08
P's values	19	07	08	18	08	18	00	13	04	23	04	17	02	08	18	04
Plaintext	t	h	i	s	i	s	a	n	e	x	e	r	c	i	s	e

(c) *Affine cipher with key = (15, 20)*
Plaintext (P) = 'this is an exercise'
Key (K) = 15

- *Encryption:* In affine cipher, the plaintext (P) is first encrypted using the multiplicative cipher and the first key (that is, 15) to produce the temporary ciphertext (C_1). Then, C_1 is again encrypted using the additive cipher and the second key (that is, 20) to produce the final ciphertext (C), as shown here:

Plaintext	t	h	i	s	i	s	a	n	e	x	e	r	c	i	s	e
P's values	19	07	08	18	08	18	00	13	04	23	04	17	02	08	18	04
C_1 = (P * 15) mod 26	25	01	16	10	16	10	00	13	08	07	08	21	04	16	10	08
C = (C_1 + 20) mod 26	19	21	10	04	10	04	20	07	02	01	02	15	24	10	04	02
Ciphertext	t	v	k	e	k	e	u	h	c	b	c	p	y	k	e	c

Hence, the corresponding ciphertext is 'tvkekeuhcbcpykec'.

- *Decryption:* First, the ciphertext (C) is decrypted using the additive cipher and the additive inverse of key 20 to produce the temporary plaintext P_1. Then, P_1 is again decrypted using the multiplicative cipher and the multiplicative inverse of key 15. The additive inverse of key 20 in Z_{26} is 6, while the multiplicative inverse of key 15 in Z_{26} is 7. Now, the decryption is performed as shown here:

Ciphertext	t	v	k	e	k	e	u	h	c	b	c	p	y	k	e	c
C's values	19	21	10	04	10	04	20	07	02	01	02	15	24	10	04	02
P_1 = (C + 6) mod 26	25	01	16	10	16	10	00	13	08	07	08	21	04	16	10	08
P = (P_1 * 7) mod 26	19	07	08	18	08	18	00	13	04	23	04	17	02	08	18	04
Plaintext	t	h	i	s	i	s	a	n	e	x	e	r	c	i	s	e

18. Encrypt the plaintext message 'ATTACK SUCCESSFUL' by using the initial key stream as 12 with the autokey cipher.

Ans.: The plaintext will be encrypted to form the ciphertext as shown here:

Plaintext	A	T	T	A	C	K	S	U	C	C	E	S	S	F	U	L
P's values (P_i)	00	19	19	00	02	10	18	20	02	02	04	18	18	05	20	11
Key stream (K_i):	12	00	19	19	00	02	10	18	20	02	02	04	18	18	05	20
C's values C_i = (P_i+K_i) mod 26	12	19	12	19	02	12	02	12	22	04	06	22	10	23	25	05
Ciphertext	M	T	M	T	C	M	C	M	W	E	G	W	K	X	Z	F

Hence, the corresponding ciphertext is 'MTMTCMCMWEGWKXZF'.

19. Given the key 'MONARCHY', apply the Playfair cipher to the plaintext 'FACTIONALISM'. Decrypt the ciphertext also.

Ans.: The given keyword = 'MONARCHY'

The corresponding keyword matrix is as follows:

M	O	N	A	R
C	H	Y	B	D
E	F	G	I/J	K
L	P	Q	S	T
U	V	W	X	Z

Encryption

The given plaintext is 'FACTIONALISM'. The different pairs of plaintext are FA, CT, IO, NA, LI and SM. These pairs are encrypted as follows:

- In the first pair, the letter F is at position (3, 2), and A is at position (1, 4) in the keyword matrix. That is, neither their rows nor their columns match. Thus, F is replaced with the letter at the intersecting position of the third row and fourth column, which is either I or J. Let us use I. Similarly, A is replaced with the letter at the intersecting position of the first row and second column, which is the letter O.
- For the next two pairs, CT and IO, neither the rows nor the columns match. Thus, using the same rule as earlier, they are replaced with DL and FA, respectively.
- In the fourth pair, NA, both letters appear in the same row. Thus, they are replaced with the letters at their immediate right positions, which are A and R.
- In the last two pairs, LI and SM, neither the rows nor the columns match. Thus, they are replaced with SE and LA, respectively.

Hence, the corresponding ciphertext is 'IODLFAARSELA'.

Decryption

The different pairs of ciphertext are IO, DL, FA, AR, SE and LA. These pairs are decrypted as follows:

- In the first pair, the letter I is at position (3, 4) and O appears at position (1, 2) in the keyword matrix. That is, neither their rows nor their columns match. Thus, I is replaced with the letter at the intersecting position of third row and second column, which is F. Similarly, O is replaced with the letter at the intersecting position of first row and fourth column, which is the letter A.
- For the next two pairs, DL and FA, neither the rows nor the columns match. Thus, using the same rule as earlier, they are replaced with CT and IO, respectively.
- In the fourth pair, AR, both letters appear in the same row. Thus, they are replaced with letters at their immediate left positions, which are N and A.
- In the last two pairs, SE and LA, neither the rows nor the columns match. Thus, they are replaced with LI and SM, respectively.

Hence, the corresponding plaintext is 'FACTIONALISM'.

20. Encrypt the plaintext message 'honesty is the best' by using a 6-character key 'CENTRE' with the Vigenere cipher.

Ans.: The encryption process using the Vigenere cipher is shown here:

Plaintext	h	o	n	e	s	t	y	i	s	t	h	e	b	e	s	t
P's values (P_is)	7	14	13	4	18	19	24	8	18	19	7	4	1	4	18	19
Key stream	C	E	N	T	R	E	C	E	N	T	R	E	C	E	N	T
K_i's values	2	4	13	19	17	4	2	4	13	19	17	4	2	4	13	19
C's values $C_i=(P_i+K_i)$ mod 26	9	18	0	23	9	23	0	12	5	12	24	8	3	8	5	19
Ciphertext	j	s	a	x	j	x	a	m	f	m	y	i	d	i	f	m

Hence, the corresponding ciphertext is 'jsaxjxamfmyidifm'.

21. Given the key 'GYBNQKURP', apply the Hill cipher to the plaintext 'ACT' to show how encryption and decryption are performed and prove authenticity.

Ans.: The given plaintext (P) = 'ACT'

Key (K) = 'GYBNQKURP'

The key used can be written as:

$$\begin{pmatrix} G & Y & B \\ N & Q & K \\ U & R & P \end{pmatrix} \text{ or } \begin{pmatrix} 6 & 24 & 1 \\ 13 & 16 & 10 \\ 20 & 17 & 15 \end{pmatrix}$$

Encryption

The plaintext ACT can be written as:

$$\begin{pmatrix} A \\ C \\ T \end{pmatrix} \text{ or } \begin{pmatrix} 0 \\ 2 \\ 19 \end{pmatrix}.$$

Thus, the ciphertext (C) is given as PK mod 26 as shown here.

$$\Rightarrow \begin{pmatrix} 6 & 24 & 1 \\ 13 & 16 & 10 \\ 20 & 17 & 15 \end{pmatrix} \begin{pmatrix} 0 \\ 2 \\ 19 \end{pmatrix} = \begin{pmatrix} 67 \\ 222 \\ 319 \end{pmatrix} \pmod{26}$$

$$= \begin{pmatrix} 15 \\ 14 \\ 7 \end{pmatrix} \text{ or } \begin{pmatrix} P \\ O \\ H \end{pmatrix}$$

Hence, the corresponding ciphertext is 'POH'.

Decryption

In order to decrypt the ciphertext, we first need to calculate the inverse of the key matrix and then multiply it with the ciphertext, that is, $P = K^{-1}C \bmod 26$. Now, the inverse of the key matrix is:

$$K^{-1} = \begin{pmatrix} 8 & 5 & 10 \\ 21 & 8 & 21 \\ 21 & 12 & 8 \end{pmatrix}$$

Thus, the plaintext can be obtained as shown here:

$$\begin{pmatrix} 8 & 5 & 10 \\ 21 & 8 & 21 \\ 21 & 12 & 8 \end{pmatrix} \begin{pmatrix} 15 \\ 14 \\ 7 \end{pmatrix} = \begin{pmatrix} 260 \\ 574 \\ 539 \end{pmatrix} \pmod{26}$$

$$= \begin{pmatrix} 0 \\ 2 \\ 19 \end{pmatrix} \text{ or } \begin{pmatrix} A \\ C \\ T \end{pmatrix}$$

Since the receiver receives the same message as sent by the sender, the authenticity of the message is proved.

22. Generate the ciphertext message using the one-time pad algorithm for the plaintext message 'higautam'.

Ans.:

Plaintext	**h**	**i**	**g**	**a**	**u**	**t**	**a**	**m**
P's values	07	08	06	00	20	19	00	12
One-Time Pad characters	b	c	z	s	v	a	x	t
One-Time Pad values	01	02	25	18	21	00	23	19
C's values	08	10	31	18	41	19	23	31
Ciphertext	i	k	f	s	p	t	x	f

Hence, the corresponding ciphertext is 'ikfsptxf'.

Multiple-choice Questions

1. Which of the following is a monoalphabetic cipher?
   (a) Caesar cipher
   (b) Autokey cipher
   (c) Vigenere cipher
   (d) All of these
2. The __________ cipher is a combination of additive and multiplicative ciphers with a pair of keys.
   (a) Affine
   (b) Caesar
   (c) Autokey
   (d) Shift
3. In the polyalphabetic cipher, the characters in plaintext have a __________ relationship with the characters in ciphertext.
   (a) One-to-one
   (b) One-to-many
   (c) Many-to-one
   (d) Many-to-many
4. The Hill cipher belongs to the category of ciphers, named __________.
   (a) Stream cipher
   (b) Block cipher
   (c) Both (a) and (b)
   (d) None of these
5. The __________ cipher can be categorized as a stream cipher.
   (a) Additive
   (b) Hill
   (c) Playfair
   (d) None of these

6. Which of the following is/are components of a modern block cipher?
   (a) Circular shift
   (b) S-box
   (c) P-box
   (d) All of these
7. __________ is based on the idea of hiding the relationship between the ciphertext and the key.
   (a) Diffusion
   (b) Confusion
   (c) Both (a) and (b)
   (d) None of these
8. The concept of product cipher was proposed by __________.
   (a) Verman
   (b) Fiestel
   (c) Lester S. Hill
   (d) Shannon
9. The Feistel cipher uses the __________ operation.
   (a) AND
   (b) NOR
   (c) XOR
   (d) OR
10. A non-Feistel cipher uses only the __________ P-box.
    (a) Compression
    (b) Expansion
    (c) Straight
    (d) None of these

Answers

1. (a)	2. (a)	3. (b)	4. (b)	5. (a)	6. (d)
7. (b)	8. (d)	9. (c)	10. (c)		

4

Symmetric-key Algorithms

1. Explain DES with its structure. Also explain its function.

Ans.: *Data Encryption Standard* (DES) is a symmetric-key block cipher that was first published in 1977 by National Institute of Standards and Technology (NIST). It was originally proposed by IBM in 1973 in response to the request for proposals for a national symmetric-key cryptosystem. This encryption standard was adopted by the US government for non-classified information and by various industries for use in security products. DES is also known as the *Data Encryption Algorithm* (DEA) by ANSI and DEA-1 by ISO.

At the sender's end, DES divides the plaintext into 64-bit blocks and encrypts each block using a 56-bit cipher key to produce a 64-bit ciphertext block. At the receiver's end, the reverse process is followed; that is, DES decrypts the 64-bit ciphertext to obtain 64-bit plaintext. Being a symmetric-key cipher, DES uses the same 56-bit cipher key for both encryption and decryption. Originally, the cipher key is of 64 bits including 8 parity bits; however, the usable bits in key are only 56.

DES involves multiple rounds to produce ciphertext, and the key used in each round (called the *round key*) is the subset of the general key, called the *cipher key*; the round keys are generated by the *round key generator*. Thus, if there are P rounds in the cipher, then the round key generator produces total P round keys (K_1, K_2,..., K_P) where K_1 is used in first round, K_2 in second round and so on.

DES Structure

Figure 4.1 shows the general structure of the DES encryption algorithm (referred to as the *DES cipher*); the design of the DES decryption algorithm (referred to as the *DES reverse cipher*) is also similar, except that the round keys are used in the reverse order from that of encryption. The whole process of producing ciphertext from plaintext comprises 19 stages. The first stage is the initial transposition, which performs keyless straight permutations that are the inverse of each other on the 64-bit plaintext block, according to a predetermined rule. The next 16 stages are the rounds that are functionally similar and, in each round, a different round key K_i of 48 bits derived from the cipher key of 56 bits is used. The second-last stage performs a swap function in which the leftmost 32 bits are exchanged with the rightmost 32 bits. The last stage, final transposition, is simply the opposite of the first stage; that is, it performs inverse transposition on the 64 bits received from the 32-bit swapper to generate a 64-bit ciphertext block. For example, if in the initial transposition stage, the input bit 2 becomes the output bit 50, then in the final transposition stage, the input bit 50 becomes the output bit 2. At the receiver's end, the decryption is performed using the same key as in encryption; however, the steps are performed in the reverse order.

The structure of one of the 16 rounds (say, i-th round) during encryption in DES is shown in Figure 4.2. It takes two inputs: the leftmost 32 bits as left input (L_i) and the rightmost 32 bits as right input (R_i), and produces two outputs, left output (L_{i+1}) and right output (R_{i+1}), each of 32 bits. The left output (L_{i+1}) is just the right input (R_i). The right output (R_{i+1}) is obtained by first applying the DES function (f) on the right input (R_i) and the 48-bit key (K_i) being used in the i-th round, denoted as $f(R_i, K_i)$, and then performing the bitwise XOR of the result of DES function and the left input (L_i). The structure of decryption round in DES is simply the opposite of the encryption round.

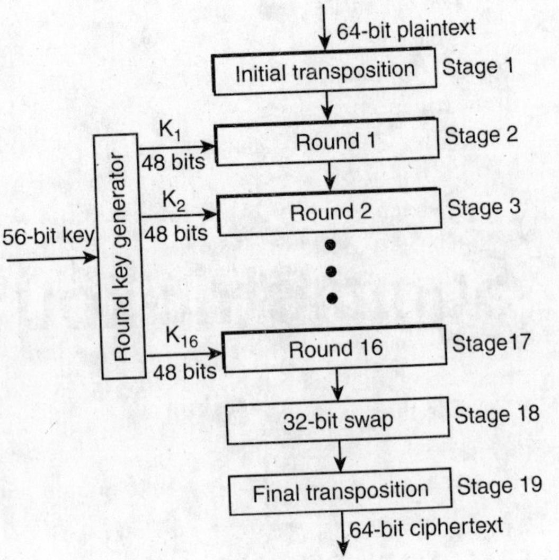

Figure 4.1 General Structure of DES Encryption

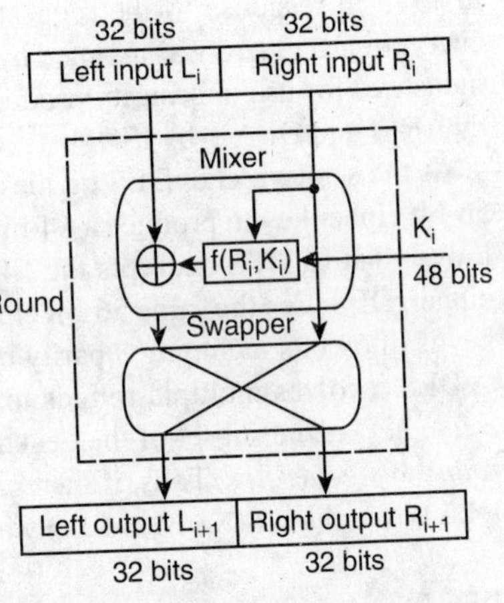

Figure 4.2 Structure of Encryption Round

DES Function

The essence of DES is the DES function, $f(R_i, K_i)$. During each round, this function takes the rightmost 32 bits and applies the 48-bit round key generated for that round on it to produce the 32-bit output. The function comprises four steps (see Figure 4.3), which are described as follows:

1. *Expansion P-box:* The right output (R_i) of 32 bits is initially fed into the expansion *P*-box, which expands it to 48 bits, because the key (K_i) used is of 48 bits. For this, the 32 bits of R_i are divided into eight blocks of 4 bits each. Each 4-bit block is then expanded to 6 bits using a predetermined rule, as explained in the following text.
   a. Copy the input bits 1, 2, 3 and 4 to output bits 2, 3, 4 and 5, respectively.
   b. Copy the input bit 4 of the previous block to output bit 1 of the block under consideration. This step is an exception to the first block.
   c. Copy the input bit 1 of the next block to output bit 6 of the block under consideration. This step is an exception to the last (eighth) block.

   Notice that in case of first block, the input bit 4 of the last block becomes the output bit 1, while in case of last block, the input bit 1 of the first block becomes the output bit 6. The resulting 48 bits are forwarded to the next step.

2. *XOR operation:* A bitwise XOR operation is performed on the 48-bit output obtained from the previous step and 48-bit round key K_i, resulting in 48 bits. These 48 bits are forwarded to the next step.
3. *S-boxes:* The 48-bit output obtained after the XOR operation is broken down into eight groups, with each group consisting of 6 bits. Each group of 6 bits is then fed to one of eight *S*-boxes. Each *S*-box follows a predetermined rule to map six inputs to four outputs and, thus, total 32 bits are obtained from eight *S*-boxes. The rule for substitution in each *S*-box is based on a table consisting of four rows and 16 columns. To perform the substitution in an *S*-box, the input bits 1 and 6 (2 bits) together define the row number, and the input bits 2, 3, 4 and 5 (4 bits) together define the column number. Now, the value at the intersection of the computed row and column number defines the 4 output bits. For example, if the input to an *S*-box is 101011, then the row number is 11 (equivalent to decimal number 3), and the column number is 0101 (equivalent to decimal number 5). Now, if the value at the intersection of third row and fifth column is 6, then the resulting output bits will be 0110.
4. *Straight P-box:* The 32 bits obtained from *S*-boxes are input to a straight *P*-box, which permutes them and produces 32 bits as output. As with the previous operations, the input bits are permuted based on the predetermined rule. For example, the input bit 7 becomes the output bit 2.

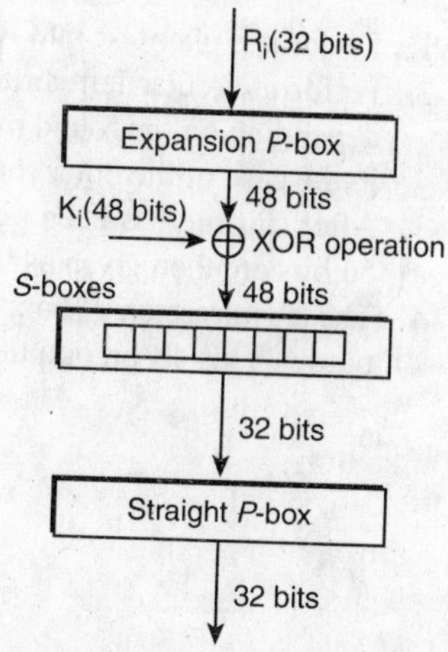

Figure 4.3 DES Function

2. Explain key generation of DES with the help of a block diagram.

Ans.: The generation of keys in DES for each round is done by *round-key generator*. The round-key generator produces sixteen 48-bit keys out of a 56-bit cipher key, one for each round. As in DES, the original key size is 64 bits, including the parity bits; therefore, the parity bits are initially dropped using the parity bit drop process before the actual key generation process starts. The *parity bit drop* process is actually a compression transposition step that drops the parity bits present at every eighth position (8, 16, 24, 32, 40, 48, 56 and 64) in the 64-bit key, generating a 56-bit key. Then the 56 bits of the key are permuted according to a predetermined rule, as shown in Table 4.1. For example, the bit 1 of the original 56-bit key becomes the eighth bit of the new 56-bit key. This 56-bit key is the actual cipher key used for key generation.

Table 4.1 Parity Drop Box Table

57	49	41	33	25	17	09	01
58	50	42	34	26	18	10	02
59	51	43	35	27	19	11	03
60	52	44	36	63	55	47	39
31	23	15	07	62	54	46	38
30	22	14	06	61	53	45	37
29	21	13	05	28	20	12	04

During each round, the round key generator uses the 56-bit cipher key and performs the following steps to generate the key for that round (see Figure 4.4).

1. Divide the plaintext into two halves of 28 bits each.
2. Perform circular left shift operation on each 28-bit half. Shifting is done either by 1 or 2 bits, depending on the round number. In case of rounds 1, 2, 9 and 16, shifting is done by 1 bit, while in the case of the other rounds, shifting is done by 2 bits.
3. After shifting has been performed, both halves are combined again to form a 56-bit part. These 56 bits are then given as input to the compression *P*-box.
4. The compression *P*-box, as its name suggests, compresses the 56-bit input to produce 48-bit output. This 48-bit output generated from the *P*-box is then used as a key for the round.

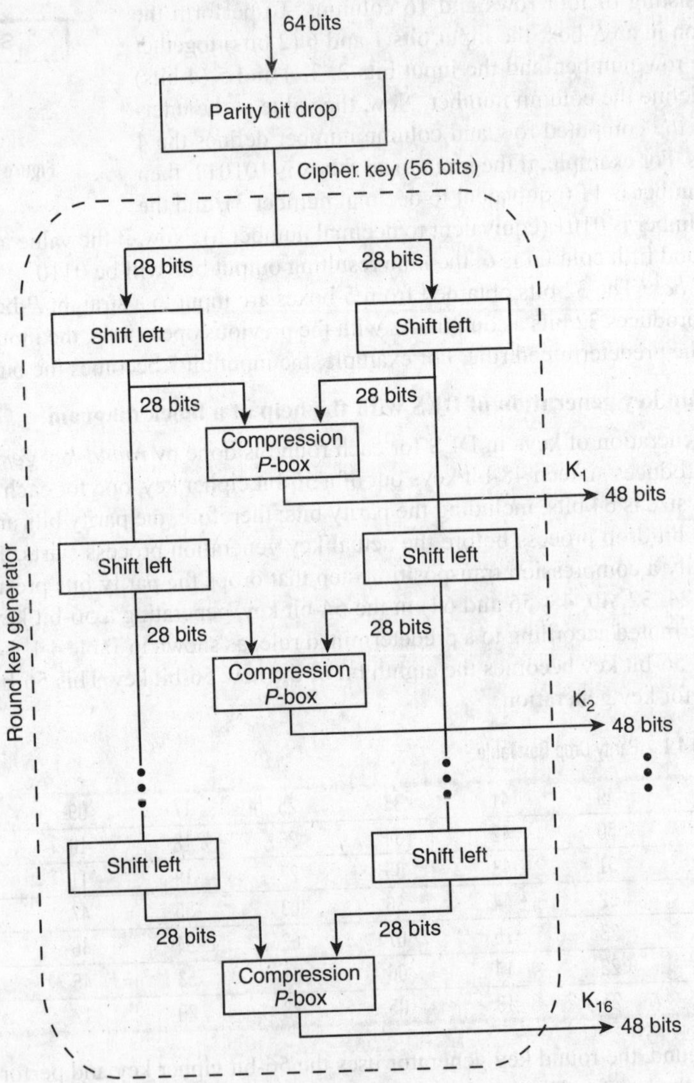

Figure 4.4 Key Generation in DES

3. Discuss the strength of DES.

Ans.: The strength of any cryptographic system is measured by the fact that how resistive it is to an attack. In case of DES, the strength of the system lies in two important aspects: key size and the use of *S*-boxes.

- *Key size:* DES uses 56-bit keys in each round, which means 2^{56} (approximately 7.2 * 10^{16}) number of keys. Therefore, a brute-force attack on DES seems practically impossible. However, if we assume that, to get the correct key, only half of the total keys are needed to be examined, a single computer performing one DES encryption per microsecond would still take more than 1000 years to break the DES.
- *Use of S-boxes:* DES uses eight *S*-boxes (substitution tables) in each round. The internal design of these substitution tables has been kept secret by IBM. Therefore, a suspicion has grown that there may be some weaknesses in the internal design of *S*-boxes that can be exploited by cryptanalysts to break the DES security. Over the years, a number of studies have appeared which suggest that there is a scope of attacking DES through *S*-boxes; however, no one has succeeded till date.

4. Comment on the weaknesses of DES.

Ans.: Although the DES cipher is widely used and is resistant to various attacks, some weaknesses are still found in it. The weaknesses have been found in two aspects of DES, in the cipher design and in the cipher key.

Weakness in the Cipher Design

The DES cipher involves a number of *S*-boxes and *P*-boxes, which suffer from certain problems. Some weaknesses found in *S*-boxes are as follows:

- In fourth *S*-box, the last 3 bits in the output can be obtained in the same way as the first bit in the output by performing complement operation on some of the bits in input.
- In a single round, the same output can be obtained if the bits in only three neighbouring *S*-boxes are changed.
- Two specific chosen inputs when given to the array of eight *S*-boxes can result in the same output.

Some weaknesses found in *P*-boxes are as follows:

- The initial and final permutation stages used in DES do not provide any security benefits.
- In the expansion permutation used within the DES function, the input bits 1 and 4 of each 4-bit series are repeated in the output.

Weakness in the Cipher Key

The cipher key used in DES has got certain shortcomings, which are described as follows:

- *Size of cipher key:* As the cipher key used in DES is of 56 bits, an intruder needs to examine 2^{56} possible keys in order to attempt a brute-force attack. If a computer with a single processor that can process about one million keys per second is used for examining the whole key domain, it will take more than 2000 years to attempt brute-force attack on DES. In 1977, this period of 2000 years reduced to 120 days when 3500 networked computers and the concept of parallel processing were used. The entire key domain was divided into several parts, and each computer had to examine only some parts. Furthermore, a secret society having 42000 members can break the cipher and thus, determine the key in 10 days only. Thus, it can be concluded that the DES with a cipher key of 56 bits is not safe enough for use.

- *Weak keys:* Out of 2^{56} keys, there are four keys that comprise either all 0s, all 1s or half 0s and half 1s. These four keys are referred to as the *weak keys*. When the round keys are created from any of the weak keys, they follow the same pattern as that of the cipher key. For example, a round key created from the weak key containing all 0s or all 1s will also comprise all 0s or 1s, respectively. This is because the cipher key is divided into two equal parts during key generation in DES. Thus, neither substitution nor permutation affects the block containing all 1s or all 0s. The disadvantage of using a weak key lies in the fact that it is the inverse of itself. That is, when a plaintext block is encrypted with a weak key and then the result is further encrypted with the same weak key, we get back the original plaintext block. Exploiting this fact, the intruder can easily attempt to decrypt the intercepted ciphertext using the weak keys. In case the result is the same after two decryptions, it means the intruder has got the key. Therefore, it is recommended that the use of weak keys be avoided.
- *Semi-weak keys:* In 2^{56} keys, there are six pairs of keys that create only two distinct round keys for total 16 rounds, and each key is used in eight rounds. These six key pairs are referred to as *semi-weak keys*. Each pair of semi-weak keys creates the same two round keys; however, they are used in 16 rounds in different order.
- *Possible weak keys:* There are 48 such keys that create only four different round keys, and each of them is repeated four times. These 48 keys are referred to as *possible weak keys*.
- *Key complement:* In 2^{56} keys, half of the keys (that is, 2^{55}) are the complement of the other half keys. That is, if half of the total keys are known, the remaining half can be obtained by simply inverting the bits (1 to 0 or 0 to 1) of the known keys. This proves to be beneficial to the intruder as now he or she has to examine only half of the key domain to attempt a brute-force attack. This is because of the fact that if the complement of plaintext is encrypted using the complement of a key, then a complement of the ciphertext is obtained.
- *Key clustering:* The situation where two or more different keys result in the same ciphertext from the same plaintext is referred to as *key clustering*. In DES, each pair of semi-weak keys is a key cluster.

5. What do you understand by differential and linear cryptanalysis of DES?

Ans.: *Differential cryptanalysis* is a chosen-plaintext attack that was introduced by Eli Biham and Adi Shamir in 1990. The basic idea of this attack is to choose a pair of plaintexts having specific differences and then analysing the corresponding ciphertext pair. The attacker examines how these differences propagate in the ciphertexts as the plaintexts pass through the rounds of DES. Using the differences in the ciphertexts, the attacker determines the probability of different possible keys and, eventually, as ciphertexts are analysed progressively, the actual cipher key emerges. The designers of DES were aware of chosen-plaintext attacks; therefore, they used *S*-boxes and 16 rounds to encrypt the plaintext in DES. Doing so makes DES invulnerable to differential cryptanalysis as breaking a DES message by differential analysis will need either 2^{47} chosen plaintexts or 2^{55} known plaintexts. Although differential cryptanalysis attacks are much powerful than brute-force attacks, finding 2^{47} chosen plaintexts or 2^{55} known plaintexts is not practically possible. Moreover, if we increase the number of rounds in DES to 20, then a differential cryptanalysis attack needs 2^{64} chosen plaintexts, which is practically impossible, because DES can only have 2^{64} possible plaintexts.

The resultant data blocks R_1, R_2, R_3 and R_4 in each round are passed to the next round. Note that the eighth round does not involve the last step (step 15); that is, it does not perform the swapping of blocks R_2 and R_3. After performing all the eight rounds, the final data blocks, R_1, R_2, R_3 and R_4, of 16 bits each are passed to the next stage – that is, output transformation.

Output Transformation

This stage applies four keys, K_{49} to K_{52}, on the input data blocks, R_1, R_2, R_3 and R_4, and produces the four ciphertext blocks, C_1, C_2, C_3 and C_4, by performing the following steps:

1. Multiply R_1 and K_{49} to obtain C_1.
2. Multiply R_2 and K_{50} to obtain C_2.
3. Multiply R_3 and K_{51} to obtain C_3.
4. Multiply R_4 and K_{52} to obtain C_4.

Finally, the four ciphertext blocks (C_1, C_2, C_3 and C_4) are combined to form a 64-bit ciphertext block.

Decryption

The decryption process of IDEA is the same as that of the encryption process; however, the sub-keys are used in the reverse order from that of encryption. The sub-keys used for decryption are the inverse of the sub-keys used for encryption.

Strength of IDEA

The IDEA algorithm is resistant to all known cryptanalysis attacks. It uses a 128-bit-long key. Therefore, to attempt a cryptanalysis attack on IDEA, the attacker needs to perform 2^{128} encryption operations, which is practically infeasible.

10. Explain the sub-key generation in the IDEA algorithm.

Ans.: As each round in the IDEA algorithm uses six sub-keys of 16-bit each and the output transformation step also needs four sub-keys, thus, a total of 52 16-bit sub-keys are required from the key length of 128 bits. For this, a sub-key generation process is used, which generates the sub-keys as follows:

- In the first round, six sub-keys of 16 bits each, that is, 96 bits, are required. Therefore, the first 96 bits of 128-bit key (say, K) are used for the first round. The rest of the key bits (97–128) remain unused and, thus, are kept for the second round.
- The second round also requires six sub-keys of 16 bits each; that is, a total of 96 bits. However, we have only 32 unused bits of the key K and, therefore, we need 64 bits more. To generate the rest of the bits, the IDEA algorithm uses the *key shifting* technique. In this technique, the original 128-bit key K is shifted left circularly by 25 bits. After shifting, the 26-th bit of the original key K becomes the first bit of the new key (say, K'), and the 25-th bit of key K becomes the 128-th bit of key K'. Now, the bits 1 to 64 of key K' and the unused 32 bits (97–128) of key K are used to form six 16-bit sub-keys for the second round.
- In the third round, we have 64 unused bits of key K' generated in the second round, and 32 bits are still required. Thus, the key shifting technique is again applied, and the key K' is left shifted by 25 bits. This process continues to obtain 96 bits in each round.

- The output transformation stage also needs four sub-keys of 16 bits each. Notice that after the eighth round, the key gets exhausted. Thus, the key is left shifted by 25 bits, and the bits 1 to 64 of the newly created key are used to generate four sub-keys (K_{49} to K_{52}) for this stage.

11. Explain Advanced Encryption Standard.

Ans.: The *Advanced Encryption Standard* (AES) is the latest and, potentially, the most secure encryption method published by NIST. It is a symmetric-key block cipher that was designed to be a significant improvement over DES/3-DES. In 1990s, the US government decided to standardize the cryptographic algorithm and to name it as AES. In response to this, a lot of proposals were submitted. After long debates, in 2000, the US government chose one of the proposals, the *Rijndael algorithm*, as AES. This algorithm is named on the surnames of the two Belgian researchers Vincent Rijmen and John Daemen. Finally, in 2001, AES was published as Federal Information Processing Standard (FIPS) 197 by NIST.

General Design of AES

AES is a non-Feistel cipher that operates on a data block of 128 bits (16 bytes) and comprises several rounds for encryption and decryption. It is available in three versions, depending on the key size and the number of rounds used. These versions include *AES-128* with key size 128 bits and 10 rounds, *AES-192* with key size 192 bits and 12 rounds and *AES-256* with key size 256 bits and 14 rounds. Despite the fact that each version uses a different key size, the round keys used in each version are always 128 bits long, which is the same size as that of the plaintext or ciphertext block. In AES, the round keys are generated using the key-expansion algorithm (explained in the next question), and the number of round keys generated is always equal to the number of rounds plus one. Figure 4.7 shows the general design for AES encryption algorithm (referred to as the *AES cipher*); the design of AES decryption algorithm (referred to as the *AES inverse cipher*) is also similar, except that the round keys are used in the reverse order from that of encryption.

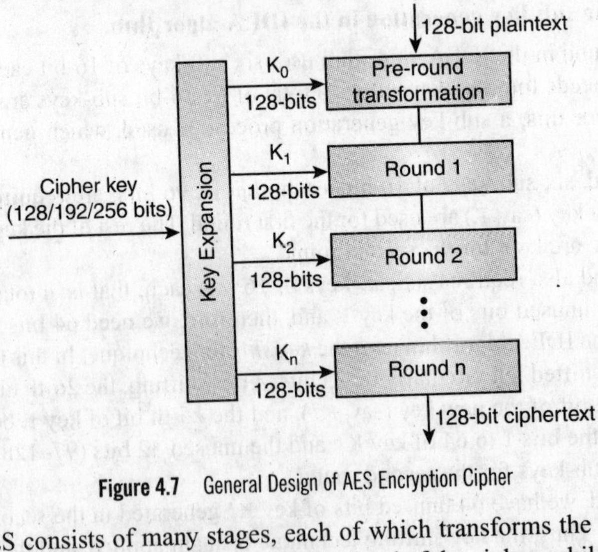

Figure 4.7 General Design of AES Encryption Cipher

Each round in AES consists of many stages, each of which transforms the 16-byte data block. In AES, the term 'data block' is used at the beginning and end of the cipher, while before and after each stage, the term 'state' is used to refer to a data block. A *state*, like a data block, is also 16-bytes long and contains the data before and after the transformation. Usually, a 16-byte state (say, S) is organized as a 4×4 bytes matrix, and each element of the matrix is referred to as $S_{i,j}$ ($0 \leq i \leq 3$ and $0 \leq j \leq 3$), where i and j denote the row number and column number, respectively.

Structure of Encryption Round

During encryption, each round, excluding the last one, involves four transformations, namely: *Substitute Bytes*, *Shift Rows*, *Mix Columns* and *Add Round Key* (see Figure 4.8). Each transformation accepts a state, changes it and creates a new state that is given as input to the next transformation or the next round. The last round in AES comprises only three transformations, except the Mix Columns transformation. Moreover, one Add Round Key transformation is applied before the first round (mentioned as pre-round transformation in Figure 4.7). Each transformation in AES is invertible in nature and, during decryption, the inverse of these transformations, namely, *Inverse Substitute Bytes*, *Inverse Shift Rows*, *Inverse Mix Columns* and *Add Round Key* (which is self-invertible), are used. Figure 4.8 shows the general structure of an encryption round in AES.

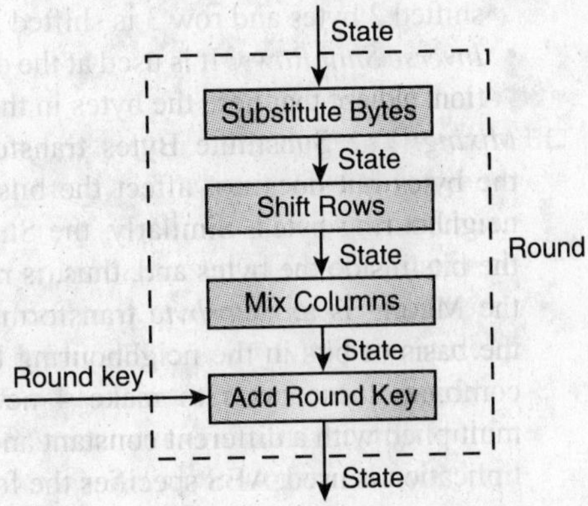

Figure 4.8 General Structure of an Encryption Round

Transformations

All the transformations performed during encryption and decryption fall under four broad categories that include *substitution*, *permutation*, *mixing* and *key adding*. These transformations are described as follows:

- *Substitution:* As with DES, AES also performs the substitution of bytes, but using a different mechanism. In AES, substitution is performed for all bytes, and that too, using only one table. This implies that if 2 bytes are the same then their transformations are also same, which is contrastive to DES where eight different *S*-boxes perform transformations. Moreover, the bytes are substituted either with the help of a transformation table or by performing the mathematical calculations in $GF(2^8)$ field. The two invertible transformations that fall under this category are as follows:
  - *Substitute Bytes:* It is the first transformation of a round used during encryption. The input to this transformation is a state organized as a 4×4 matrix of bytes. The bytes in the matrix are substituted one at a time. Thus, there are 16 distinct byte-to-byte transformations. To substitute the bytes using a transformation table, each byte is treated as two hexadecimal digits, where the first digit (left one) specifies the row and the second digit (right one) specifies the column of the substitution table. The value (two hexadecimal digits) at the intersection of the row and the column in the transformation table is the new byte with which the given byte is to be replaced.

- *Inverse Substitute Bytes:* It is used at the decryption side and is the inverse of the Substitute Bytes transformation.

- *Permutation:* AES also permutes the bytes. It performs a byte-level permutation (unlike DES, which works on the bit level), such that the order of bits in each byte does not change in the resultant bytes. The two invertible transformations that fall under this category are as follows:
  - *Shift Rows:* It is used at the encryption side. In this transformation, the bytes in the rows of the input state matrix are shifted to the left, and the number of bytes to be shifted depends on the row number. For example, the row 0 is not shifted at all, the row 1 is shifted 1 byte, row 2 is shifted 2 bytes and row 3 is shifted 3 bytes.
  - *Inverse Shift Rows:* It is used at the decryption side and is similar to the Shift Rows transformation, except that here the bytes in the rows are shifted to the right.
- *Mixing:* The Substitute Bytes transformation is an *intrabyte* transformation as it transforms the bytes but does not affect the bits inside the bytes. It also does not take into account the neighbouring bytes. Similarly, the Shift Rows transformation permutes only the bytes but not the bits inside the bytes and, thus, is referred to as a *byte-exchange* transformation. In contrast, the Mixing is an *interbyte* transformation in which the bits inside the bytes are changed on the basis of bits in the neighbouring bytes. Mixing transformation takes 4 bytes at a time and combines these bytes to make 4 new bytes. In the combination process, each byte is first multiplied with a different constant and, then, all the 4 bytes are mixed. For mixing, matrix multiplication is used. AES specifies the following two invertible transformations that fall under this category:
  - *Mix Columns:* It is used at the encryption side. This is a column-level transformation that takes one column of input state matrix at a time and transforms it to a new column. For transforming the columns, a constant square matrix is used. The square matrix is multiplied by each column of state matrix resulting into a column. Notice that the bytes multiplication operation is performed in $GF(2^8)$ field and the bytes addition operation is performed by simply XORing the bits within bytes.
  - *Inverse Mix Columns:* It is used at the decryption side and is similar to Mix Columns transformation except that it uses the inverse of the constant square matrix used in Mix Columns transformation.
- *Key adding:* This is the only transformation that makes use of the round key (generated from cipher key) and, thus, is considered an important transformation. To perform key adding transformation, the 128-bit round key is considered as four 32-bit words, and further, each 32-bit word is treated as a column matrix. A self-invertible transformation that falls under this category is as follows:
  - *Add Round Key:* Like Mix Columns transformation, it also operates on one column at a time; however, it uses matrix addition operation rather than matrix multiplication. Each column of the state matrix is XORed with the corresponding key word (column matrix) to produce the new column. This transformation is used in both encryption and decryption.

12. What do you mean by key expansion in AES? Explain the key expansion process in AES-128.

Ans.: *Key expansion* is a process used in AES to generate the round keys from the given cipher key. In AES, the number of round keys generated by this process is always one greater than the number of rounds. That is, if there are n rounds, the key expansion generates (n+1) keys (say, K_0 to K_n), out of which the first round key K_0 is used in the Add Round Key transformation before the first round, and the remaining keys (K_1 to K_n) are used in the corresponding rounds. In addition, the key expansion generates each round key word-by-word, where each word is an array of 4 bytes. Thus, the total number of words created in n rounds is equal to 4(n+1), denoted as $d_0, d_1, \ldots, d_{4(n+1)-1}$.

Key Expansion in AES-128

In AES-128, there are 10 rounds, and the cipher key is 128 bits long. Therefore, the number of keys generated is 11 (K_0 to K_{10}), and the number of words created is 44 (d_0 to d_{43}). The cipher key of 128 bits is treated as an array of 16 bytes (say, r_0 to r_{15}) – that is, four 32-bit words. Before we describe the steps involved in key expansion, we need to know the two routines, `RotWord()` and `SubWord()`, as well as round constant `RCon`, which are used in the process.

- `RotWord()`: The `RotWord` (which stands for *rotate word*) routine performs a similar function as that of the Shift Rows transformation, with the exception that it is applied to only one row. It takes a 4-byte word, and shifts each byte of the word to the left with wrapping.
- `SubWord()`: The `SubWord` (which stands for *substitute word*) routine performs a similar function as that of the Substitute Bytes transformation, with the exception that it is applied to only 4 bytes (that is, a single word). It takes each byte of a 4-byte word and substitutes it with another byte with the help of transformation table.
- `RCon`: `RCon` (which stands for *round constants*) is a 4-byte value where the leftmost byte is non-zero and the rightmost 3 bytes are always zero. As the name implies, this value is fixed for each round. Table 4.2 lists the round constants for 10 rounds of AES-128.

Table 4.2 Round Constants for AES-128

Round	RCon
1	$(01\ 00\ 00\ 00\ 00)_{16}$
2	$(02\ 00\ 00\ 00\ 00)_{16}$
3	$(04\ 00\ 00\ 00\ 00)_{16}$
4	$(08\ 00\ 00\ 00\ 00)_{16}$
5	$(10\ 00\ 00\ 00\ 00)_{16}$
6	$(20\ 00\ 00\ 00\ 00)_{16}$
7	$(40\ 00\ 00\ 00\ 00)_{16}$
8	$(80\ 00\ 00\ 00\ 00)_{16}$
9	$(1B\ 00\ 00\ 00\ 00)_{16}$
10	$(36\ 00\ 00\ 00\ 00)_{16}$

The steps involved in creating 44 words (d_0 to d_{43}) from the original cipher key of 16 bytes (r_0 to r_{15}) are as follows (see Figure 4.9):

1. The 16 bytes of the cipher key (that is, r_0 to r_{15}) form the first four words d_0, d_1, d_2 and d_3. That is, $d_0 := r_0r_1r_2r_3$, $d_1 := r_4r_5r_6r_7$, $d_2 := r_8r_9r_{10}r_{11}$ and $d_3 := r_{12}r_{13}r_{14}r_{15}$.

2. Create the remaining 40 words using the following process.

```
for (i = 4 to 43) do
{
  if (i mod 4) = 0 then
  {
    s: = SubWord(RotWord(d_{i-1}))
    t_i: = s ⊕ RCon_{i/4}
    d_i: = t_i ⊕ d_{i-4}
  }
  else
    d_i: = d_{i-1} ⊕ d_{i-4}
}
```

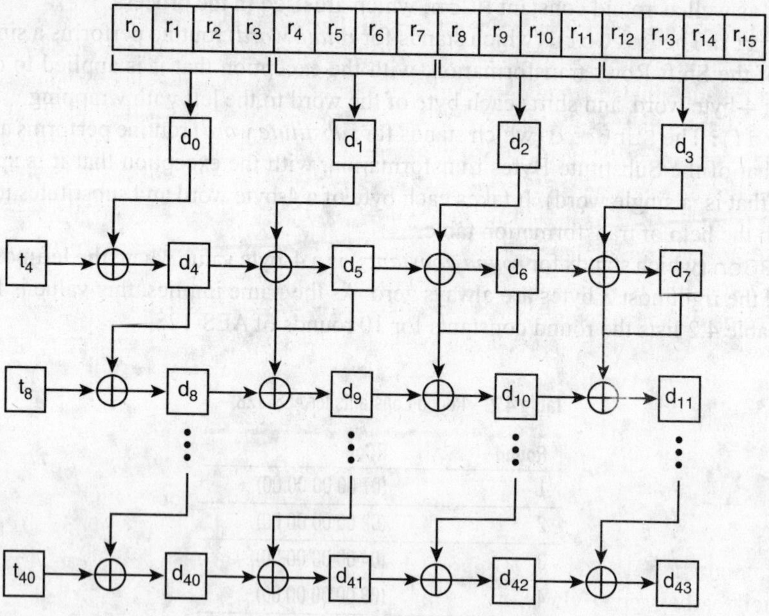

Figure 4.9 Key Expansion in AES-128

13. How is the key expansion in AES-192 and AES-256 different from that in AES-128?

Ans.: AES-192 and AES-256 employ a similar key expansion as that of AES-128, however, with a few differences. In AES-192, the cipher key is 192 bits long and is treated as an array of 24 bytes (r_0 to r_{23}), that is, six 32-bit words. As there are 12 rounds, the key expansion creates 52 words of round key (d_0 to d_{51}), and these words are generated in groups of six. The differences between key expansion in AES-192 and AES-128 are as follows:

1. The 24 bytes of cipher key (that is, r_0 to r_{23}) form the first six words (d_0 to d_5) of the round key.
2. For the remaining words (d_i, i = 6 to 51), if (i mod 6) = 0 then $d_i := t_i \oplus d_{i-6}$; else, $d_i := d_{i-1} \oplus d_{i-6}$.

On the other hand, in AES-256, the cipher key is 256 bits long and is treated as an array of 32 bytes (r_0 to r_{31}), that is, eight 32-bit words. As there are 14 rounds, the key expansion creates 60 words of round key (d_0 to d_{59}) and these words are generated in the groups of eight. The differences between key expansion process in AES-256 and AES-128 are as follows:

1. The 32 bytes of the cipher key (that is, r_0 to r_{31}) form the first eight words (d_0 to d_7) of the round key.
2. For the remaining words (d_i, i = 8 to 59)
   - if(i mod 8) = 0 then $d_i := t_i \oplus d_{i-8}$; else, $d_i := d_{i-1} \oplus d_{i-8}$.
   - if(i mod 4) = 0, but (i mod 8) ≠ 0, then $d_i :=$ SubWord(d_{i-1}) $\oplus d_{i-8}$.

14. What do you mean by mode of operation in block ciphers? Explain block cipher modes of operation.

Ans.: Modern block ciphers such as DES and AES perform symmetric-key encipherment, thus providing data security. Both DES and AES have been devised to encipher/decipher fixed-size blocks of 64 and 128 bits, respectively. However, in real-life applications, the data to be enciphered is generally of variable size. Thus, some technique is needed to enhance the strength of block ciphers such as DES and AES and to adapt them to such applications so that data of any size can be enciphered. Such technique is referred to as the *mode of operation*. There are four commonly used block cipher modes of operations that have been suggested by NIST. These modes are discussed in the following sections.

Electronic Code Book (ECB) Mode

This is the simplest mode of operation in which the entire plaintext message is divided into m blocks (P_1, P_2,…, P_m), with each block containing n (usually n = 64) bits. While breaking the message, if the last block contains less than n bits, padding is used to make it equal to the other blocks.

During encryption, one n-bit block of plaintext (say, P_i) is taken at a time and encrypted using a key K to produce the corresponding n-bit ciphertext block (say, C_i). Each block is encrypted independently of the other blocks, and the same key (say, K) is used for encrypting all the blocks. During decryption also, one block is decrypted at a time, and the same key K is used for decrypting the blocks. Figure 4.10 shows the encryption and decryption processes in the ECB mode.

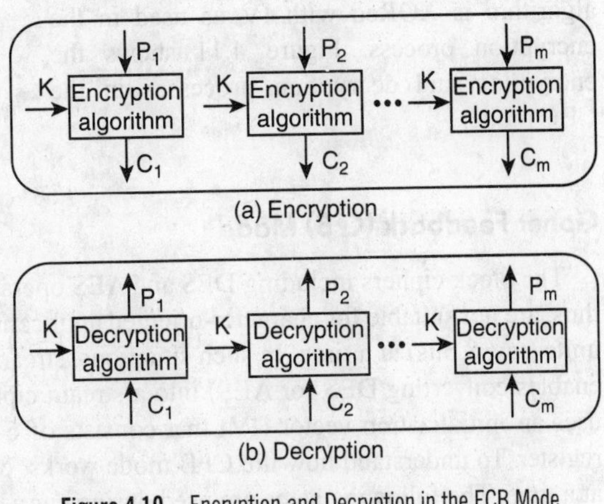

Figure 4.10 Encryption and Decryption in the ECB Mode

In the ECB mode, since all blocks are encrypted independent of each other, a bit error in one block during transmission will not affect any other block; however, it may cause errors in many bits within the same block. In addition, as the same key is used for encrypting all the blocks, if an n-bit block repeats in the plaintext message, the corresponding ciphertext block also repeats in the ciphertext. That is, two same plaintext blocks always result in the same ciphertext blocks. This makes the ECB mode suitable for sending only short messages, such as an encryption key, for example. For long messages, this mode may not be secure, as there are more chances of repetition in long messages.

Cipher Block Chaining (CBC) Mode

This mode of operation overcomes the problem of the ECB mode by ensuring that the same plaintext blocks will not result in the same ciphertext blocks. For this, in the CBC mode, a plaintext block is encrypted based on the previous ciphertext block. In other words, each ciphertext block depends on the corresponding current plaintext block, as well as on all the previous plaintext blocks. Like the ECB mode, the same key (say, K) is used for encrypting all the blocks.

During encryption, each plaintext block (except the first one) is first XORed with the previous ciphertext block, and then encrypted. As there is no ciphertext block prior to the first block, a data block called *initialization vector* (IV) is used for this. The value of this vector is randomly generated and is agreed upon by the sender and the receiver. During decryption, each ciphertext block is first decrypted using the same key (K) that was used for encryption, and then the decrypted result is XORed with the previous ciphertext block to obtain the corresponding plaintext block. In case of the first ciphertext block, the output of the decryption algorithm is XORed with IV, as used in the encryption process. Figure 4.11 shows the encryption and decryption processes in the CBC mode.

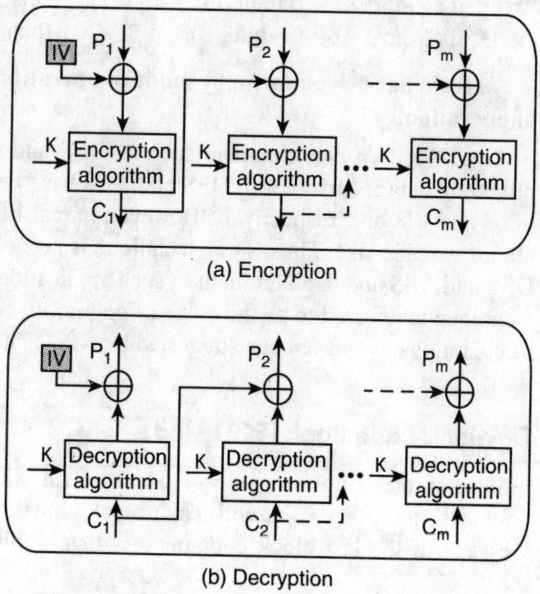

Figure 4.11 Encryption and Decryption in the CBC Mode

Cipher Feedback (CFB) Mode

The block ciphers including DES and AES operate on 64 and 128 blocks of data, respectively, and thus, are not suitable for character-oriented applications where we need to encrypt/decrypt the smaller units (say, 8 bits) at a time. In such situations, stream ciphers prove useful. The CFB is the mode that enables converting DES (or AES) into a stream cipher. As with the CBC mode, the CFB mode also uses an initialization vector (IV) that consists of 64 bits. The contents of IV are stored in the shift register. To understand how the CFB mode works, consider that d bits are to be encrypted/decrypted at a time. The following steps are used during encryption (see Figure 4.12):

1. Encrypt IV, which is stored in the shift register using the block cipher such as DES with key K, to produce an encrypted IV.
2. Take the r leftmost bits of encrypted IV and XOR them with r bits of the plaintext to be encrypted, thus producing an r-bit ciphertext (say, C). Send the ciphertext C to the receiver.
3. Shift the contents of IV stored in the shift register left by r positions, and fill the rightmost r positions with r bits of C.
4. Repeat steps 1 to 3 until the whole plaintext message is encrypted.

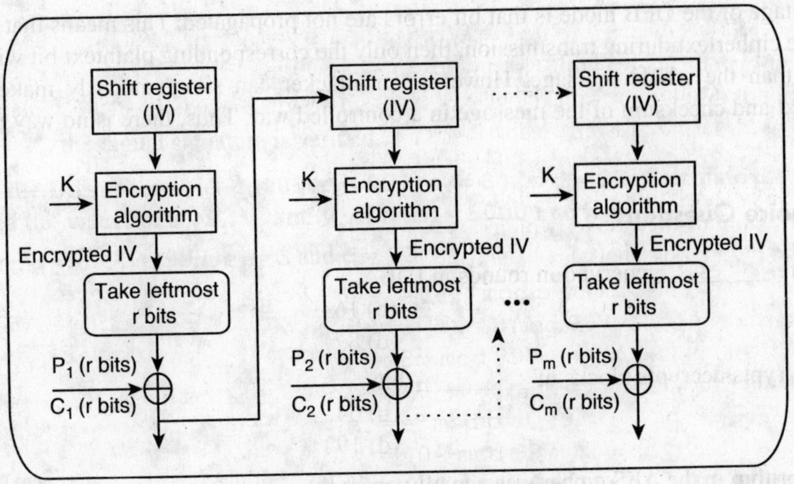

Figure 4.12 Encryption in the CFB Mode

During decryption, the same process is used, except that now the XOR operation is performed on the received ciphertext and the output of encryption algorithm to produce the plaintext. It should be noted that the encryption algorithm, and not the decryption algorithm, is used during decryption also.

Output Feedback (OFB) Mode

This mode is similar to the CFB mode, except that in this mode, instead of feeding ciphertext as an input to the shift register in the next stage of the encryption process, the output of IV encryption (that is, encrypted IV) is fed into the shift register. Thus, the ciphertext does not take any part in the encryption process. Figure 4.13 shows the encryption process in the OFB mode.

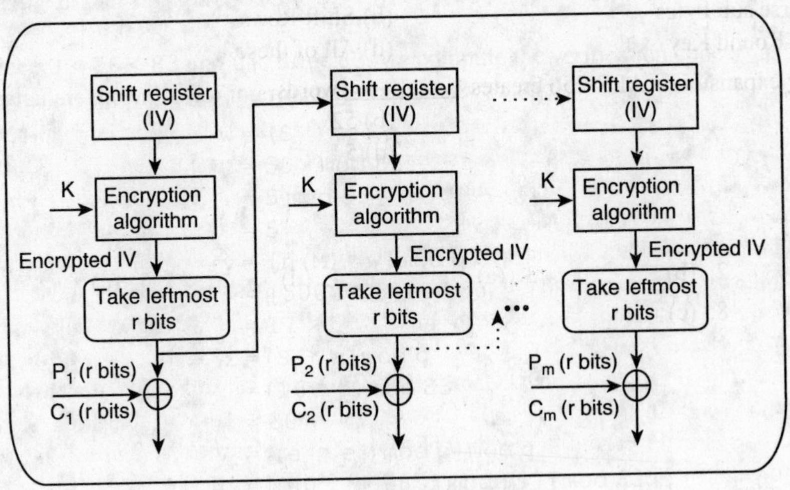

Figure 4.13 Encryption in the OFB Mode

An advantage of the OFB mode is that bit errors are not propagated. This means that if a bit error occurs in the ciphertext during transmission, then only the corresponding plaintext bit will be erroneous, rather than the whole message. However, an attacker can simultaneously make changes to the ciphertext and checksum of the message in a controlled way. Thus, there is no way to detect this change.

Multiple-choice Questions

1. There are ________ encryption rounds in IDEA.
   (a) 5 (b) 16
   (c) 10 (d) 8
2. DES encrypts/decrypts blocks of ________ bits.
   (a) 128 (b) 64
   (c) 56 (d) 192
3. The algorithm in the AES cipher was actually given by ________.
   (a) Rijndael (b) IDEA
   (c) Blowfish (d) None of these
4. Which of the following modes of operations does not make use of an initialization vector?
   (a) Cipher block chaining (b) Output feedback
   (c) Cipher feedback (d) Electronic codebook
5. Each round in DES uses ________ *S*-boxes.
   (a) Five (b) Ten
   (c) Eight (d) Six
6. Which of the following services is based on the IDEA algorithm?
   (a) PGP (b) S/MIME
   (c) SET (d) SSL
7. Which of the following transformations belong to permutation?
   (a) Inverse sub-bytes (b) Shift Rows
   (c) Add Round Key (d) All of these
8. The key expansion in AES-256 creates ________ words.
   (a) 44 (b) 52
   (c) 60 (d) 54

Answers

1. (d) 2. (b) 3. (a) 4. (d) 5. (c) 6. (a)
7. (b) 8. (c)

5

Number Theory

1. What are prime numbers and relatively prime numbers?

Ans.: Any positive integer greater than 1 is a *prime number* if and only if it is divisible by only two integers, 1 and itself. For example, the numbers 2, 3, 5, 7, 11, 13, 17 and 19 are all prime numbers, whereas the numbers 4, 6, 8 and 10 are composite (means not prime), because they have more than two divisors.

Two positive integers a and b are said to be *relatively prime*, or *co-prime*, if gcd(a, b)=1. In other words, two numbers are said to be relatively prime if they have no common factors except the integer 1. For example, the integers 14 and 15 are relatively prime; however, the integers 14 and 16 are not relatively prime because they have a common factor other than the integer 1. Note that the integer 1 is relatively prime with any integer. Also, if n is a prime number, all integers ranging from 1 to n−1 are relatively prime to n.

2. State and prove Fermat's theorem.

Ans.: *Fermat's theorem*, also called *Fermat's little theorem*, plays an important role in public-key cryptography. The theorem states that if p is a prime number and x is a positive integer not divisible by p, then:

$$x^{p-1} \equiv 1 \pmod{p}$$

In other words, we can say that:

$$x^{p-1} \bmod p = 1$$

Proof

Consider a set of integers $Z_p=\{1, 2, ..., p-1\}$ where each element of Z_p is relatively prime to p.

If all elements of Z_p are multiplied by x, and the result is mapped to Z_p using modular arithmetic, we get another set (say, S), as shown here:

$$S = \{x \bmod p, 2x \bmod p, ..., (p-1)x \bmod p\}$$

As x is not divisible by p, none of the elements of S is zero. Also, no two elements of S are equal. Thus, we can say that the set S contains the elements of Z_p, that is, {1, 2, ..., p-1} in some order. On multiplying the elements in both the sets and taking the result modulo p, we get:

$$[x*2x*...*(p-1)x] \equiv [1*2*...*(p-1)] (\text{mod } p)$$
$$\Rightarrow [1*2*...*(p-1)]*x^{p-1} \equiv [1*2*...*(p-1)] (\text{mod } p)$$
$$\Rightarrow (p-1)!*x^{p-1} \equiv (p-1)! \ (\text{mod } p) \quad (1)$$

As p and (p-1) are relatively prime, the term (p-1)! can be cancelled out from both sides. Thus, equation (1) becomes:

$$x^{p-1} \equiv 1 \ (\text{mod } p)$$

Hence, proved.

There is another version of Fermat's theorem which states that, if p is a prime number and x is a positive integer, then:

$$x^p \equiv x \ (\text{mod } p)$$

3. Explain Euler's totient function.

Ans.: *Euler's totient function*, also called *Euler's phi function* [denoted as $\phi(n)$], has an important role in cryptography. The value of this function is the number of positive integers that are smaller than n and relatively prime to n. The set of these numbers is represented by Z_n.

A set of rules is to be followed while calculating the value of $\phi(n)$ in the set Z_n. These rules are as follows:

Rule 1: $\phi(1) = 1$
Rule 2: $\phi(p) = p-1$, if p is a prime number
Rule 3: $\phi(m * n) = \phi(m) * \phi(n)$, if m and n are relatively prime
Rule 4: $\phi(p^e) = p^e - p^{e-1}$, if p is prime

To compute $\phi(n)$, suppose that we have two prime numbers p and q, such that $p \neq q$ and $n = pq$. Thus, we can write:

$$\phi(n) = \phi(pq)$$
$$\Rightarrow \phi(p) * \phi(q) \text{ [using } \textit{Rule 3}\text{]}$$
$$\Rightarrow (p-1) * (q-1) \text{ [using } \textit{Rule 2}\text{]}$$

For example, for n = 21

$$\phi(21) = \phi(3 * 7)$$
$$\Rightarrow \phi(3) * \phi(7)$$
$$\Rightarrow (3-1) * (7-1)$$
$$\Rightarrow 2 * 6 = 12$$

From the preceding example, it is clear that there are 12 integers that are smaller than the number 21 and relatively prime to 21.

4. State and prove Euler's theorem with the help of an example.

Ans.: *Euler's theorem* is also known as *Fermat-Euler theorem* or *Euler's totient theorem*. This theorem has two forms. The first form of Euler's theorem states that for every positive integer x that is relatively prime to n,

$$x^{\phi(n)} \equiv 1 \ (\text{mod } n)$$

Proof

If n is a prime number, then $\phi(n) = n-1$. Thus, the preceding equation becomes $x^{n-1} \equiv 1 \pmod{n}$, which is true by the Fermat's theorem, discussed in **Question 2**. Now, consider the case when n is not prime.

Let us consider a set $R = \{a_1, a_2, \ldots, a_{\varphi(n)}\}$, where each a_i is less than n and relatively prime to n. Multiplying each element of the set R by x and taking the result mod n, we get another set S, as shown here:

$$S = \{(xa_1 \bmod n), (xa_2 \bmod n), \ldots, (xa_{\phi(n)} \bmod n)\}$$

The set S is a permutation of R, because of the following reasons:

- As a_i and x are relatively prime to n, xa_i must also be relatively prime to n. Thus, all the elements of S are positive integers that are less than n and relatively prime to n.
- The set S does not contain any duplicate elements. That is, if $xa_i \bmod n = xa_j \bmod n$, then $a_i = a_j$.

Therefore, we can write that:

$$\prod_{i=1}^{\phi(n)} (xa_i \bmod n) = \prod_{i=1}^{\phi(n)} a_i$$

$$\Rightarrow \prod_{i=1}^{\phi(n)} xa_i \equiv \prod_{i=1}^{\phi(n)} a_i \pmod{n}$$

$$\Rightarrow x^{\phi(n)} * \prod_{i=1}^{\phi(n)} a_i \equiv \prod_{i=1}^{\phi(n)} a_i \pmod{n}$$

$$\Rightarrow x^{\phi(n)} \equiv 1 \bmod n$$

Hence, proved.

The alternative form of Euler's theorem states that:

$$x^{\phi(n)+1} \equiv x \bmod n$$

Unlike the first form, this form does not require x be relatively prime to n.

5. What is primality testing? What are its categories?

Ans.: In cryptographic algorithms, we often need to create large prime numbers. The selection of such numbers is a very challenging task. Thus, an algorithm is needed that can efficiently check whether a given large number is prime or composite. That is, we need an algorithm that can efficiently perform primality test on numbers. The algorithms for checking the primality are divided into two categories: *deterministic* and *probabilistic*.

- *Deterministic algorithms:* As the name suggests, these algorithms determine whether a given number is prime or not. They accept a number (say, p) as input and output the result, either that p is prime or that p is composite. There are two types of deterministic algorithms, which are as follows:
  - *Basic algorithm:* A simple way to check whether a number p is prime or not is to divide p by all values m (from 2 to p−1) and check whether p is fully divisible by any value of m. If so, then p is composite; else, it is prime.

- *Divisibility algorithm:* In this algorithm, instead of testing up to p−1, testing up to only $\sqrt{p}$ is sufficient. The reason behind this is that if p is composite, then it can be factored into two values, and at least one of the values must be less than or equal to $\sqrt{p}$. Thus, if the number p is divisible by any of the prime numbers less than $\sqrt{p}$, then it is composite.

❑ *Probabilistic algorithms:* As the name suggests, these tests are based on the probability theory and are used to check the probability of a number being prime. These algorithms are also referred to as *randomized algorithms*. They accept an integer p and output the probability of p being prime. There are two types of tests based on the probability theory.

- *Fermat's primality test:* This is a probabilistic test that checks whether a number is prime or not. We check the probability of the Fermat's little theorem to be true or false. As we know that the theorem states that if p is prime and x is relatively prime to p such that $1 < x < p \in Z_p$, then:

$$x^{p-1} \equiv 1 \pmod{p}$$

To test whether p is prime or not, we pick a random number x from Z_p and check whether equality holds. If equality does not hold, then p is composite, whereas if equality holds for many values of x, then p is said to be *probably prime* or *pseudoprime*. Usually, it is not possible to check the equality for all values of x. In case we pick such a value of x for which the equality holds, but p is composite, then x is known as a *Fermat liar*. In contrast, if we do pick a value for x such that the equality fails and p is also composite, then x is known as *Fermat witness* for the compositeness of p.

- *Miller-Rabin test:* It is also a probabilistic test to check whether a number taken at random is prime or not. This test returns the result as *composite* if p is not prime, or as *inconclusive* if p may or may not be a prime number. We check the probability of the number being *composite* or *inconclusive* with the help of an algorithm given by Miller and Rabin.

6. Give the Miller-Rabin algorithm for testing primality.

Ans.: The *Miller-Rabin algorithm* (also known as the *Rabin-Miller test*) is used to test a large number for primality. It is a polynomial-time algorithm with a run-time complexity of $O((\log n)^3)$.

As we know, a positive odd integer p can be written in the power of 2 as follows:

$$p-1 = 2^k q$$

Where, q is an odd number that is obtained by dividing (p−1) by 2, and k is the number of times and k > 0.

For example, let p = 37. Then, p−1 = 36, which can be written as $36 = 2^2 * 9$. Here, 9 is obtained when 36 is divided twice by 2.

In Miller-Rabin algorithm, we take into account two basic properties of prime numbers, which are as follows.

1. If p is a prime number and x is a positive integer $(1 < x < p)$, then $x^2 \bmod p = 1$ if and only if $x \bmod p = 1$ or $x \bmod p = -1$. As in modular arithmetic, $-1 \bmod p = (p-1)$; therefore, $x \bmod p = -1$ means $x \bmod p = (p-1)$. As we know, $(x \bmod p) * (x \bmod p) = x^2 \bmod p$. Hence, whether $x \bmod p = 1$ or $x \bmod p = -1$, we always get $x^2 \bmod p = 1$.
2. If p is a prime number greater than 2, we can say that $p-1 = 2^k q$ where k > 0 and q is odd, then any one of the following conditions is true:
   - $x^q \bmod p = 1$ or $x^q \equiv 1 \pmod{p}$

- One of the numbers from $(x^q, x^{2q}, x^{4q}, \ldots, x^{2^{(k-1)}q}, x^{2^k q})$ is congruent to -1 modulo p. This implies that there is some j in the range $(1 \le j \le k)$ such that:

$$x^{2^{(j-1)}q} \bmod p = -1 \quad \text{or} \quad x^{2^{(j-1)}q} \bmod p = p-1.$$

After considering these two properties, we can come to the conclusion that a number p can be prime if either the first element of the list $(x^q, x^{2q}, x^{4q}, \ldots, x^{2^{(k-1)}q}, x^{2^k q})$ modulo p is equal to 1 or if some element in this list (say, $x^{2^{(j-1)}q}$) modulo p is equal to $p-1$. If neither of the conditions is satisfied, the number p is not prime (that is, it is composite).

Here, it is important to note that if the condition is satisfied, it does not necessarily mean that p is prime. That is, even if the condition is satisfied, p may or may not be prime. For example, let $p = 2047$. Then $p-1$, that is, 2046, can be written as $2*1023$, yielding $k = 1$ and $q = 1023$. Now, as $2^{1023} \bmod 2047 = 1$, 2047 should be prime; however, it is not. Thus, it is clear that even though a number may satisfy a condition, it may not be prime.

Miller-Rabin algorithm

Let p be an integer to be checked for primality. The algorithm returns the result as *composite* if p is not prime and *inconclusive* if p may or may not be a prime number.

```
1. Find integers k and q where k > 0 and q is odd such that (p-1 = 2^k q).
2. Choose a random integer x such that 1< x < p-1
3. S:= x^q mod p
4. If S = 1, then print('inconclusive') and exit
5. for j = 0 to k-1
   {
     S:= x^(2^j q) mod p          //equivalent to S:= S^2 mod p
     if S = p-1
          print('inconclusive') and exit
   }
6. print('composite')
```

7. Describe and illustrate the Chinese Remainder Theorem.

Ans.: *Chinese Remainder Theorem* (CRT) is so named as it was discovered by the Chinese mathematician Sun-Tsu in around 100 AD. It is used to solve a set of congruent equations with a single variable but different moduli, which are relatively prime. Consider such a set of equations as shown here:

$$a = x_1 \bmod m_1$$
$$a = x_2 \bmod m_2$$
$$\vdots$$
$$a = x_k \bmod m_k$$

All these equations have a unique solution if the moduli for the equations are pair-wise relatively prime, that is, $\gcd(m_i, m_j) = 1$. In case the moduli are not relatively prime but satisfy other conditions, then even we can have the solution. In cryptography, we prefer to solve the equations with relatively prime moduli.

The solution to the set of simultaneous equations can be obtained by performing the following steps:

1. Find the common modulus, $M = m_1 * m_2 * \ldots * m_k$.
2. Find $M_1 = M/m_1$, $M_2 = M/m_2$, ..., $M_k = M/m_k$.
3. Find the multiplicative inverse of $M_1, M_2, \ldots, M_k$ using the corresponding moduli $m_1, m_2, \ldots, m_k$. Let the inverses be $M_1^{-1}, M_2^{-1}, \ldots, M_k^{-1}$.
4. The solution to the simultaneous equations is:

$$a = (x_1 * M_1 * M_1^{-1} + x_2 * M_2 * M_2^{-1} + \ldots + x_k * M_k * M_k^{-1}) \bmod M$$

8. Define the following terms:

(a) Finite multiplicative group

(b) Order of the group

(c) Order of an element

(d) Primitive roots of a group

(e) Cyclic group

Ans.: (a) *Finite multiplicative group:* A finite multiplicative group is often used in cryptography. It is represented as $G = \langle Z_n^*, * \rangle$

Where:

G = finite multiplicative group

Z_n^* = a set containing integers between 1 and n−1 that are relatively prime to n

$*$ = the multiplication operation

The identity element (e) of the finite multiplicative group G is equal to 1.

(b) *Order of the group:* As we know, the order of a group is the number of elements in the group. For a finite multiplicative group $G = \langle Z_n^*, * \rangle$, the order of the group is $\phi(n)$, where $\phi(n)$ is the Euler's totient function.

(c) *Order of an element:* For a finite multiplicative group $G = \langle Z_n^*, * \rangle$, the order of an element (say, a), represented as Ord(a), is the smallest integer i such that $a^i \equiv e \pmod{n}$, where e is the identity element of the group G. Here, the value of e is 1.

(d) *Primitive roots of a group:* For a finite multiplicative group $G = \langle Z_n^*, * \rangle$, the primitive roots are the elements that have the order equal to $\phi(n)$. The number of primitive roots in a group is equal to $\phi(\phi(n))$.

(e) *Cyclic group:* If a finite multiplicative group $G = \langle Z_n^*, * \rangle$ has primitive roots, it is called a *cyclic group*. Each primitive root of the cyclic group can be used to generate the elements of the set Z_n^*, thus termed as *generator*. If x is a generator, then elements can be created using x^a modulo n, where a is an integer ranging from 1 to $\phi(n)$, as shown here:

$$Z_n^* = \{x^1 \bmod n, x^2 \bmod n, x^3 \bmod n, \ldots, x^{\phi(n)} \bmod n\}$$

Notice that a finite multiplicative group $G = \langle Z_p^*, * \rangle$ is always cyclic if p is a prime number.

9. Write a short note on discrete logarithmic problems.

Ans.: In cryptography, exponentiation and modular logarithm are often used. Exponentiation and logarithm are reverse of each other. Whenever exponentiation is used to encrypt the plaintext or decrypt the ciphertext, the opponent can use logarithm to attack. Thus, it is required to identify how difficult it is to reverse the exponentiation. An approach to determine this is to use the concept of *discrete logarithm*.

Consider a finite multiplicative group $G = <Z_p^*, *>$, where p is prime. The elements of this group are the integers from 1 to p−1. In addition, the group is cyclic, as p is prime and thus has primitive roots. The primitive roots of such a group can be considered as the base of the logarithm. Thus, in case the group has m primitive roots, the calculation can be performed in m different bases.

Let us consider a as a primitive root of group G. Then, an element (say, y) of Z_p^* can be created as:

$$y = a^x \bmod p$$

Where, x is an integer ranging from 1 to $\phi(p)$ (which is p−1, in this case). Suppose we are given the value of y, and we are to find the value of x. Such type of problem is referred to as a *discrete logarithmic problem*, and the solution to this problem is given as:

$$x = \log_a y \bmod p$$

That is, we need to find the log of y in base a, and then take the result mod p.

10. Find out the result of 3^{12} mod 11.

Ans.: We can write:

$$3^{12} \bmod 11 = (3^{11} * 3) \bmod 11$$
$$\Rightarrow (3^{11} \bmod 11) * (3 \bmod 11) \quad (1)$$

Now, according to second version of Fermat's theorem, $x^p \equiv x \pmod p$ or $x^p \bmod p = x$. Thus, we get $(3^{11} \bmod 11) = 3$. Also, $(3 \bmod 11) = 3$. Putting both these values in equation (1), we have:

$$3^{12} \bmod 11 = 3 * 3$$
$$\Rightarrow 9$$

11. Find out the result of 5^{12} mod 13.

Ans.: We can write:

$$5^{12} \bmod 13 = 5^{13-1} \bmod 13$$

Now, according to Fermat's theorem for a prime number p, which states that $x^{p-1} \bmod p = 1$, we have:

$$5^{13-1} \bmod 13 = 1, \text{ as 13 is a prime number.}$$

12. Find $\phi(7)$.

Ans.: As 7 is a prime number, according to *Rule 2* of the Euler's totient function $[\phi(n) = n-1]$, we have:

$$\phi(7) = 7-1$$
$$\Rightarrow 6$$

This implies that there are six positive integers that are less than 7 and relatively prime to 7. These integers include 1, 2, 3, 4, 5 and 6.

13. Find $\phi(10)$.

Ans.: The integer 10 is a multiple of 5 and 2, therefore, we can write:

$$\phi(10) = \phi(5*2)$$

As 5 and 2 are relatively prime, by applying *Rule 3* of Euler's totient function [$\phi(m * n) = \phi(m) * \phi(n)$], we can write:

$\phi(10) = \phi(5) * \phi(2)$

$\Rightarrow (5-1) * (2-1)$ [using *Rule 2* of Euler's totient function, $\phi(n) = n-1$]

$\Rightarrow 4 * 1$

$\Rightarrow 4$

14. Check whether 89 is a prime.

Ans.: To check 89 for primeness, we can apply the divisibility test, where we check whether 89 is divisible by any of the prime numbers less than $\sqrt{89}$. Now, the integral value of $\sqrt{89}$ is 9 and the prime numbers less than 9 are {2, 3, 5, 7}. As 89 is not divisible by any of these numbers, it is a prime.

15. Apply Miller-Rabin's algorithm and use base 2 to test whether the number 561 passes the test.

Ans.: Using Miller-Rabin algorithm, explained in **Question 6**, we can test the number 561 as follows:

Step 1: $561-1 = 2^4 * 35$. Thus, $p = 561$, $k = 4$ and $q = 35$.

Step 2: $x = 2$ (Given)

Step 3: $S = x^q \bmod p$

$\Rightarrow 2^{35} \bmod 561$

$\Rightarrow 263$

Step 4: As $263 \neq 1$, we move to the next step.

Step 5: For $j = 1$, $S = x^{2q} \bmod p$

$\Rightarrow 2^{70} \bmod 561 = 166$

As $166 \neq 560$ (that is, $p-1$), we pick the next value of j (which is 2) and repeat the preceding step.

For $j = 2$, $S = x^{4q} \bmod p$

$\Rightarrow 2^{140} \bmod 561 = 67$

As $67 \neq 560$, we pick the next value of j (which is 3) and repeat the preceding step.

For $j = 3$, $S = x^{8q} \bmod p$

$\Rightarrow 2^{280} \bmod 561 = 1$

As for no value of j, S is equal to 560. Thus, 561 is composite.

16. Solve the following simultaneous congruence using Chinese Remainder Theorem to find the value of a.

$$a \equiv 2 \bmod 3$$
$$a \equiv 3 \bmod 5$$
$$a \equiv 2 \bmod 7$$

Ans.: Applying Chinese Remainder Theorem, explained in **Question 7**, the solution to the given equations is obtained as follows:

Step 1: Given $m_1 = 3$, $m_2 = 5$, $m_3 = 7$

Thus, the common modulus, M = 3*5*7 = 105

Step 2: Compute M_1, M_2 and M_3.

$M_1 = M/m_1 = 105/3 = 35$
$M_2 = M/m_2 = 105/5 = 21$
$M_3 = M/m_3 = 105/7 = 15$

Step 3: Compute the multiplicative inverse of M_1; M_2 and M_3 in modulo m_1, m_2 and m_3, respectively.

$M_1^{-1} = 2$ as $(2*35) \bmod 3 = 1$
$M_2^{-1} = 1$ as $(1*21) \bmod 5 = 1$
$M_3^{-1} = 1$ as $(1*15) \bmod 7 = 1$

Step 4: The solution to the simultaneous equations is as follows:

$a = (2*35*2 + 3*21*1 + 2*15*1) \bmod 105$
$\Rightarrow 233 \bmod 105$

Thus, the value of a is 23.

17. Find the order of all the elements in G = <Z_7^*, *>. Also find the primitive roots in the group G.

Ans.: For the group G = <Z_7^*, *>, the set Z_7^* contains those integers between 1 and 6 that are relatively prime to 7. That is, $Z_7^* = \{1, 2, 3, 4, 5, 6\}$. The order of this group = $\phi(7) = 6$.

For each element a of the set Z_7^*, we will find out for which value of i (from 1 to 6), the condition $a^i \equiv 1 (\bmod n)$, that is, $a^i \bmod n = 1$, holds true. That value of i will be the order of the element.

1. For a = 1,
   $1^1 \bmod 7 = 1$
   Thus, the order of element 1, that is, Ord(1) = 1.
2. For a = 2,
   $2^1 \bmod 7 = 2 \neq 1$
   $2^2 \bmod 7 = 4 \bmod 7 = 4 \neq 1$
   $2^3 \bmod 7 = 8 \bmod 7 = 1$
   Thus, the order of element 2, that is, Ord(2) = 3.
3. For a = 3,
   $3^1 \bmod 7 = 3 \neq 1$
   $3^2 \bmod 7 = 9 \bmod 7 = 2 \neq 1$
   $3^3 \bmod 7 = 27 \bmod 7 = 6 \neq 1$
   $3^4 \bmod 7 = 81 \bmod 7 = 4 \neq 1$
   $3^5 \bmod 7 = 243 \bmod 7 = 5 \neq 1$
   $3^6 \bmod 7 = 729 \bmod 7 = 1$
   Thus, the order of element 3, that is, Ord(3) = 6.

4. For a = 4,
   $4^1 \bmod 7 = 4 \bmod 7 = 4 \neq 1$
   $4^2 \bmod 7 = 16 \bmod 7 = 2 \neq 1$
   $4^3 \bmod 7 = 64 \bmod 7 = 1$
   Thus, the order of element 4, that is, Ord(4) = 3.

5. For a = 5
   $5^1 \bmod 7 = 5 \neq 1$
   $5^2 \bmod 7 = 25 \bmod 7 = 4 \neq 1$
   $5^3 \bmod 7 = 125 \bmod 7 = 6 \neq 1$
   $5^4 \bmod 7 = 625 \bmod 7 = 2 \neq 1$
   $5^5 \bmod 7 = 3125 \bmod 7 = 3 \neq 1$
   $5^6 \bmod 7 = 15625 \bmod 7 = 1$
   Thus, the order of element 5, that is, Ord(5) = 6.

6. For a = 6,
   $6^1 \bmod 7 = 6 \neq 1$
   $6^2 \bmod 7 = 36 \bmod 7 = 1$
   Thus, the order of element 6, that is, Ord(6) = 2.

Only the elements 3 and 5 have the order equal to $\phi(7)$, that is, 6, and therefore the primitive roots of the group G are 3 and 5.

18. Find the value of x in the group $G = (Z_7^*, *)$ for the following cases with the help of the given table.

(a) $4 \equiv 3^x \bmod 7$
(b) $6 \equiv 5^x \bmod 7$

a	1	2	3	4	5	6
$x = \log_3 a$	6	2	1	4	5	3
$x = \log_5 a$	6	4	5	2	1	3

Ans.: For the group $G = (Z_7^*, *)$, $\phi(7) = 6$ and $Z_7^* = \{1, 2, 3, 4, 5, 6\}$. The given equations are of the form $a = b^x \bmod n$. These equations can be solved using the table for each Z_7^* and different bases, as provided in the question.

(a) $4 \equiv 3^x \bmod 7$
Here, a = 4. Thus, $x = \log_3 4 \bmod 7$

From the given table, it is clear that $\log_3 4 = 4$. Therefore,
$x = 4 \bmod 7$
$\Rightarrow 4$

(b) $6 \equiv 5^x \bmod 7$
Here, a = 5. Thus, $x = \log_5 6 \bmod 7$

From the given table, it is clear that $\log_5 6 = 3$. Therefore,
$x = 3 \bmod 7$
$\Rightarrow 3$

Multiple-choice Questions

1. What is the value of $\phi(1)$?
   (a) Zero
   (b) One
   (c) Not defined
   (d) None of these
2. The gcd of 14 and 15 is __________.
   (a) One
   (b) Two
   (c) Three
   (d) Four
3. Two positive integers a and b are said to be relatively prime if __________.
   (a) Their gcd is 1
   (b) They have no common prime factors
   (c) If 1 is their only common divisor
   (d) All of these
4. Which of the following is used for testing primality?
   (a) Fermat's primality test
   (b) Miller-Rabin
   (c) Divisibility test
   (d) All of these
5. Chinese remainder theorem is given by __________
   (a) Fermat
   (b) Euler
   (c) Sun-Tsu
   (d) Miller and Rabin
6 The number of primitive roots in a group is computed by __________
   (a) $\phi(\phi(n))$
   (b) $\phi(n)$
   (c) Ord(n)
   (d) None of these

Answers

1. (b) 2. (a) 3. (d) 4. (d) 5. (c) 6. (a)

6

Asymmetric-key Algorithms

1. What are the requirements of asymmetric-key cryptography?
Or
What are the characteristics that an asymmetric-key cryptographic algorithm must possess?

Ans.: Asymmetric-key cryptography requires the use of two different keys: the *public key* for encryption and *private key* for decryption. The public key is known to everyone, whereas the private key is known to its owner only. Diffie and Hellman laid out some requirements that must be fulfilled by the algorithms used for asymmetric-key cryptography. These requirements are listed below:

- It should be easy for the receiver to generate the pair of keys (public and private).
- It should be easy for the sender to generate the ciphertext from the original message (that is, the plaintext) with the help of the receiver's public key.
- It should be easy for the receiver to decrypt the ciphertext generated by the sender by using its private key in order to recover the original message.
- It should be infeasible for an intruder to determine the private key of the receiver, even if he or she knows the public key of the receiver.
- It should be infeasible for an intruder to determine the original message even if he or she knows the public key of the receiver as well as the ciphertext.
- It should be possible to use any of the two keys (public or private) for encryption and decryption. That is, it should be possible to encrypt the message with any one of the keys and decrypt it using the other.

2. Explain the RSA cryptosystem.

Ans.: In 1978, a group at MIT discovered a strong method for public-key encryption. It is known as *RSA*, the name derived from the initials of its three discoverers Ron *R*ivest, Adi *S*hamir, and Len *A*dleman. RSA cryptosystem is the most widely accepted asymmetric-key algorithm; in fact, most of the practically implemented security systems are based on RSA. The algorithm requires keys of at least 1024 bits for good security. This algorithm is based on some principles from number theory, which states that determining the prime factors of a large number is extremely difficult.

RSA Key Generation

Let A and B be two users who wish to communicate. Suppose that A wants to send a message securely to B. To encrypt the message, A needs to know B's public key. Thus, B uses the following steps to generate his or her public and private keys.

1. Choose two large distinct prime numbers, p and q (about 1024 bits), such that $p \neq q$.
2. n: = p*q
3. ϕ(n): = (p−1) * (q−1)
4. Choose a number E such that $1 < E < \phi(n)$, and such that E is relatively prime to $\phi(n)$. The public (encryption) key is (E,n), which is announced publicly.
5. Find another number D such that $E * D = 1 \bmod \phi(n)$, that is, $D = E^{-1} \bmod \phi(n)$. In other words, D is the inverse of E modulo ϕ(n). The private (decryption) key is D, which is kept secret.

An important property of RSA algorithm is that the roles of E and D can be interchanged. As the number theory suggests, it is very hard to find the prime factors of a large number n, and hence it is extremely difficult for an intruder to determine the private key D using just E and n.

RSA Encryption and Decryption

In RSA, modular exponentiation is used for performing encryption and decryption. For example, if A has to send a message to B using B's public key (E,n), A encrypts the plaintext (P) to produce the ciphertext (C), as shown here:

$$C = P^E \bmod n$$

After B has received the ciphertext (C), he or she decrypts the ciphertext using its private key (D) to get back the original plaintext (P) as shown here.

$$P = C^D \bmod n$$

3. Discuss the different attacks on RSA.

Ans.: Although RSA is a secure algorithm used for encryption in public-key cryptography, there are still some weaknesses that enable an attacker to crack the security of the algorithm. There are several attacks that have been predicted on the basis of weak plaintext, parameter selection or inappropriate implementation. These attacks are discussed as follows:

- *Factorization attack:* This attack is possible if the value of n is small, so that the intruders can easily factorize n and obtain the value of p and q (as $n = p \times q$). As the value of e is public, it may further result in obtaining the value of ϕ(n) and d (as $d = e^{-1} \bmod (p-1)(q-1)$). Thus, by using all these values, an intruder can now decrypt any encrypted plaintext and crack the security. To prevent such an attack, n must be more than 300 decimal digits, so that it becomes infeasible to factorize such a long value of n.
- *Chosen-ciphertext attack:* This attack tries to get the plaintext from the ciphertext by using the multiplicative property of RSA. Suppose the sender sends the ciphertext (C) to the receiver and an intruder intercepts it. Now, the intruder sends fake ciphertext, say Y, to the receiver by choosing a random integer X. As the receiver is unaware about the interception of the original ciphertext, he or she decrypts the fake ciphertext by performing $Y^d \bmod n$ to get Z. Thus, an intruder can now easily get the plaintext (P), as $P = Z * X^{-1} \bmod n$. That is, an intruder needs to find only

the multiplicative inverse of X to get the original plaintext. Therefore, the name of attack is *chosen-ciphertext attack*, as only the particular ciphertext was chosen to know the corresponding plaintext.

- *Timing attack:* This is a cipher-text-only attack that was unveiled by Paul Kocher. In this attack, an intruder determine a private key by keeping track of how long a computer takes to decrypt the encrypted plaintext. That is, variable timing in evaluation helps an intruder find the value of each bit in d. This means that an intruder can now perform bit-by-bit analysis of the exponential. Such an attack can be prevented if random delays are added to exponentiation, such that the underlying hardware takes a random amount of time to process each. In addition, the concept of *blinding* can also be used. In this concept, the ciphertext is multiplied by a random number before evaluation. Thus, an intruder will be unable to decipher the ciphertext bits and, therefore, bit-by-bit analysis can be prevented.
- *Plaintext attack:* In this attack, an intruder already knows something about the plaintext. This helps the intruder to also know about the fact that the ciphertext is the permutation of the plaintext. Thus, an intruder can now compute all the possible messages until the result is equal to the ciphertext intercepted.
- *Common modulus attack:* In this attack, a common modulus is used by a group of people. That is, a whole group agrees for a trusted third party to select the values of two prime numbers p and q, computes n and $\phi(n)$ and then creates exponents (e_i, d_i) for each person belonging to the group. By doing this, any person who is a member of the group can decrypt the ciphertext by factoring n and can also compute the receiver's private exponent (d_r). Therefore, to prevent such attack, the modulus must not be shared, and each person in the group must calculate his or her own modulus.

4. Discuss the uses of public-key cryptography in relation to key distribution.

Ans.: One of the major problems in secret-key cryptography is that of key distribution, which can be overcome by the use of public-key cryptography. The two aspects that must be taken into account for using public-key cryptography include the distribution of public keys and the use of public-key encryption for the distribution of secret keys.

Distribution of Public Keys

There are several schemes that have been used for the distribution of public keys. These schemes are as follows:

- *Public announcement:* The main focus of public-key encryption is on the fact that the public key should be public; that is, a user can send his or her public key to any other user or broadcast it to a large community. Though this approach is convenient, it has some drawbacks. The main problem is that of forgery. That is, anyone can forge the key while it is being transmitted. For example, someone could pretend to be user A and send a public key to another user or broadcast it to many users. Until the original user A comes to know about this forgery and alerts other users, the forger is able to read all the messages intended for user A.
- *Public directory:* As the public announcement scheme for the distribution of public keys was not too secure and there were chances of forgery, a new scheme was introduced, in which a dynamic directory having the name and public key entry for each user is maintained and distributed by some trusted authority. This approach assumes that the public key of the authority is known to

everyone, however the corresponding private key is known only to the authority. Each user has to register his or her public key with the directory authority. The authority either publishes the entire directory periodically in a widely circulated newspaper, or the user can access the directory electronically. The user can replace its existing key with a new one as per his or her choice. Although this scheme is more secure than public announcement, it has some weaknesses. If anyone is able to compute the private key of the directory authority, the person would get the authority to pass around the fake public keys and, later, may pretend to be a genuine user and eavesdrop on the messages being sent to any other user. The fake user may also read or alter the records kept by the authority.

- *Public-key authority:* In public directory scheme, if the private key of the authority is stolen, then it may result in loss of data. Thus, to achieve stronger security for public-key distribution, a tighter control needs to be provided over the distribution of public keys from the directory. In this case also, a central authority maintains the dynamic directory of the public keys of all the users. The user knows only the public key of the authority, while the corresponding private key is secret to the authority.

  To understand how the public-key authority scheme works, consider two users A and B who wish to communicate securely. To enable communication, the following steps are used.

  1. A sends a timestamped message containing a request for the current public key of B to the public-key authority.
  2. The authority responds by sending A a message that is encrypted using the private key of authority (say, $P_{authority}$). The user A attempts to decrypt the message using the authority's public key. If the message gets decrypted, A is assured that the message has been sent by the authority itself. The message sent by the authority contains the following:
     - B's public key (say, PUB_B), which can be used by A to send messages to B.
     - The original request sent by A, so that A can match the message received from the authority with its corresponding request, and also verify that the request was not altered before reaching the authority.
     - The original timestamp, so that A can verify whether the message is a new one containing the current public key of B, or an old message containing any other public key.
  3. A stores B's public key and uses it to encrypt the message destined for B containing an identifier of A (say, I_A) and a nonce N_1, which uniquely identifies this transaction.
  4. B also follows the same method to retrieve A's public key from the authority. It stores the A's public key for future use. Now, both A and B have got the public keys of each other and, thus, may start exchange messages.
  5. B sends a message to A, encrypting it with the public key of A (PUB_A). The message contains A's nonce N_1 as well as B's nonce N_2. As the message could have been decrypted by B only, the inclusion of N_1 in the message assures A that the corresponding user is B.
  6. A returns N_2, encrypted with B's public key (PUB_B), to assure B that the corresponding user is A.

  Note that the first four steps need not to be followed each time, as the users A and B can store the public keys of each other for future use. This technique is known as *caching*. However, the users should periodically request for fresh or new copies of the public keys.

- *Public-key (or digital) certificates:* A better approach where a user can exchange keys without communicating to the public-key authority is to use digital certificates—an electronic document that signifies the association between the user and his/her public key. A *certificate authority*, such as a government agency or some trusted institution, issues a certificate to each user, which contains a public key and the identifier of the key owner. The certificate is signed by the certificate authority. A user can present his or her public key to the authority to get the certificate. The user can then publish his or her certificate. Now, any other user wishing to get the public key can obtain the certificate and verify its validity by means of the attached trusted signature. The user can also send his or her key information to another user by transmitting the certificate. Users can easily verify that the certificate has been generated by the authority and that it is not a fake certificate. Moreover, only the certificate authority can create or update the certificates.

Distribution of Secret Keys using Public-key Cryptography

The public-key encryption can be exclusively used for providing distribution of secret keys that are to be used for conventional encryption. There are certain schemes for this, which are described as follows:

- *Simple method:* In this method, a session is created between the two users who wish to communicate (say, A and B). When A wants to communicate with B, he or she first creates a pair of public and private keys. Then, A transmits to B a message that contains the public key and A's identifier. B creates a secret key, encrypts it with the public key of A, and sends it to A. A recovers the secret key by decrypting the received encrypted message using his or her private key. At this point, both A and B know the secret key. After exchanging the secret key, A discards both the public and private keys, and B discards the public key. Now, both A and B can securely communicate using conventional encryption and the secret key.

  The main advantage of this technique is that no keys exist before the start of the communication and none exists after the communication ends. Therefore, the risk of compromising the keys is minimal, and the communication is secure from eavesdropping. Note that the technique is well suited when the only threat is eavesdropping, as it does not provide confidentiality and assure authenticity of the message.

- *Distribution with confidentiality and authentication:* This method provides protection against both active and passive attacks. To prevent the transmission of the message from attacks, assuming that A and B have already exchanged their public keys by any of the earlier-discussed schemes, the following steps take place:

  1. A sends a message to B, encrypted with the public key of B, say PUB_B. The message contains an identifier of A (say, I_A) and a nonce N_1, which is used to identify this transaction uniquely.
  2. B sends a message to A encrypted with the public key of A (say, PUB_A). The message contains A's nonce N_1 as well as B's nonce N_2. Since only B could have decrypted the message sent by A, the inclusion of B's nonce in the message assures A that the corresponding user is B. Similarly, A sends B's nonce N_2, encrypted with B's public key, to assure B that the corresponding user is A.
  3. A chooses a secret key (say, SCR_A), encrypts it with its private key (PRV_A) and sends a message m, encrypted with B's public key (PUB_B), as shown here:

  $$m = E_{PUB_B}[E_{PRV_A}[SCR_A]]$$

  Encrypting the message m with B's public key ascertains that only B can read it, and encrypting the message with A's private key ascertains that only A could have sent it.

4. Now, B decrypts the message by computing $D_{PUB_A}[D_{PRV_B}[m]]$, thus recovering the secret key. This method ensures both confidentiality and authenticity in the exchange of a secret key.

- *Hybrid method:* This method uses the key distribution centre (KDC), in which a secret master key is shared with each user. The role of KDC is to distribute the session secret keys, encrypted using the master key. A public-key scheme is used for the distribution of the session key. Generally, the applications in which session keys often change, the use of public-key encryption for distributing the secret session keys could degrade the overall system's performance. This is because relatively high computational efforts are required for the public-key's encryption and decryption.

  The main advantage of this three-level hierarchy is that public-key encryption is rarely used to update the master key between a user and a KDC. Moreover, the scheme is compatible with existing KDC schemes and, thus, can be overlaid on existing schemes with minimal changes required.

5. Discuss Diffie-Hellman key exchange algorithm. Also discuss about its security.

Ans.: Diffie-Hellman key exchange is the first published public-key algorithm that was published in 1976 by Whitefield Diffie and Martin Hellman. This algorithm was devised for the exchange of secret keys between the communicating users in a secure manner. It allows two users to securely exchange a key that can be further used for encryption of messages. Notice that this algorithm can be used only for the exchange of keys, and not for encryption and decryption.

Diffie-Hellman key exchange algorithm enables two users to establish a symmetric session (secret) key without requiring the use of KDC. This is what is referred to as the *symmetric-key agreement*. Once both the communicating parties have agreed (exchanged) on the common secret key, then a symmetric-key encryption algorithm can be used for encryption and decryption of messages.

Diffie-Hellman algorithm

Consider two users A and B who want to communicate with each other securely over an insecure network. Initially, both A and B need to agree upon a key that is to be used for encryption and decryption of the messages. For this, they can follow the Diffie-Hellman key exchange algorithm, which is given below:

1. Select two numbers p and q by the mutual agreement of A and B, such that p is prime, q is a primitive root of p and $q < p$. There is no need to keep these two numbers secret.
2. A selects a random number X_A (less than p), which becomes his or her private key. Then it computes its public key, Y_A, as shown here:

$$Y_A = q^{X_A} \bmod p$$

   A sends its public key Y_A to B.

3. B selects a random number X_B (less than p), which becomes his or her private key. Then, it computes its public key, Y_B, as shown here:

$$Y_B = q^{X_B} \bmod p$$

   B sends its public key Y_B to A.

4. After exchanging the public keys, both A and B compute the common secret key (K). A generates the secret key as shown here:

$$K = (Y_B)^{X_A} \bmod p$$

B generates the secret key as shown here:

$$K = (Y_A)^{X_B} \bmod p$$

Proof of algorithm

To show that both A and B have computed the same secret key, we need to prove that the calculation of K by A and B produce the identical results.

$$\begin{aligned} K &= (Y_B)^{X_A} \bmod p \\ &= (q^{X_B} \bmod p)^{X_A} \bmod p \\ &= (q^{X_B})^{X_A} \bmod p \quad \text{[using the rule of modular arithmetic]} \\ &= (q^{X_A})^{X_B} \bmod p \\ &= (q^{X_A} \bmod p)^{X_B} \bmod p \quad \text{[using the rule of modular arithmetic]} \\ &= (Y_A)^{X_B} \bmod p \end{aligned}$$

Hence, proved.

Security of the Diffie-Hellman algorithm

In Diffie-Hellman algorithm, the private keys X_A and X_B are secret, while the numbers p and q and the public keys Y_A and Y_B are known to everyone. Thus, an opponent has p, q, Y_A and Y_B to work with. To determine the key using the available information, the opponent has to use the discrete logarithm. For example, if the opponent wants to find the private key of user A, then he or she has to perform the following calculation:

$$X_A = \text{dlog}_{q,p}(Y_A)$$

After computing X_A, the opponent can compute the common secret key (K) in the same way that A computed it. Since it is difficult to compute the discrete logarithm in comparison to computing exponentials modulo a prime number, the security of the Diffie-Hellman algorithm depends on this fact. In case of large prime numbers, it is infeasible to compute the discrete logarithm and, thus, to break the security of the Diffie-Hellman algorithm.

5. List some advantages of the Diffie-Hellman algorithm.

Ans.: Some advantages of the Diffie-Hellman key exchange algorithm are as follows:

- Secret keys are generated as and when required. Thus, they need not be stored for a long time, thereby making them less vulnerable to attacks.
- No pre-existing infrastructure is required for key exchange. The communicating parties just have to agree upon the values of global variables p and q.

6. What are the limitations of the Diffie-Hellman algorithm?

Ans.: Although the Diffie-Hellman key exchange algorithm allows two communicating parties to securely exchange the key over an insecure network, there are a number of weaknesses to this algorithm, which are given below:

- It does not provide any information regarding the identities of the users exchanging the key. In other words, it does not authenticate the communicating users.
- It is vulnerable to *man-in-the-middle-attack*, where a third user (say, C) pretends to be user B while communicating with A and pretends to be user A while communicating with B, thereby intercepting their messages. This attack is discussed in the next question.

- It involves a lot of computations and, thus, is subject to *clogging attacks*. In this attack, an opponent requests for a large number of keys, thus keeping the victim busy in doing unnecessary calculations rather than doing the real work.

7. Explain the man-in-the-middle attack.

Ans.: As the Diffie-Hellman algorithm does not authenticate the users exchanging the keys, it is vulnerable to man-in-the-middle attacks, also referred to as the *bucket brigade attack*. To understand this attack, consider that A and B are two users who want to communicate and, thus, exchange their keys using the Diffie-Hellman algorithm. Let C be an opponent who wants to intercept the communication between A and B. Now, the man-in-the-middle attack proceeds as follows:

1. A sends a message containing its public key (Y_A) to B.
2. C intercepts this message, stores A's public key and sends a new message containing its public key (Y_C) and A's user ID to B.
3. On receiving the message, B saves the C's public key (Y_C) with A's user ID.
4. B sends a message containing its public key (Y_B) to A.
5. The opponent C intercepts this message, stores B's public key (Y_B) and sends a new message containing its public key (Y_C) and B's user ID to A.
6. On receiving the message, A saves C's public key (Y_C) with B's user ID.
7. A computes the secret key K_1 based on its private key X_A and C's public key Y_C as shown here:

$$K_1 = (Y_C)^{X_A} \bmod p$$

8. B computes the secret key K_2 based on its private key X_B and C's public key Y_C, as shown here:

$$K_2 = (Y_C)^{X_B} \bmod p$$

9. C computes K_1 using its private key X_C and Y_A and computes K_2 using X_C and Y_B as shown here:

$$K_1 = (Y_A)^{X_C} \bmod p$$
$$K_2 = (Y_B)^{X_C} \bmod p$$

At this point, A and B think that they have shared a common secret key; however, actually A and C have shared the key K_1, whereas B and C have shared the key K_2. The opponent C is now able to trap all the messages coming from A to B and B to A, without letting A and B know that their communication is shared with C. This happens in the following way:

1. A sends a message m encrypted with key K_1 to B.
2. C intercepts the encrypted message and decrypts it to obtain the original message.
3. C sends either the same message (m) or a modified message (m') to B, encrypted using the key K_2.

B receives the message assuming that it has come from A. A similar thing happens when B sends a message to A. This way, C comes in the middle of the communication between A and B and, therefore, the attack is named so.

8. What is the ElGamal encryption system? Explain its encryption and decryption processes.

Ans.: The ElGamal encryption system is a public-key cryptosystem based on the concept of Diffie-Hellman key agreement. It was discovered by Taher ElGamal in 1984. It is based on the discrete logarithm problem. To understand this problem, consider that p is a large prime number, q is an integer and e_1 is a primitive root in the group $G = \langle Z_p^*, * \rangle$. Now, it is easy to compute $e_2 = e_1^q \bmod p$ by using fast exponential algorithms. However, if e_1, e_2 and p are given, then it is difficult to calculate $q = \log(e_1 * e_2) \bmod p$. This is what is known as the *discrete logarithm problem*. Thus, the security of ElGamal depends on the complexity of computing discrete logarithms.

The Elgamel encryption system consists of three different components, and separate algorithms are defined for them. The components are *key generator*, *encryption algorithm* and *decryption algorithm*.

ElGamal key generation

Suppose A and B are the communicating parties, and A wishes to send a message to B using the ElGamal encryption system. For this, A needs to know the public key of B. Thus, B uses the following steps to generate his or her private and public keys.

1. Choose a large prime number p.
2. Choose a random number q in the group $G = \langle Z_p^*, * \rangle$, that is, $1 \le q < p$.
3. Choose a primitive root e_1 in the group $G = \langle Z_p^*, * \rangle$.
4. $e_2 := e_1^q \bmod p$.
5. Announce (e_1, e_2, p) as the public key.
6. Retain q as the private key and keep it secret.

After knowing the public key of B, anyone can now send a message to B using its public key.

ElGamal encryption

Suppose the user A wants to send an encrypted message to B. For this, A uses the B's public key (e_1, e_2, p) and the following steps to convert the plaintext P to ciphertexts C_1 and C_2.

1. Choose a random number d in the group $G = \langle Z_p^*, * \rangle$.
2. $C_1 := e_1^d \bmod p$.
3. $C_2 := (P * e_2^d) \bmod p$.
4. Send C_1 and C_2.

ElGamal decryption

After receiving the ciphertext (C_1 and C_2), the recipient B uses its private key q to decrypt the ciphertext and, thus, obtain the original plaintext P, as shown here:

$$P = [C_2 (C_1^q)^{-1}] \bmod p$$

Proof of decryption

We can also verify the ElGamal decryption expression $[C_2 (C_1^q)^{-1}] \bmod p$ to be equivalent to P. Putting the values of C_1 and C_2 in the ElGamal decryption expression, we get:

$$\begin{aligned}
[C_2 (C_1^q)^{-1}] \bmod p &= [((P * e_2^d) \bmod p) * ((e_1^d \bmod p)^q)^{-1}] \bmod p \\
&\Rightarrow [((P * e_2^d) \bmod p) * (e_1^{qd} \bmod p)^{-1}] \bmod p \\
&\Rightarrow [((P * e_2^d) \bmod p) * (e_1^{-qd} \bmod p)] \bmod p \\
&\Rightarrow [((P * (e_1^q \bmod p)^d) \bmod p) * (e_1^{-qd} \bmod p)] \bmod p \\
&\quad \ldots\ldots. [\text{as } e_2 = e_1^q \bmod p] \\
&\Rightarrow [(P * e_1^{qd}) * (e_1^{-qd})] \\
&\Rightarrow P
\end{aligned}$$

9. Discuss the different attacks on the ElGamal algorithm.

Ans.: Although the ElGamal algorithm can be used for key exchange, encryption, decryption and authentication of small messages, it has certain weaknesses that may help an attacker to crack the security of the algorithm. Generally, the ElGamal cryptosystem is subject to two types of attacks, which are as follows:

- *Modulus attack:* In case the value of `modulus p` is small, it will be much easier for an attacker to solve the discrete logarithm problem. For example, the attacker can easily solve the discrete logarithm problem $q = \log_{e_1 e_2} \bmod p$ and obtain the value of q. It can store the value of q and use it to decrypt any message sent to the recipient. The attacker can do so as long as the recipient uses the same keys. The attacker can also easily solve the discrete logarithm problem $d = \log_{e_1} C_1 \bmod p$ and get the value of random number d used by the sender. Thus, to avoid this attack, it is recommended to use large values, at least of 1024 bits, for `modulus p`.
- *Known-plaintext attack:* If the sender uses the same value of q to encrypt two different plaintexts, P_1 and P_2, the attacker can determine P_2 if he or she knows P_1. Let $C = P_1 * e_2^q \bmod p$ and $C' = P_2 * e_2^q \bmod p$. Now, the attacker can determine P_2 using the following steps:

  1. $e_2^q := C' * P_1^{-1} \bmod p$
  2. $P_2 := C' * (e_2^q)^{-1} \bmod p$

  Thus, to avoid this attack, it is recommended that the sender use a different value of q to encrypt each plaintext.

10. Write a short note on elliptic curves.

Ans.: An *elliptic curve* can be defined by an equation in two variables with coefficients. The general form of an elliptic curve is given as:

$$y^2 + b_1xy + b_2y = x^3 + a_1x^2 + a_2x + a_3$$

Where x, y are the variables, while a_1, a_2, a_3, b_1 and b_2 are the coefficients.

There are three kinds of elliptic curves, which are as follows:

- *Elliptic curves over real numbers:* When we talk about elliptic curves over real numbers, we use a special class of elliptic curves, of the form given here:

$$y^2 = x^3 + ax + b$$

  Here, the variables x and y take values of real numbers and the coefficients a and b are the real numbers as well.
- *Elliptic curves over finite field GF(p):* In elliptic curves over finite field GF(p), the variables and coefficients are bound to be the elements of the finite field. Here, the elliptic curve is denoted as $E_p(a,b)$, where p is the modulus and all calculations are made using `modulo p`. The elliptic curve $E_p(a,b)$ over finite field GF (p) is represented as:

$$y^2 \bmod p = (x^3 + ax + b) \bmod p$$

  Notice that the value of x lies between 0 and p.
- *Elliptic curves over finite field GF(2^n):* The elliptic curves over finite field GF (2^n), denoted as $E_{2^n}(a,b)$, are of the form given here:

$$y^2 + xy = x^3 + ax^2 + b$$

  Where the variables x and y and the coefficients a and b are the elements of finite field GF (2^n), and all calculations are performed in GF (2^n).

11. What is the elliptic curve cryptosystem?

Ans.: The *elliptic curve cryptosystem* (ECC) is a public-key cryptosystem based on the theory of elliptic curves over finite field, and was unveiled by Neal Koblitz and Victor S. Miller in 1985. It involves both groups and logarithmic problems, and provides a higher rate of security at smaller key size, which is not possible using ElGamel and RSA.

In ECC, the plaintext is first encoded in the form of P(x, y) point and then further encrypted or decrypted.

ECC with Diffie-Hellman key exchange

Consider that A and B are two users who wish to communicate and, thus, exchange the secret key using ECC. The exchange of key between A and B proceeds as follows:

1. Choose a large integer p, such that p is either a prime or in the form 2^n.
2. Choose the elliptic curve coefficients a and b for the cubic equations of the form $y^2 \bmod p = (x^3 + ax + b) \bmod p$ or $y^2 + xy = x^3 + ax^2 + b$. This defines $E_p(a,b)$, the elliptic group of points.
3. Choose a base point $G = (x_1, y_1)$ in $E_p(a,b)$, whose order is a very large value, m.
4. A chooses an integer $X_A < m$, which becomes his or her private key. Then, A calculates his or her public key Y_A, as shown here:

   $$Y_A = X_A * G$$

   The public key Y_A is a point in $E_p(a,b)$.
5. B chooses an integer $X_B < m$, which becomes his or her private key. Then, B calculates his or her public key Y_B, as shown here:

   $$Y_B = X_B * G$$

   The public key Y_B is a point in $E_p(a,b)$.
6. A calculates the secret key K using his or her private key X_A and the public key of B (that is, Y_B), as shown here:

   $$K = X_A * Y_B$$

7. Similarly, B calculates the secret key K using his or her private key X_B and public key of A (that is, Y_A), as shown here:

   $$K = X_B * Y_A$$

Proof of algorithm

To prove that both A and B have generated the same secret key, we need to show that the calculation of K by both users yield the same result.

$$\begin{aligned} K &= X_A * Y_B \\ &\Rightarrow X_A * (X_B * G) \\ &\Rightarrow X_B * (X_A * G) \\ &\Rightarrow X_B * Y_A \end{aligned}$$

Hence, proved.

ECC encryption

When A has to send a message (say, P_m) to B, A first chooses a random integer (say, r). Then, A encrypts the message using B's public key Y_B and the base point G to produce the ciphertext C_m, containing the pair of points as shown here:

$$C_m = \{r * G,\ P_m + r * Y_B\}$$

ECC decryption

On receiving the ciphertext C_m, B decrypts the ciphertext to obtain the original plaintext P_m. For this, it multiplies the first point in C_m (that is, r * G) with its private key X_B, and then subtracts it from the second point (that is, $P_m + r * Y_B$), as shown here:

$$P_m + r * Y_B - X_B * (r * G)$$
$$\Rightarrow P_m + r * (X_B * G) - X_B * (r * G)$$
$$\Rightarrow P_m$$

Security of ECC

A encrypts the message P_m with $r * Y_B$ (r is only known to A) and r * G; therefore, the attacker needs the value of r, G and r * G to decrypt the message, which is not so easy.

12. Encrypt the plaintext 6 using RSA public key encryption algorithm. Use prime numbers 11 and 3 to compute the public key and private key. Also, decrypt the cipher text using the private key.

Ans.: According to the RSA algorithm explained in **Question 2**, we have:

$$p = 11 \text{ and } q = 3$$
$$\text{Thus, } n = p * q$$
$$\Rightarrow 11 * 3 = 33$$
$$\phi(n) = (p-1) * (q-1)$$
$$\Rightarrow (11-1) * (3-1)$$
$$\Rightarrow 10 * 2 = 20$$

We choose D = 3 (a number relatively prime to 20, that is, gcd (20,3) = 1)

$$\text{Now, } E * D = 1 \bmod n$$
$$\Rightarrow E * 3 = 1 \bmod 20$$
$$\Rightarrow E = 7$$

As we know, the public key consists of (E,p), and the private key consists of (D,p). Therefore, the public key is (7, 33), and the private key is (3, 33).

The plaintext 6 can be converted into ciphertext using the public key (7, 33), as shown here:

$$C = P^E \bmod n$$
$$\Rightarrow 6^7 \bmod 33$$
$$\Rightarrow 30$$

If we apply the private key to the ciphertext 30, we get the original plaintext, as follows:

$$P = C^D \bmod n$$
$$\Rightarrow (30)^3 \bmod 33$$
$$\Rightarrow 6$$

13. In the Diffie-Hellman key exchange algorithm, let the prime number be 353 and one of its primitive root be 3. Let the users A and B select their secret keys $X_A = 97$ and $X_B = 233$. Compute:

(i) The public keys of A and B

(ii) The common secret key

Ans.: According to the Diffie-Hellman key exchange algorithm explained in **Question 5**, we have:

$$p = 353$$
$$q = 3$$
$$X_A = 97$$
$$X_B = 233$$

(i) Public key of A

$$Y_A = q^{X_A} \bmod p$$
$$\Rightarrow 3^{97} \bmod 353$$
$$\Rightarrow 40$$

Public key of B

$$Y_B = q^{X_B} \bmod p$$
$$\Rightarrow 3^{233} \bmod 353$$
$$\Rightarrow 248$$

(ii) Common secret key

$$K = (Y_B)^{X_A} \bmod 353$$
$$\Rightarrow (248)^{97} \bmod 353$$
$$\Rightarrow 160$$

14. A is using the ElGamal encryption system to transmit a message to B, with p = 11, primitive root in G is 2, private key of A is 3 and the plaintext is 7.

(i) Calculate e_2 and public key of A

(ii) If B chooses d = 4, then calculate C_1, C_2

Ans.: According to the ElGamal encryption system explained in **Question 8**, we have:

$$q = 3$$
$$p = 11$$
$$m = 7$$
$e_1 = 2$ (e_1 is the primitive root in group G)

(i) As we know, $e_2 = e_1^q \bmod p$

$$\Rightarrow 2^3 \bmod 11$$
$$\Rightarrow 8 \bmod 11$$
$$\Rightarrow 8$$

Thus, the public key of A = $(e_1, e_2, p) = (2, 8, 11)$

(ii) Given, d = 4

$$C_1 = e_1^d \bmod p$$
$$\Rightarrow 24 \bmod 11$$
$$\Rightarrow 16 \bmod 11$$
$$\Rightarrow 5$$
$$C_2 = (m * e_2^d) \bmod p$$
$$\Rightarrow (7 * 8^4) \bmod 11$$
$$\Rightarrow 7 * 4096 \bmod 11$$
$$\Rightarrow 28672 \bmod 11$$
$$\Rightarrow 6$$

Thus, the ciphertexts are $C_1 = 5$ and $C_2 = 6$.

15. Using elliptic curve encryption/decryption scheme, key exchange between users A and B is accomplished. The cryptosystem parameters are elliptic group of points $E_{11}(1, 6)$ and point G on the elliptic curve is G = (2, 7). B's secret key is $X_B = 7$.

(i) Find out B's public key Y_B.

(ii) A wishes to encrypt the message $P_m = (10, 9)$ and chooses the random value r = 3. Determine the ciphertext C_m.

(iii) How will B recover P_m from C_m?

Ans.: Given G = (2, 7)

B's private key, $X_B = 7$

(i) B's public key, Y_B, can be computed as:

$$Y_B = X_B * G$$
$$\Rightarrow 7 * (2, 7)$$
$$\Rightarrow (7, 2)$$

(ii) Given, $P_m = (10, 9)$ and r = 3. Thus, the ciphertext C_m can be computed as:

$$C_m = \{r * G, P_m + r * Y_B\}$$
$$\Rightarrow \{3 * (2, 7), (10, 9) + 3 * (7, 2)\}$$
$$\Rightarrow \{(8, 3), (10, 9) + (3, 5)\}$$
$$\Rightarrow \{(8, 3), (10, 2)\}$$

(iii) B can recover P_m from C_m using its private key (X_B) as follows:

$$P_m = (10, 2) - X_B * (8, 3)$$
$$\Rightarrow (10, 2) - 7 * (8, 3)$$
$$\Rightarrow (10, 2) - (3, 5)$$
$$\Rightarrow (10, 2) + (3, 6)$$
$$\Rightarrow (10, 9)$$

Multiple-choice Questions

1. In asymmetric-key cryptography, how many keys are required for each communicating party?

(a) 2 (b) 3

(c) 4 (d) 1

2. In asymmetric-key cryptography, the private key must be ________.
   (a) Shared with anyone
   (b) Distributed
   (c) Kept secret
   (d) None of these
3. In asymmetric-key cryptography, if A wants to communicate with B, then B must know ________.
   (a) A's private key
   (b) A's public key
   (c) B's private key
   (d) B's public key
4. If a sender encrypts the message with his or her private key, it achieves ________.
   (a) Confidentiality
   (b) Confidentiality and authentication
   (c) Confidentiality but not authentication
   (d) Authentication
5. To decrypt a message that is encrypted using RSA, we need the ________.
   (a) Sender's private key
   (b) Sender's public key
   (c) Receiver's private key
   (d) Receiver's public key
6. Which method provides a higher level of security with a small-sized key?
   (a) RSA
   (b) ElGamal
   (c) Elliptic curve cryptography
   (d) Diffie-Hellman key agreement
7. Which of the following is the first secure key exchange algorithm?
   (a) RSA
   (b) ElGamal
   (c) Elliptic curve cryptography
   (d) Diffie-Hellman key agreement

Answers

1. (a)	2. (c)	3. (b)	4. (b)	5. (c)	6. (c)
7. (d)					

7

Message Authentication and Hash Functions

1. What do you mean by message authentication?

Ans.: *Message authentication* refers to the mechanism used to ensure that the integrity of the received message has been preserved – that the message has not been altered during transmission. It also assures the receiver that the message has originated from the intended sender and not from any intruder. Thus, a message is said to be authentic if the message has not been altered and has come from the actual sender.

2. What types of attacks are addressed by message authentication?

Ans.: The messages transmitted across a network are subject to various attacks. The types of attacks that are addressed by message authentication are as follows:

- *Masquerade:* This attack happens when the messages from a fraud source are put into the network; an intruder impersonates an authorized entity and creates fake messages, which are sent to the recipient. This attack also includes the fake acknowledgements corresponding to the received or failed messages by some other entity except the intended recipient.
- *Modification of the message:* This attack involves making certain modifications in the contents of the captured message or changing the sequence of messages being transmitted between the communicating parties. An intruder may insert, delete or transpose the contents of the message, or he or she may reorder the messages being sent in order to cause an unauthorized effect.
- *Timing modification:* This attack involves delaying or replaying the messages being transmitted. The term 'replay' means capturing a copy of the message sent by the original sender and retransmitting it later to bring about an unauthorized result. In a connection-oriented application, the entire session can be delayed or replayed, whereas in a connection-less application, the individual messages can be delayed or replayed.

3. Discuss various types of authentication functions?

Ans.: Each authentication mechanism involves the use of a function to produce a value to be used for authenticating a message. This value is known as the *authenticator*. The authenticator enables the recipient of the message to verify the authenticity of the message.

The authentication functions that are used to produce an authenticator fall under three classes, which are as follows:

- *Message encryption:* In this class, the authenticator of the message is the ciphertext that is produced after encrypting the entire plaintext.
- *Message authentication code (MAC):* In this class, the authenticator of the message is a fixed-length value that is generated by applying a function on the message and the secret key.
- *Hash function:* In this class, a hash function (also called *message digest algorithm*) is applied on a variable-length message to produce a fixed-length output that acts as the authenticator of the message.

4. Write a short note on message authentication code?

Ans.: *Message authentication code* (MAC) is a piece of information used to authenticate a message being transmitted between two communicating parties. A *MAC algorithm* is applied on an arbitrary-length message to be authenticated and the common secret key shared between the parties to generate a small fixed-size block of data called *cryptographic checksum* (or `MAC`). The calculated `MAC` is concatenated with the original message, and the message plus `MAC` are then sent to the receiver.

Let `A` and `B` be two parties that share a common secret key `K`. When `A` wants to send a message (say, `M`) to `B`, it computes `MAC` by applying the MAC algorithm (say, `C`) on message `M` and secret key `K`, as shown here:

$$\texttt{MAC} = \texttt{C(K,M)}$$

After `MAC` has been computed, `A` sends the message `M` and `MAC` to `B` through the network. On receiving, `B` distinguishes the message `M` from `MAC` and applies the same MAC algorithm `C` on the message `M` and the secret key `K` to generate `MAC'`. Then, `MAC'` and `MAC` are compared to determine whether they are the same. If so, `B` is assured that the message `M` has not been altered, because if it was changed by an attacker, then `MAC'` would not match with `MAC`; the attacker cannot change `MAC` to correspond to the changed message, as he or she is not aware of the secret key `K`. In addition, `B` is also assured that the message `M` has actually come from `A`, since nobody else could have created a message with the proper `MAC` without having knowledge of the secret key `K`. Notice that in case the messages being transmitted between `A` and `B` also comprise sequence numbers, then `B` can also be assured about the proper sequence, as the attacker cannot change the sequence number successfully.

Figure 7.1 depicts the use of MAC to authenticate a message at the sender's end and to verify the authenticity of the message at the receiver's end.

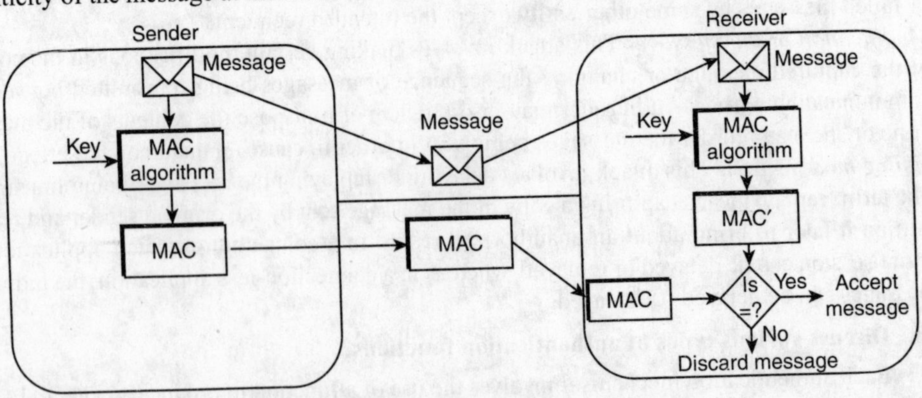

Figure 7.1 Message Authentication using MAC

MAC is different from message encryption in the sense that the MAC algorithm is not required to be reversible as it should be for decryption at the receiver's end. Generally, the MAC function is a many-to-one function whose domain comprises messages of any length, while the range comprises all possible MACs and keys. For an n-bit MAC, there are 2^n possible MACs and m possible messages, where $m >> 2^n$. For a k-bit key, there are 2^k possible keys. For example, if the messages being transmitted are of 100 bits and the MAC is of 10 bits, then there are 2^{100} different messages and 2^{10} different MACs. Thus, it can be said that, on average, each MAC is generated by $2^{100}/2^{10} = 2^{90}$ different messages. Furthermore, if the key used is of 10 bits, then there are 2^{10} different mappings between all the messages and the MACs.

MAC is widely helpful in some situations, which are as follows:

- When the same message has to be broadcasted to several destinations, it would be desirable to assign to one destination the responsibility of checking the authenticity of the message. Thus, the plaintext message and the message authentication code must be sent to all the destinations. Since the responsible destination is aware of the secret key, it verifies whether the message is authentic. In case some violation occurs, it alerts other destinations.
- When the receiving side is heavily loaded and cannot decrypt all the messages, then messages can be authenticated on a selective basis. That is, the messages are chosen randomly for verification.
- When it is more important to authenticate messages rather than keeping them secret.

5. Write down the purpose of hash function along with a simple hash function.

Ans.: A *hash function* (or *one-way hash function*) is a variation of MAC used for message authentication. Like MAC, it takes a variable-length message as input and produces a fixed-length output referred to as the *hash code* or *hash value* or a *message digest*. However, unlike MAC, a hash function does not require a secret key and, thus, is also called a *non-key message digest*. Formally, the hash code (h) can be expressed as:

$$h = H(M)$$

Where,

M = message (string) of any length

H = hash function

$H(M)$ = a fixed-length string (hash code).

At the sender's end, the hash code is computed and concatenated with the message. The message plus hash code are then sent to the receiver through the network. At the receiving end, the receiver separates the message from the hash code and again applies the hash function on it to produce a new hash code. If the recomputed hash code is the same as the received hash code, the message is authenticated.

A secret key is not given as an input to hash function. Thus, hash code plays the role of a 'signature' for the data being sent from the sender to the receiver through the network. In addition, the hash function takes into account all bits of the message; therefore, a change to any bit of the message results in a change to the hash code.

Simple Hash Function

All the hash functions consider the input message as a sequence of blocks where each block is of m bits. They process the input message one block at a time iteratively and produce an m-bit hash code.

One of the simple hash functions takes the bitwise XOR of every block of the input message to produce the hash code. This can be expressed as follows:

$$h_i = b_{i1} \oplus b_{i2} \oplus b_{i3} \oplus \ldots \oplus b_{in}$$

Where,
h_i = i^{th} bit of the hash code with $1 \le i \le m$
n = number of m-bit blocks in the input message
b_{ik} = i^{th} bit of the kth block with $1 \le k \le n$.

The preceding operation is known as *longitudinal redundancy check* (LRC), and it generates a simple parity corresponding to each bit position. It effectively ensures data integrity for randomly selected input; however, it proves less effective in case of predictable formatted data. To improve the effectiveness, an alternate simple hash function is used that circular-shifts (or rotates) the hash value by one bit after processing each block. This hash function uses the following steps to produce an m-bit hash code from an input message consisting of m-bit blocks.

1. Set all the m bits of hash code to zeros.
2. For each successive m-bit block, perform the following:
   i. Shift left the current value of hash code by one bit.
   ii. Take the XOR of new hash code and the block.

6. What characteristics (requirements) are needed in secure hash function.

Ans.: A hash function takes as input a variable-length message, a file or any block of data and produces a hash code, referred to as the *fingerprint* of the message, file or block of data. If M is a variable-length message and H is the hash function, then the hash code (h) can be expressed as:

$$h = H(M)$$

The hash function must possess the following properties in order to be used for message authentication.

1. The hash function should be applicable on a block of data of any size.
2. The output produced by the hash function should always be of fixed length.
3. For any given message or block of data, it should be easier to generate the hash code. That is, given a message M, H(M) should be easily computable. This property is important to make the hardware and software implementation feasible.
4. Given a hash code, it should be nearly impossible to determine the corresponding message or block of data. That is, if h is given, one should not be able to determine M such that H(M) = h. This is referred to as *one-way property*. This property is of prime importance when a secret value is being used in the authentication technique. Though the secret value is not sent through the network, the attacker can still easily find out the secret value if the used hash function does not show the one-way property.
5. Given a message or block of data, it should not be computationally feasible to determine another message or block of data generating the same hash code as that of the given message or block of data. That is, if M_1 is given, there is no other M_2 (where $M_1 \neq M_2$) such that $H(M_1) = H(M_2)$. This property is referred to as *weak collision resistance*.
6. No two messages or blocks of data, even being almost similar, should be likely to have the same hash code. That is, it is virtually impossible to determine a pair (M_1, M_2) such that $H(M_1) = H(M_2)$. This property is referred to as *strong collision resistance*.

From these six properties, if the first five properties are satisfied, then the hash function is called a *weak hash function*, and if all the six properties are satisfied, then it is called a *strong hash function*. This is because the sixth property protects the hash function from the birthday attack.

7. Describe the birthday attack against any hash function.

Ans.: When two different messages on applying the same hash function yield the same hash code, it is known as *collision*. A specific type of cryptographic attack that is performed against hash functions in order to discover collisions in them is referred to as *birthday attack*. This attack is based on the principle of *Birthday Paradox*, according to which, in a group of 23 randomly chosen people, the probability of finding two people sharing the same birthday is more than 50%. In case the number of people increases to 57, this probability becomes more than 99%. Thus, it can be concluded that the probability of finding a pair with same birthday in a group increases with increase in number of people in the group and, at a certain point, it may reach 100%.

In a birthday attack against a given hash function H, the goal of the attacker is to find two input messages, say M_1 and M_2, such that $H(M_1) = H(M_2)$; this is what is referred to as collision. To detect the collision, the attacker may continue to evaluate the hash function H for different randomly selected inputs until he or she gets the same output more than once. In case a hash function H produces N different outputs with same probability and N is quite large, then it can be expected to get a pair of different inputs M_1 and M_2 such that $H(M_1) = H(M_2)$ after we evaluate the function for approximately $1.25\sqrt{N}$ different inputs on average.

To estimate the expected number of values that we must choose before detecting the first collision, let us take q values at random from the set of N values, with repetitions allowed. Further, assume that $p(q; N)$ denotes the probability that at least one value is chosen more than once. The approximate value of this probability can be given as shown here:

$$p(q; N) \approx 1 - e^{-q(q-1)/(2N)} \approx 1 - e^{-q^2/(2N)}$$

If $n(p; N)$ denotes the least number of values that must be chosen such that the probability for detecting a collision is at least p, then we can find the approximate value of $n(p; N)$ by inverting the preceding expression as shown here:

$$n(p; N) \approx \sqrt{2N \ln\left(\frac{1}{1-p}\right)}$$

For 50% probability of detecting collision (that is, $p = 0.5$), we get

$$n(0.5, N) \approx 1.1774\sqrt{N}$$

Now, the expected number of values that must be selected before detecting the first collision, denoted as $Q(N)$, can be approximated as shown here:

$$Q(N) \approx \sqrt{\left(\frac{\pi}{2}\right) N}$$

For example, if we use a 64-bit hash code, then there will be approximately 1.8×10^{19} different outputs. If all of these are equally probable (the best case), then an attacker would require approximately 5.1×10^9 attempts to generate a collision using brute force. This value is called *birthday bound*. In general, for an m-bit hash code, the birthday bound can be approximated as $2^{m/2}$.

8. Write a short note on iterated hash functions?

Ans.: To ensure message integrity, the hash functions are used that produce a fixed-length message digest from a variable-length message. To accomplish this efficiently, iterations are used in the hash function. In place of using hash functions with variable-length input, the hash functions with fixed-length input can also be created and used the required number of times. Such a fixed-size input hash function is termed as a *compression function*. This function takes as input an m-bit string and produces an n-bit string as output such that $n < m$. This scheme is known as *iterated cryptographic hash function*.

There are two different approaches that can be used in designing iterated hash functions. In the first approach, the cryptographic hash functions employ a compression function that is made from the scratch and has been designed for that specific purpose. Examples of such cryptographic hash functions include all versions of message digest (MD) algorithm such as MD2, MD4 and MD5 as well as all versions of secure hash algorithm (SHA) such as SHA-1, SHA-224, SHA-256, SHA-384 and SHA-512. On the other hand, in the second approach, the cryptographic hash functions use a symmetric-key block cipher such as triple-DES or AES as the compression function. Notice that the role of block ciphers here is to perform only encryption and not decryption. An example of a cryptographic hash function based on this approach is Whirlpool.

9. Explain MD5 algorithm with the help of a block diagram.

Ans.: *MD5* (*message digest, version 5*) is a cryptographic hash algorithm developed by Ron Rivest in 1991. It came into existence after its four predecessors, all of which were developed by Rivest. The original hash algorithm was named MD. Then came MD2, which was quite weak. Therefore, Rivest started working on MD3. However, due to some technical deficiency, MD3 was never released. This led Rivest to the release of MD4, which too worked for a short period of time and ultimately, it was replaced by MD5. MD5 is quite fast and has been resistant to collision till now.

Figure 7.2 shows the block diagram for generating message digest using MD5. The algorithm takes a variable-length message as input and produces a fixed-length message digest. It processes the given input in blocks of 512 bits, which are again divided into 16 blocks of 32 bits each. The output obtained is a set of four blocks of 32 bits each, that is, total 128 bits.

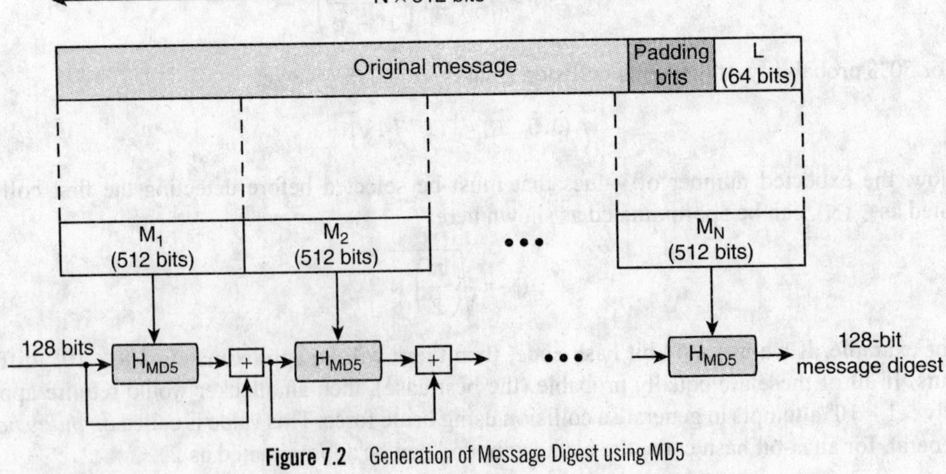

Figure 7.2 Generation of Message Digest using MD5

The following steps are involved in the working of MD5.

Step 1: Append Padding Bits

In the initial step, the padding bits are added to the end of the original message. This is done as to make the number of bits in the message equal to 64 bits less than an integral multiple of 512. For example, if the original message is of 1900 bits, then 84 bits are padded to make the length of the message 1984 bits. The reason behind adding 84 bits is that when we add 64 to 1984, we get 2048, which is an exact multiple of 512 (512*4 = 2048). Padding bits comprise a single one bit followed by the required number of zero bits. It is mandatory to add padding bits even if the length of the original message plus 64 is already an exact multiple of 512. For example, if the original message is of 448 bits (448 + 64 = 512), even then 512 padding bits need to be added. Thus, the number of padding bits may vary from 1 to 512 bits, and the length of the message after adding padding bits can be 448 bits, 960 bits, 1472 bits, and so on.

Step 2: Append Length

The next step is to calculate the length of the message excluding the padding bits. For example, if the original message is 1900 bits long, and the length of message after adding padding bits is 1984 bits, then here the length is considered as 1900 and not 1984. The length (say, `L`) is expressed as a 64-bit value, and these 64 bits are added at the end of the message, plus the padding bits. In case the message is too long to be expressed as a 64-bit value, then we need to take the length modulo 2^{64}. After appending the length, we get a message whose length is an exact multiple of 512. Now, the digest of this message is to be found.

Step 3: Divide the Input Message into 512-bit Blocks

In this step, the input message is divided into `N` 512-bit blocks, denoted as $M_1, M_2, \ldots, M_N$. For example, in our case, the 2048-bit message will be divided into four blocks of 512 bits each.

Step 4: Initialize MD Buffer

A 128-bit buffer is used to hold the intermediate and final results of the hash function while computing the message digest. This buffer is represented as four 32-bit registers (`A`, `B`, `C`, `D`). Each of these registers is initialized with a 32-bit integer in hexadecimal (initial hash values), as shown here:

A = 01 23 45 67
B = 89 AB CD EF
C = FE DC BA 98
D = 76 54 32 10

The MD5 algorithm treats the registers `A`, `B`, `C` and `D` as a single 128-bit register `ABCD`.

Step 5: Process Blocks

Each 512-bit block of the message is now processed as follows:

a. Copy the contents of `A`, `B`, `C` and `D` into four corresponding 32-bit variables H_0, H_1, H_2 and H_3 as shown here:

$$H_0 = A$$
$$H_1 = B$$
$$H_2 = C$$
$$H_3 = D$$

b. The 512-bit block is divided into 16 sub-blocks of 32 bits each, denoted as, $S_1, S_2, \ldots, S_{16}$ or in general as S_i where $1 \le i \le 16$.

c. Now, the compression function, labelled as H_{MD5} in Figure 7.2, is applied on the 512-bit block. The compression function comprises four rounds where each round takes three inputs: all the 16 32-bit sub-blocks of the current 512-bit block, the register ABCD and an array of constants T (see Figure 7.3). The array T consists of 64 elements of 32 bits each, represented as $T_1, T_2, \ldots, T_{64}$ or in general as T_j where $1 \le j \le 64$. As there are total four rounds, 16 values of array T are used in each round. Each round updates the contents of the register ABCD by performing the MD5 algorithm steps.

d. Each round contains 16 iterations, one per each sub-block, that is, there are total 64 iterations in MD5 for one 512-bit block. Each iteration involves certain operations to update the contents of the register ABCD.

After performing all the 64 iterations for one 512-bit block, each of the four registers (A, B, C and D) is incremented by the value it had before the processing of that block, as shown here:

$$A = A + H_0$$
$$B = B + H_1$$
$$C = C + H_2$$
$$D = D + H_3$$

This incremented value of A, B, C and D (128 bits together) becomes one of the inputs to the first round of the next 512-bit block. Notice that addition is performed using modulo 2^{32}.

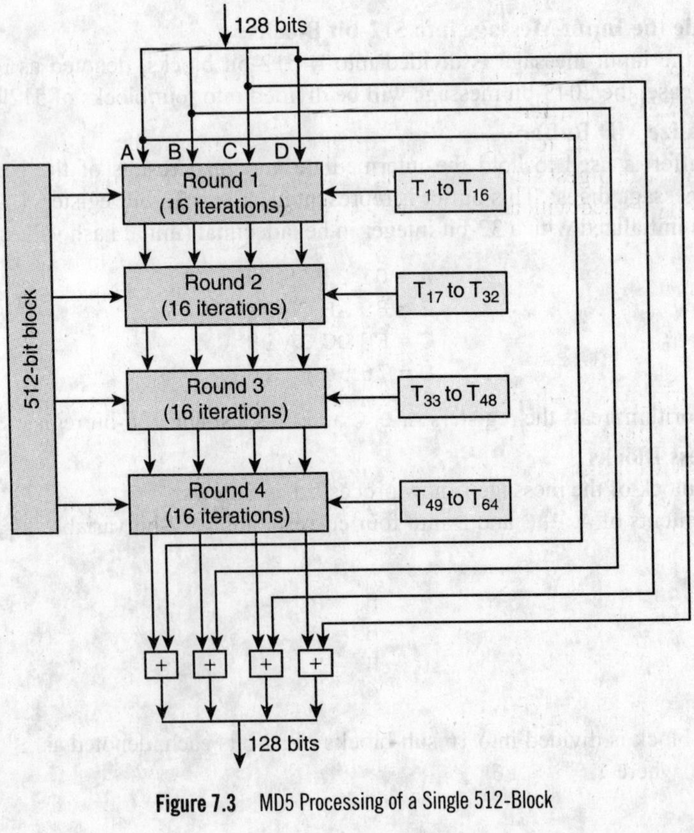

Figure 7.3 MD5 Processing of a Single 512-Block

Single MD5 Iteration: Each iteration in MD5 goes through the following steps (see Figure 7.4).

i. Apply a function F on registers B, C and D. The function F differs for each round.
ii. Add the contents of register A to the output of the previous step.
iii. Add the message sub-block S_i to the output of the previous step.
iv. Add the constant T_j to the output of the previous step.
v. Perform circular left shift operation by m bits on the output of the previous step. Notice that the value of m and T_j differ for each iteration, as defined by MD5.
vi. Add the contents of register B to the output of the previous step.
vii. Store the contents of register D into a 32-bit temporary variable (say, Temp).
viii. Copy the contents of register C to register D.
ix. Copy the contents of register B to register C.
x. Copy the output of step (vi) to register B.
xi. Copy the value of variable Temp to register A.

After performing these steps, we get new ABCD for the next iteration.

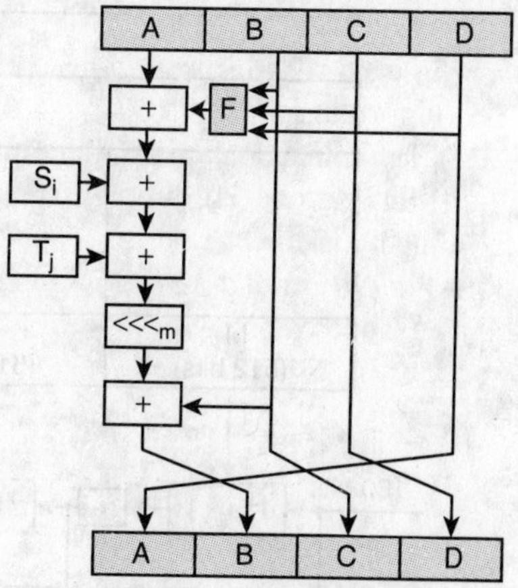

Figure 7.4 Single MD5 Iteration

Mathematical representation of a single MD5 iteration can be given as:

$$ABCD = (D, ((A + F(B, C, D) + S_i + T_j) <<<_m) + B, B, C)$$

Where,

F = a non-linear function different for each round

$S_i = S_{q \times 16 + i}$, the ith 32-bit sub-block in the qth 512-bit block of the message

T_j = a 32-bit constant

$<<<_m$ = circular left shift by m bits

+ = addition modulo 2^{32}.

Function F: The function F is different in each of the four rounds, while the rest of the steps are the same. The function F involves some Boolean operations on the variables B, C and D in the four rounds, as shown here:

Round 1: $(B \wedge C) \vee ((!B) \wedge D)$

Round 2: $(B \wedge D) \vee (C \wedge (!D))$

Round 3: $B \oplus C \oplus D$

Round 4: $C \oplus (B \vee (!D))$

Step 6: Output

After all the 512-bit blocks of the message have been processed, the contents of the register ABCD form the 128-bit message digest.

10. Explain the working of SHA-1.

Ans.: *Secure Hash Algorithm* (SHA), also referred to as *Secure Hash Standard* (SHS), was developed by the National Security Agency (NSA). In 1993, it was published by the National Institute of Standards and Technology (NIST) as a Federal Information Processing Standard (FIPS PUB 180). In 1995, a revised version of SHA was issued as FIPS PUB 180-1, which was given the name SHA-1. SHA-1 has been designed such that it is computationally infeasible to determine the original message from a given message digest, as well as to determine two messages generating the same message digest.

Figure 7.5 shows the block diagram for generating a message digest using SHA-1. Like MD5, the SHA-1 algorithm takes an input message with a maximum length of 2^{64} bits and processes the input in 512-bit blocks. However, it produces a message digest of 160 bits, unlike MD5.

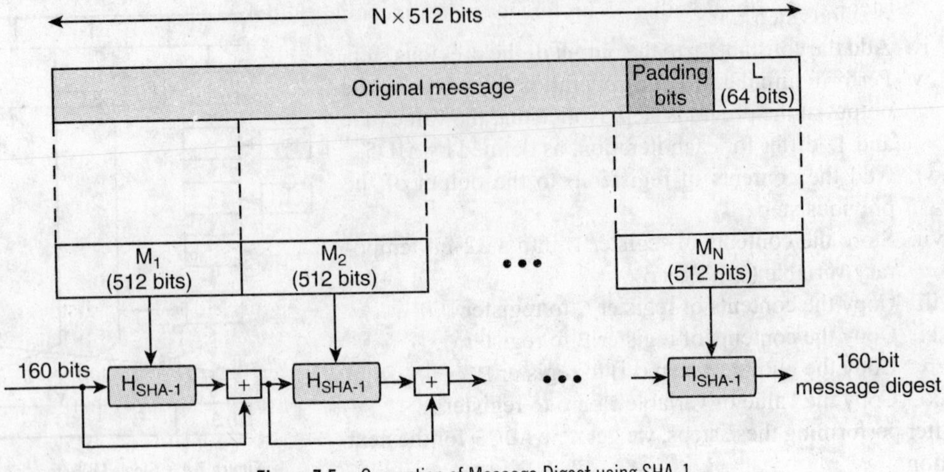

Figure 7.5 Generation of Message Digest using SHA-1

The working of SHA-1 involves the following steps:

Step 1: Append Padding Bits

In the initial step, the padding bits are added to the end of the original message. This is done as to make the number of bits in the message equal to 64 bits less than an integral multiple of 512. For example, if the original message is of 1900 bits, then 84 bits are padded to make the length of the message 1984 bits. The reason behind adding 84 bits is that when we add 64 to 1984, we get 2048, which is an exact multiple of 512 (512*4 = 2048). Padding bits comprise a single one bit followed by the required number of zero bits. It is mandatory to add padding bits even if the length of the original message plus 64 is already an exact multiple of 512. For example, if the original message is of 448 bits (448 + 64 = 512), even then 512 padding bits need to be added. Thus, the number of padding bits may vary from 1 to 512 bits, and the length of the message after adding padding bits can be 448 bits, 960 bits, 1472 bits and so on.

Step 2: Append Length

The next step is to calculate the length of message excluding the padding bits. For example, if the original message is 1900 bits long, and the length of message after adding the padding bits is 1984 bits, then here the length is considered as 1900 and not 1984. The length (say, `L`) is expressed as a 64-bit value, and these 64 bits are added at the end of the message plus padding bits. In case the message is too long to be expressed as a 64-bit value, then we need to take the length modulo 2^{64}. After appending the length, we get a message whose length is an exact multiple of 512. Now, the digest of this message is to be found.

Step 3: Divide the Input Message into 512-bit Blocks

In this step, the input message is divided into `N` 512-bit blocks, denoted as $M_1, M_2, \ldots, M_N$. For example, in our case, the 2048-bit message will be divided into four blocks of 512 bits each.

Step 4: Initialize Hash Buffer

A 160-bit buffer is used to hold the intermediate and final results of the hash function while computing the message digest. This buffer is represented as five 32-bit registers (`A`, `B`, `C`, `D`, `E`). Each of these registers is initialized with a 32-bit integer in hexadecimal (initial hash values), as shown here:

```
A = 67 45 23 01
B = EF CD AB 89
C = 98 BA DC FE
D = 10 32 54 76
E = C3 D2 E1 F0
```

The SHA-1 algorithm treats the registers `A`, `B`, `C`, `D` and `E` as a single 160-bit register `ABCDE`.

Step 5: Process Blocks

Each 512-bit block of message is now processed. Initially, the contents of the five registers `A`, `B`, `C`, `D` and `E` are copied to five 32-bit variables H_0, H_1, H_2, H_3 and H_4, respectively. Then, the 512-bit block is divided into 16 sub-blocks of 32 bits each. Now, the compression function, labelled as H_{SHA-1} in Figure 7.5, is applied on the 512-bit block. The compression function consists of four rounds, with each round consisting of 20 iterations. That is, a total of 80 iterations are performed to process one 512-block. As shown in Figure 7.6, each of the four rounds takes three inputs: all the 16 32-bit

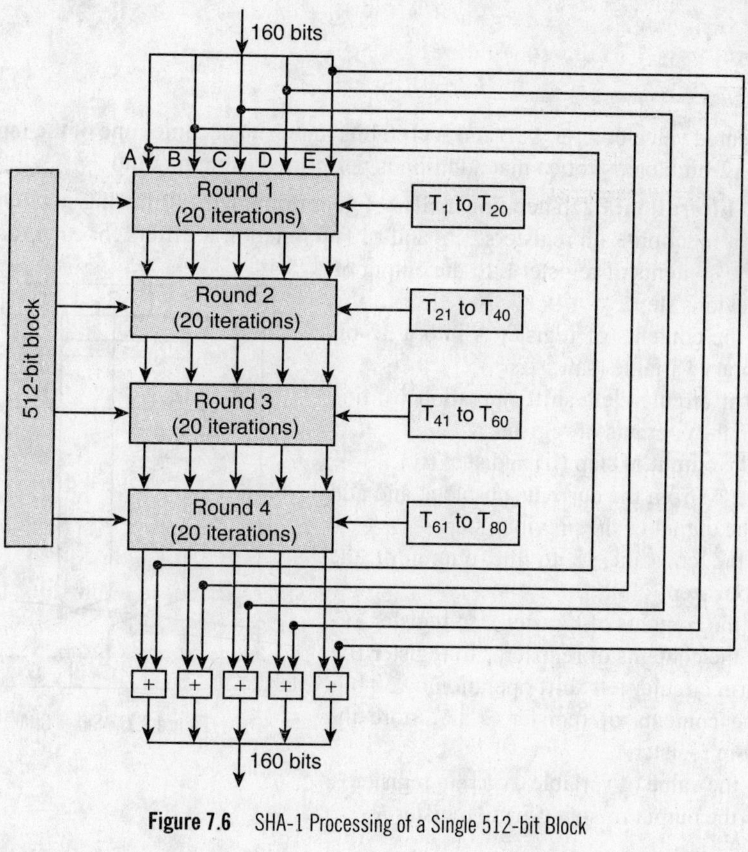

Figure 7.6 SHA-1 Processing of a Single 512-bit Block

sub-blocks of the current 512-bit block, the register ABCDE and an additive constant T_i where $1 \le i \le 80$. Unlike MD5, in SHA-1, we have only four values defined for T_i, one value per round, as shown in Table 7.1.

Table 7.1 Values of T_i

Round	Value of i	Value of T_i (in hexadecimal)
1	$1 \le i \le 20$	5A 92 79 99
2	$21 \le i \le 40$	6E D9 EB A1
3	$41 \le i \le 60$	8F 1B BC DC
4	$61 \le i \le 80$	CA 62 C1 D6

Each iteration of SHA-1 involves certain operations to update the contents of the register ABCDE. After performing all the 80 iterations for one 512-bit block, each of the five registers (A, B, C, D and E) is incremented by the value it had before the processing of that block, as shown here:

$$A = A + H_0$$
$$B = B + H_1$$
$$C = C + H_2$$
$$D = D + H_3$$
$$E = E + H_4$$

This incremented value of A, B, C, D and E (160 bits together) becomes one of the inputs to the first round of next 512-bit block. Notice that addition is performed using modulo 2^{32}.

Single SHA-1 Iteration: Each iteration in SHA-1 goes through the following steps (see Figure 7.7).

i. Apply a function F on registers B, C and D. The function F differs for each round.
ii. Add the contents of register E to the output of the previous step.
iii. Store the contents of register A into a 32-bit temporary variable (say, Temp).
iv. Perform circular left shift operation by five bits on the contents of register A.
v. Add the output of step (ii) and step (iv).
vi. Derive W_i from the current sub-block and add it to the output of the previous step.
vii. Add the constant T_i to the output of the previous step.
viii. Copy the contents of register D to register E.
ix. Copy the contents of register C to register D.
x. Perform circular left shift operation by 30 bits on the contents of register B and store the result in register C.
xi. Copy the value of variable Temp to register B.
xii. Copy the output of step (vii) to register A.

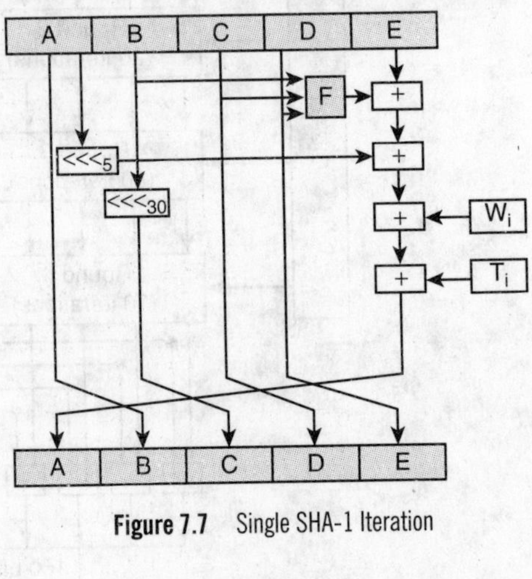

Figure 7.7 Single SHA-1 Iteration

After performing the preceding steps, we get new ABCDE for the next iteration.
Mathematical representation of a single SHA-1 operation can be given as:

$$ABCDE = ((E + F(B, C, D) + <<<_5 (A) + W_i + T_i), A, <<<_{30} (B), C, D)$$

Where,

F = a non-linear function different for each round
W_i = a 32-bit block derived from current 32-bit sub-block S_i based on rules (see Table 7.2)
T_i = one of the five 32-bit additive constants
$<<<_m$ = circular left shift by m positions
+ = addition modulo 2^{32}.

Table 7.2 Values of W

Value of i	Value of W_i
$1 \le i \le 16$	Same as M_i
$17 \le i \le 80$	$<<<_1 (W_{i-16} \oplus W_{i-14} \oplus W_{i-8} \oplus W_{i-3})$

Function F: The function F is different in each of the four rounds, while the rest of the steps are the same. The function F involves some Boolean operations on the variables B, C and D in the four rounds, as shown here:

Round 1: $(B \wedge C) \vee ((!B) \wedge D)$
Round 2: $B \oplus C \oplus D$
Round 3: $(B \wedge C) \vee (B \wedge D) \vee (C \wedge D)$
Round 4: $B \oplus C \oplus D$

Step 6: Output

After all the 512-bit blocks of the message have been processed, the contents of the register ABCDE form the 160-bit message digest.

11. Differentiate between SHA-1 and MD5.

Ans.: Both SHA-1 and MD5 are message digest algorithms. The design and functionality of SHA-1 and MD5 are almost similar. However, there are certain key differences between them. Some of these differences are listed in the Table 7.3.

Table 7.3 Differences between SHA-1 and MD5

SHA-1 Algorithm	MD5 Algorithm
It generates a message digest of 160 bits.	It generates a message digest of 128 bits.
It uses little-endian scheme to interpret the message as a sequence of 32-bit words. In this scheme, the most significant byte of a 32-bit word is stored in the low-address byte position.	It uses big-endian scheme, where the least significant byte of a 32-bit word is stored in the low-address byte position.
It undergoes four rounds, each having 20 iterations, that is, a total of 80 iterations are used. Moreover, it requires a 160-bit buffer and, thus, is slower in operation than MD5.	It undergoes four rounds, each having 16 iterations, that is, a total of 64 iterations are used. Moreover, it requires a 128-bit buffer and, thus, is faster in operation than SHA-1.

(Continued...)

Table 7.3 (...Continued)

SHA-1 Algorithm	MD5 Algorithm
It requires 21^{60} operations for finding the original message from the given message digest and 2^{80} operations to find two messages generating the same message digest.	It requires 21^{28} operations for finding the original message from the given message digest and 2^{64} operations to find two messages generating the same message digest.
It is not vulnerable to cryptanalytic attack.	It is vulnerable to cryptanalytic attack.
It is more secure than MD5.	It is less secure as compared to SHA-1.

12. Explain Whirlpool cryptographic hash function.

Ans.: *Whirlpool* is a cryptographic hash function designed by Vincent Rijmen and Paulo S.L.M. Barreto. It is one of the hash functions that have been supported by New European Schemes for Signatures, Integrity, and Encryption (NESSIE). It is based on the use of a symmetric-key block cipher instead of a compression function as used in MD5 and SHA. The Whirlpool cipher is a modified version of the Advanced Encryption Standard (AES) cipher.

Whirlpool Hash Function

Figure 7.8 shows the block diagram for generating a message digest using Whirlpool (the triangular hatch in the figure indicates key input). The algorithm takes as input a message with a maximum length of up to 2^{256} bits, processes the input in 512-bit blocks and returns a 512-bit hash code as output. The steps involved in the working of the Whirlpool hash function are as follows:

1. *Append padding bits:* In the initial step, the padding bits are added to the end of the original message. This is done so as to make the length of the message an odd multiple of 256. For example, if the original message is of 600 bits, then 168 bits are padded to make the length of the message 768 bits (768 = 256*3). Padding bits comprise a single one bit followed by the required number of zero bits. It is mandatory to add padding bits even if the length of the original message is already of the desired length. For example, if the original message is of 256 bits, even then 512 padding

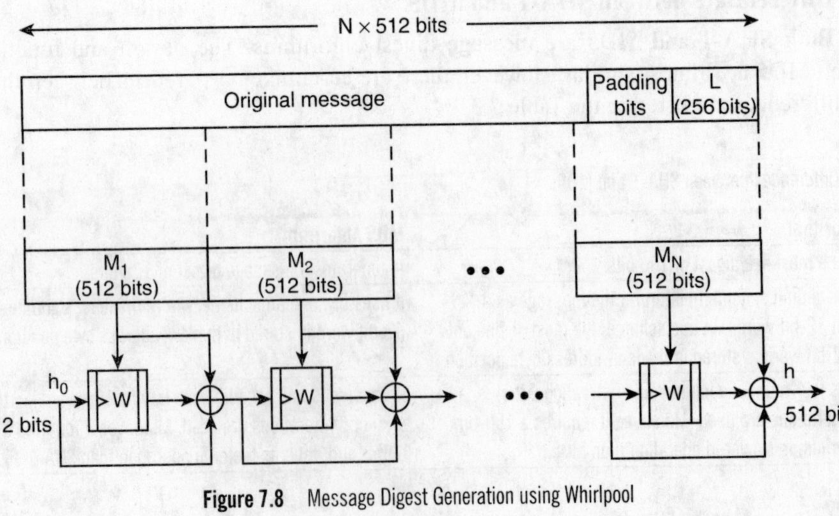

Figure 7.8 Message Digest Generation using Whirlpool

bits need to be added to make the length equal to 768 bits. Thus, the number of padding bits may vary from 1 to 512 bits.

2. *Append length:* The next step is to calculate the length of the message excluding the padding bits. The length (say, `L`) is expressed as a 256-bit value, and these 256 bits are added at the end of the message plus padding bits. After appending the length, we get a message whose length is an even multiple of 256 or an integral multiple of 512.
3. *Divide the message into 512-bit blocks:* The message is divided into `N` 512-bit blocks, $M_1, M_2, \ldots, M_N$. Each of these blocks is treated as an array of 8-bit bytes (that is, total 64 bytes). A byte matrix of size 8 × 8 is used to hold the intermediate and final hash values. The matrix is initialized with zero bits.
4. *Process message blocks:* Each message block of 512 bits is processed through the Whirlpool cipher (`W`) and, finally, a 512-bit message digest (`h`) is generated. To process the first message block, the 512-bit message digest (h_0) is initialized with all zeros and is used as the cipher key for encrypting the first message block. The ciphertext produced after encrypting each block is XORed with the previous cipher key and previous plaintext block. The result obtained is used as the cipher key for encrypting the next 512-bit block. This process continues, and the final ciphertext block after the last XOR operation becomes the final 512-bit message digest `h`.

Whirlpool Cipher

The Whirlpool cipher (`W`) is a non-Feistel cipher that operates on 512-bit blocks (64 bytes). It consists of 10 rounds and uses a key size of 512 bits. The cipher uses a total of 11 round keys ($K_0, K_1, \ldots, K_{10}$), with each key of 512 bits. The round keys are generated using the key expansion algorithm. The general design of the Whirlpool cipher is shown in Figure 7.9.

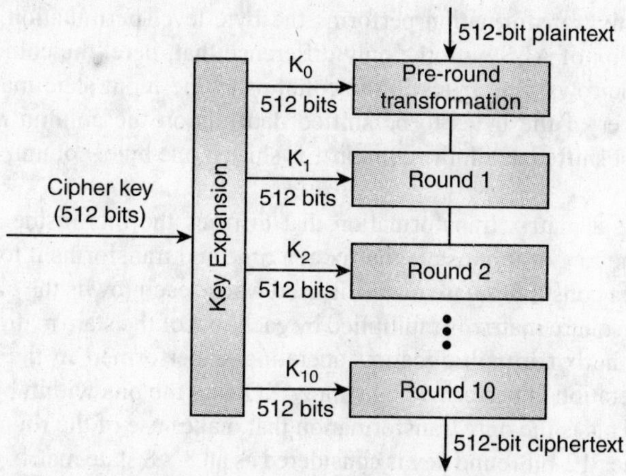

Figure 7.9 General Design of Whirlpool Cipher

State and blocks: Each round in the Whirlpool cipher consists of many stages, where each stage transforms the 512-bit (64-byte) data block. As with AES, the Whirlpool cipher also uses the term 'block' at the beginning and end of the cipher and the term 'state' before and after each stage. The only difference is that here the size of state and block is 512 bits. Each 512-bit block is treated as a row matrix of 64 bytes, and a state is treated as a square matrix of 8 × 8 bytes. The transformation from block to state and vice versa is performed row wise, unlike in AES cipher.

Structure of each round: Each round involves four transformations; namely, *Substitute Bytes*, *Shift Columns*, *Mix Rows* and *Add Round Key* (see Figure 7.10). Moreover, one Add Round Key transformation is applied before the first round (mentioned as pre-round transformation in Figure 7.9). Each transformation accepts a state, changes it and creates a new state, which is given as input to the next transformation or the next round.

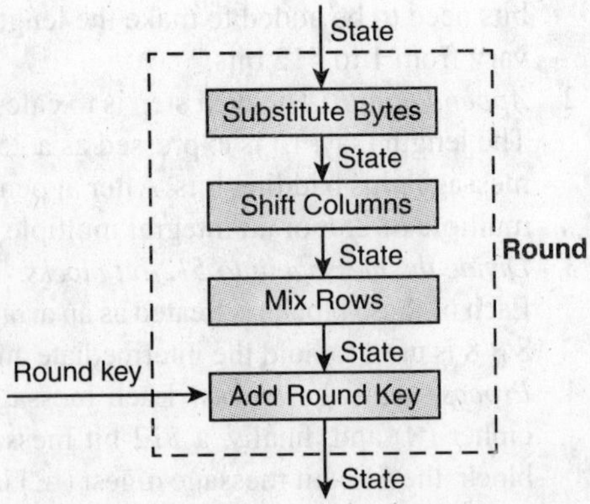

Figure 7.10 Structure of each Round in Whirlpool Cipher

The transformations involved in each round are described as follows:

- *Substitute Bytes:* This is the first transformation of a round that performs substitution of bytes. The input to this transformation is an 8 × 8 byte state matrix. The bytes in the matrix are substituted one at a time; thus, there are 64 distinct byte-to-byte transformations. The bytes are substituted either with the help of a substitution table or by performing the mathematical calculations in $GF(2^4)$ field. To substitute the bytes using a substitution table, each byte is treated as two hexadecimal digits, where the first digit (left one) specifies the row and the second digit (right one) specifies the column of the substitution table. The value (two hexadecimal digits) at the intersection of the row and the column in the substitution table is the new byte with which the given byte is to be replaced. Notice that, in this transformation, the contents of each byte is changed; however, the order of bytes in the matrix does not change.
- *Shift Columns:* This transformation performs the byte-level permutation. It is similar to Shift Rows transformation of AES with the only difference that, here, the columns of the matrix are shifted, and not the rows. The bytes in the columns of the input state matrix are shifted to the left and the number of the bytes to be shifted depends on the column number. For example, the column 0 is not shifted at all, the column 1 is shifted one byte, column 2 is shifted two bytes, and so on.
- *Mix Rows:* This is a matrix transformation that diffuses the bits inside the bytes of the state matrix. It takes one row of input state matrix at a time and transforms it to a new row. For transforming the rows, a constant square matrix is used whose each row is the circular right shift of its previous row. The square matrix is multiplied by each row of the state matrix, resulting in another row. Notice that the bytes multiplication operation is performed in the $GF(2^8)$ field, and the bytes addition operation is performed by simply XORing the bits within bytes.
- *Add Round Key:* This is the only transformation that makes use of the round key. To perform this transformation, the 512-bit round key is considered as an 8 × 8 state matrix. Each byte of the input state matrix is added with the corresponding byte of round key state matrix in the $GF(2^8)$ field, resulting in a new byte.

13. What is HMAC? What are its design objectives? Explain its working.

Ans.: *Hash-based MAC* (HMAC) is a message authentication code derived from a cryptographic hash function such as MD5 and SHA-1. The basic idea behind HMAC is to use a secret key in the existing message digest algorithms (hash functions). It has been issued as a standard (FIPS 198) by NIST. As algorithms such as MD5 and SHA-1 do not rely on the secret key, HMAC has been selected as mandatory-to-implement MAC for IP security. It is also used in other Internet protocols, such as Secure Socket Layer (SSL).

HMAC can work with any existing message digest algorithms (hash functions). It considers the message digest produced by the embedded hash function as a black box. It then uses the shared symmetric key to encrypt the message digest, thus, producing the final output, that is, MAC.

Design Objectives of HMAC

HMAC was issued as RFC 2104, which defines the following objectives for HMAC.

- To use the existing hash functions such as MD5 and SHA-1 without modification.
- To be able to easily replace an existing hash function in case a fast hash function is available or needed.
- To maintain the original performance of the function till the time it is possible.
- To use the keys and to handle them in a simple and efficient manner.
- To better understand the cryptographic analysis of the strength of the authentication mechanism used in embedded hash function.

HMAC Implementation

The implementation of HMAC is very complex. Before discussing the algorithm, let us define the variables used in the algorithm.

H = embedded cryptographic hash function such as MD5 or SHA
IV = initial value to the hash function
M = input message
q = number of input blocks in M
n = length of the message digest (or hash value)
b = number of bits in a block
M_i = i^{th} block of input message with $1 \le i \le q$
K = shared symmetric key (secret key)
K_{pad} = secret key K padded with 0s on the left to make the length b bits
I_{pad} = input pad, a constant having value 00110110 (36 in hex) repeated b/8 times
O_{pad} = output pad, a constant having value 01011100 (5C in hex) repeated b/8 times

Mathematically, the HMAC operation can be expressed as:

$$\text{HMAC}(K, M) = H[(K_{pad} \oplus O_{pad}) \| H[(K_{pad} \oplus I_{pad}) \| M]]$$

Figure 7.11 depicts the HMAC operation. Initially, the given input message M is divided into q blocks, $M_1, M_2, \ldots, M_q$, with each block having b bits. Then, the following steps are performed to produce the n-bit message digest.

1. *Add padding bits to secret key* K: Add the required number of zeros to the left of secret key K to make it a b-bit string, K_{pad}. It is recommended that the original size of secret key K should not be greater than n, the length of the message digest.
2. *XOR* K_{pad} *with* I_{pad}: Apply XOR operation on b-bit K_{pad} obtained from the previous step and the constant I_{pad} to create a b-bit block, say S_1.
3. *Append* M *to* S_1: Append the input message M (equivalent to q b-bit blocks) to the output of the previous step, that is, S_1. The result is q+1 blocks of b bits each.

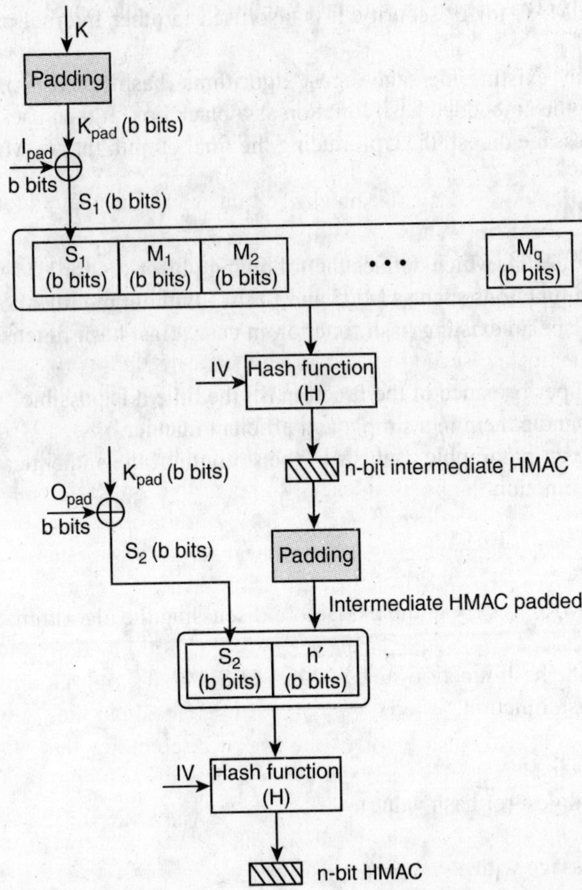

Figure 7.11 HMAC Structure

4. *Apply hash function:* Apply the selected hash function H on the stream containing q+1 blocks, generated in the previous step, to produce n-bit digest, referred to as the intermediate HMAC. The n-bit IV is also given as input to the hash function.
5. *Add padding bits to intermediate HMAC:* Add the required number of zeros to the left of n-bit intermediate HMAC to produce h′ with length equal to b bits.
6. *XOR K_{pad} with O_{pad}:* Apply XOR operation on b-bit K_{pad} and the constant O_{pad} to create a b-bit block, say S_2.
7. *Append h′ to S_2:* Append the b-bit intermediate HMAC (h′) obtained from step 5 to the output of the previous step, that is, S_2.
8. *Apply hash function:* Apply the same hash function H with an n-bit IV as input on the output of the previous step to produce a final n-bit message digest.

14. Discuss the security of HMAC.

Ans.: The security of HMAC depends on the cryptographic strength of the embedded hash function, the size of secret key used and the length of the message digest produced. In essence, the probability of attacking HMAC successfully is equal to either of the following attacks on the embedded hash function.

- The intruder can calculate the output of compression function without having the knowledge of IV, which is selected at random and kept secret.
- The intruder determines the collisions in the hash function even if the IV is secret and random.

To attempt the first attack, the compression function can be viewed as a hash function that is applied on a message containing only one b-bit block. The intruder selects a random value of n bits (i.e. the length of the message digest produced) and uses it in place of IV. However, to perform this attack on the hash function, either a brute-force attack on the secret key or a birthday attack is to be attempted, because HMAC involves the secret key also while computing the hash value. Attempting a brute-force attack on the secret key requires the intruder to perform 2^n operations.

On the other hand, to attempt the second attack, the intruder needs to determine two messages, M_1 and M_2, such that when the hash function H is applied on them, they yield the same output, that is, $H(M_1) = H(M_2)$. This is the birthday attack, and it requires the intruder to perform $2^{n/2}$ operations in case the hash code is of n bits. For example, if the MD5 algorithm, which produces 128-bit hash code, is used as the embedded hash function, the intruder has to perform 2^{64} operations in order to attempt birthday attack on the hash function. Performing so many operations does not seem infeasible with today's technology. However, it does not necessarily mean that MD5 is unsuitable to HMAC. The reason behind this is explained in the following text.

The intruder can attack MD5 by selecting some set of messages and generating the corresponding hash codes to determine the collisions. As the intruder knows the hash function as well as the default IV to MD5, he or she is able to work offline on some dedicated computing facility. However, when MD5 is used in HMAC, the intruder cannot determine the messages and their corresponding hash codes offline. This is because HMAC also involves the use of a secret key that is not known to the intruder. Therefore, the intruder needs to observe a series of messages being generated by HMAC using the same key and then attempt to attack these known messages. For a 128-bit hash code in MD5, this requires observing 2^{64} blocks generated using the same key. To observe so many blocks on a 1-Gbps link, one would need approx 1,50,000 years to succeed. Thus, the use of MD5 is acceptable to HMAC as far as speed is concerned.

Multiple-choice Questions

1. A ________ is used to verify the integrity and authenticity of a message.
   (a) Decryption algorithm (b) Message digest
   (c) MAC (d) Both (b) and (c)
2. Which of the following is the latest version of the SHA algorithm?
   (a) SHA-512 (b) SHA-256
   (c) SHA-128 (d) SHA-1
3. The purpose of hash function is to ensure ________.
   (a) Message integrity (b) Message authentication
   (c) Both (a) and (b) (d) None of these
4. Choose the odd one out.
   (a) RC5 (b) Blowfish
   (c) ECC (d) MAC

5. When two different messages yield the same message digest, it is called ________.
   (a) Attack
   (b) Collision
   (c) Hash
   (d) None of these
6. Which of the following is based on the use of asymmetric-key block cipher?
   (a) SHA-1
   (b) MD5
   (c) RIPEMD
   (d) Whirlpool
7. An attacker needs to perform ________ operations in order to determine collision in SHA-1.
   (a) 2^{64}
   (b) 2^{80}
   (c) 2^{256}
   (d) 2^{72}

Answers

1. (c) 2. (a) 3. (a) 4. (d) 5. (b) 6. (d)
7. (b)

8

Digital Signatures and Authentication Protocols

1. What is digital signature? Discuss the various services it provides.

Ans.: A *digital signature* is an authentication mechanism that allows the sender to attach an electronic code with the message in order to ensure its authenticity and integrity. This electronic code acts as the signature of the sender and, hence, is named *digital signature*. Digital signatures use the public-key cryptography technique. The sender uses his or her private key and a signing algorithm to create a digital signature, and the signed document can be made public. The receiver, on the other hand, uses the public key of the sender and a verifying algorithm to verify the digital signature.

Digital signatures are analogous to physical handwritten signatures and provide the following security services.

- *Message authentication:* A normal message authentication scheme protects the two communicating parties against attacks from a third party (intruder). However, a secure digital signature scheme protects the two parties against each other also. Suppose A wants to send a signed message (message with A's digital signature) to B through a network. For this, A encrypts the message using his or her private key, which results in a signed message. The signed message is then sent through the network to B. Now, B attempts to decrypt the received message using A's public key in order to verify that the received message has really come from A. If the message gets decrypted, B can believe that the message is from A. However, if the message or the digital signature has been modified during transmission, it cannot be decrypted using A's public key. From this, B can conclude that either the message transmission has tampered with, or that the message has not been generated by A.
- *Message integrity:* Digital signatures also provide message integrity. If a message bears a digital signature, then any change in the message after the signature is attached will invalidate the signature. That is, it is not possible to get the same signature if the message is changed. Moreover, there is no efficient way to modify a message and its signature such that a new message with

a valid signature is produced. These days, a hash function is used in the signing and verifying algorithms that help in preserving the integrity of the message.

- *Nonrepudiation:* Digital signatures also ensure nonrepudiation. For example, if A has sent a signed message to B, then in future A cannot deny about the sending of the message. B can keep a copy of the message along with A's signature. In case A denies, B can use A's public key to generate the original message. If the newly created message is the same as that initially sent by A, it is proved that the message has been sent by A only. In the same way, B can never create a forged message bearing A's digital signature, because only A can create his or her digital signatures with the help of that private key.
- *Message confidentiality:* Digital signatures do not provide message confidentiality, because anyone knowing the sender's public key can decrypt the message. Thus, to achieve message confidentiality, we need to encrypt the message along with the signature using either the secret-key encryption or public-key encryption scheme. For example, if we use the public-key encryption scheme, then at A's end, first the message is encrypted using A's private key and then a second encryption is performed using the B's public key. Similarly, at B's end, first the message is decrypted using B's private key and then a second decryption is performed using A's public key. With this mechanism, only B can decrypt the encrypted message received from A because only B knows his or her private key.

2. Describe the digital signature process with the help of a suitable diagram.

Ans.: The digital signature process is shown in Figure 8.1. Suppose user A wants to send a signed message to B through a network. To achieve this communication, these steps are followed:

(i) A uses his private key (E_A), applied to a signing algorithm, to sign the message (M).
(ii) The message (M) along with A's digital signature (S) is sent to B.
(iii) On receiving the message (M) and the signature (S), B uses A's public key (D_A), applied to the verifying algorithm, to verify the authenticity of the message. If the message is authentic, B accepts the message; otherwise it is rejected.

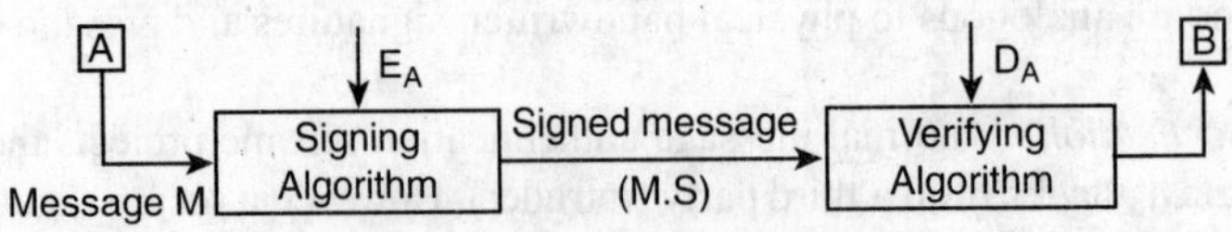

Figure 8.1 Digital Signature Process

3. How is the use of private and public keys in digital signatures different from that in public-key cryptography?

Ans.: The private and public keys used in public-key cryptography are different from the private and public keys used in digital signatures. In the former case, the public and private keys of the receiver are used for encryption and decryption of the message, respectively. That is, the sender encrypts the message using the receiver's public key, and the receiver decrypts the message using his own private key. However, in digital signatures, the private and public keys of the sender are used to create and verify the digital signature, respectively. That is, the sender creates a digital signature using his or her own private key, and the receiver verifies it using the sender's public key.

4. Can we use a secret (symmetric) key in the digital signature process? Justify your answer.

Ans.: We cannot use a secret (symmetric) key to create and verify digital signatures, due to the following two reasons.

- In symmetric-key cryptosystem, a secret key K is shared between two users only, say A and B. Now, if A wants to send another message to C, then he or she has to use another secret key.
- B could create a forged signed message using the secret key K that is shared between A and B, and send that message to C pretending that it has come from A.

5. What are the essential properties and requirements for a digital signature?

Ans.: A digital signature is used in those situations where there is a lack of trust between the sender and the receiver. For example, suppose a user A transfers funds to B electronically. Now, B in future increases the amount of funds transferred and claims that the larger amount had arrived from A. Thus, to achieve secure communication between the two users and to resolve their disputes if any, digital signature must have the following properties:

- It must be able to verify the author and the date and time of the signature.
- It must be able to authenticate the contents of the message at the time of the signature.
- There must be some third (trusted) party who can verify the digital signature to resolve disputes between the sender and receiver.

Thus, we can say that the authentication function is included within the digital signature function. Based on the these properties, we can list out the following requirements for a digital signature:

- The signature must be in the form of a bit pattern and relative to the message being signed.
- The signature must contain some information that is unique to the sender, so that forgery and denial can be avoided.
- The process of creating the digital signature must be comparatively easy.
- The process of recognizing and verifying the digital signature must also be comparatively easy.
- A high computational effort must be required to forge a digital signature. That is, it must be infeasible for an intruder to create a new message for an existing signature or to create a fake digital signature for an existing message.
- The copy of a digital signature must be retained in some storage mechanism.

6. Discuss the different kinds of attacks on digital signatures.

Ans.: There are three kinds of attacks possible on digital signatures, namely, *key-only*, *known message* and *chosen-message attack*. To get an idea of these attacks, consider A and B as the communicating parties and C as the opponent.

- *Key-only attack:* In this type of attack, the intruder knows only the public information of A. With the help of this information, the intruder tries to create A's digital signature. He then forges the message by putting the newly created A's signature and sends the signed message to B pretending that it has come from A. It is similar to the ciphertext-only attack discussed in Chapter 2.
- *Known-message attack:* In this type of attack, the intruder has access to some messages signed by A. That is, he or she already has one or more message–signature pairs. With the help of these known message–signature pairs, the intruder tries to create another message and forge A's digital signature on it. This attack is similar to the known-plaintext attack discussed in Chapter 2.
- *Chosen-message attack:* In this type of attack, the intruder manages to let A sign one or more messages for him. In other words, the intruder himself chooses a message–signature pair.

Later, he creates a new message with the contents he or she wants and forges A's digital signature on it, and sends it to B pretending that it has come from A. This attack is similar to the chosen-plaintext attack discussed in Chapter 2.

7. Discuss the different approaches proposed for the digital signature function.

Ans.: A digital signature cannot be a constant and must be a function of the entire document it signs. There are several approaches that have been proposed for the digital signature function. These approaches are categorized into two types: *direct* and *arbitrated.*

Direct digital signature

In the direct digital signature approach, the signed document is directly passed from the sender to the receiver. That is, no third party is involved in carrying out this communication, because it is assumed that the receiver knows the public key of the sender and, hence, can easily verify the authenticity of the message. There are two ways of creating a digital signature—one, by encrypting the whole message with the sender's private key, and another, by taking the hash of the message and then encrypting it with the sender's private key. Message confidentiality can be achieved by further encrypting the message and the signature with the receiver's public key in case of public-key encryption or shared key in case of symmetric-key encryption.

Though there is no third party directly involved in carrying out the communication between the sender and receiver, in case of disputes, the third party may be involved in resolving the conflicts. The third party views both the message and its signature. If the signature function is applied on the encrypted message, then the third party also needs to know the decryption key to read the plaintext message. However, if the signature function is applied on the plaintext message, then the recipient can simply store the plaintext message and its signature, so that it can be used in future for resolving disputes. Thus, it is better to apply the digital signature function on the message before encrypting it.

The main problem with the direct digital signature scheme is that if the sender wants to deny the sending of a particular message, he or she can claim that his or her private key is stolen or lost and that someone has forged the signatures. Since no trusted third party is directly involved in the communication, it is difficult to verify whether the key was actually stolen, or if the sender is lying. This type of threat can be controlled to some extent by two ways:

- The sender whose key has been stolen can immediately report to a central authority, or
- The sender can include a timestamp (date and time) in each signed message.

The latter solution can still be compromised. For example, if the private key of the sender A is actually stolen at time (t), then some intruder (say, X) can create A's signature and send a forged signed message to B including a timestamp before or equal to t.

Arbitrated digital signature

In the arbitrated digital signature approach, a third party known as the *trusted arbiter* is directly involved in the process. Every signed message sent by the sender to the receiver goes through the arbiter. The arbiter performs two functions. First, it verifies the integrity (origin and content) of the signed message and signature by applying a certain number of tests. Second, it attaches the date and time of creation of the message, and forwards the message to its final destination. This scheme is based on the assumption that both the sender and receiver completely trust the arbiter's claim that he or she verifies the message to the level of his or her satisfaction and will not alter the data in any way.

The main advantages of the arbitrated digital signature approach are as follows:

- Both the communicating parties cannot share any kind of information before communication, thus preventing the chances of any kind of fraud.
- Any incorrectly dated message cannot be sent to the receiver.
- The contents of the message from A to B are hidden from the trusted third party and others.

8. Write a short note on the RSA digital signature scheme.

Ans.: In addition to the encryption and decryption of a message, the RSA approach can also be used for signing and verifying the message. In this case, it is known as the *RSA digital signature scheme.* At the sender's end, the message M to be signed is given as input to a function, which produces the digital signature S with the help of sender's private key. The sender then transmits both the message and the signature to the receiver. At the receiver's end, the digital signature S is given as input to a function, which computes the copy of the message (M′) with the help of sender's public key. Now, the receiver compares the received and the computed message. If M and M′ are congruent, the receiver accepts the message, otherwise rejects it. The RSA digital signature scheme is shown in Figure 8.2.

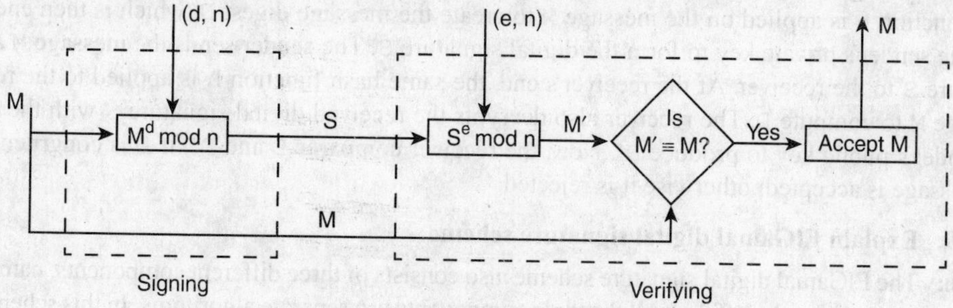

Figure 8.2 RSA Digital Signature Scheme

The key generation, signing and verifying algorithms for the RSA digital signature scheme are described as follows:

Key generation: The sender generates his or her private and public key as follows:

(i) The sender chooses two prime numbers p and q and computes the following:

$$n = p * q$$

$$\phi(n) = (p-1)(q-1)$$

(ii) He then chooses $e(1 < e < \phi(n))$, the public exponent, and computes his private key d such that:

$$e * d = 1 \bmod \phi(n)$$

Signing: The sender creates his digital signature S using his private key d as follows:

$$S = M^d \bmod n$$

where M is the message to be signed.

Verifying: The receiver receives the message M and signature S, and computes a copy of the message using the sender's public key (e, n) as follows:

$$M' = S^e \bmod n$$

The receiver then compares M′ with M. If $M' \equiv M$, the message is accepted; otherwise, it is rejected.

To prove the RSA digital signature scheme, we need to show that $M' \equiv M(\text{mod } n)$.

As,

$$M' \equiv S^e(\text{mod } n) \qquad (1)$$

And,

$$S \equiv M^d(\text{mod } n)$$

Thus, we can write equation (1) as

$$M' \equiv M^{d*e}(\text{mod } n)$$

Since $\quad d*e = 1 \text{ mod } \phi(n)$

Therefore, $\quad M' \equiv M\,(\text{mod } n)$

Hence, proved.

RSA digital signature scheme on a message digest

The RSA digital signature scheme can also be applied on a message digest. In this case, a strong hash function h is applied on the message M to create the message digest D, which is then encrypted with the sender's private key to form the digital signature S. The sender sends the message M and the signature S to the receiver. At the receiver's end, the same hash function h is applied to the received message M to compute D. The receiver also decrypts the received digital signature S with the help of the sender's public key to produce D′. Now, the receiver compares D and D′, if D is congruent to D′, the message is accepted; otherwise it is rejected.

9. Explain ElGamal digital signature scheme.

Ans.: The ElGamal digital signature scheme also consists of three different components, namely, *key generation*, *signing* and *verifying*. All the three components use separate algorithms. In this scheme, four functions are used, in which one function is common in both the signing and verification process, however, with different inputs. Thus, in total, only three different functions are used in the whole process.

In the signing process, two functions F_1 and F_2 are used to create two different digital signatures S_1 and S_2, respectively. The sender transmits the message M and the signatures S_1 and S_2 to the receiver. On receiving the message and the two signatures, the receiver computes two verification codes V_1 and V_2 with the help of the functions F_1 and F_3, respectively. Now, the receiver compares two codes V_1 and V_2; if both are congruent, the message is accepted; otherwise it is rejected. The ElGamal digital signature scheme is shown in Figure 8.3.

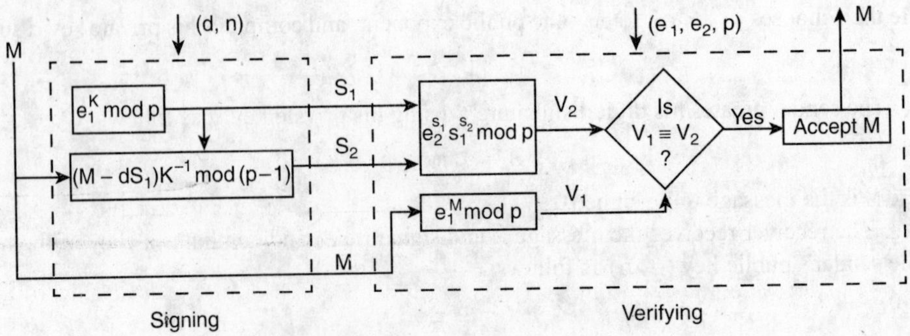

Figure 8.3 ElGamal Digital Signature Scheme

The key generation, signing and verifying algorithms for ElGamal digital signature scheme are described as follows:

Key generation: The sender generates his or her private and public keys as follows:

(i) The sender chooses a large prime number p, such that the discrete log problem is difficult in Z_p^*.

(ii) The sender then chooses his or her private key d, such that $1 \leq d < p-1$, and computes $e_2 = e_1^d \bmod p$, where e_1 is a primitive root Z_p^*. The public key of A is (e_1, e_2, p), and the private key is d.

Signing: To create the signature, the sender chooses a random number k, such that $0 < k < q$, and then computes the value of S_1 and S_2 as follows:

$$S_1 = e_1^k \bmod p$$

(S_1 is independent of the message M)

$$S_2 = [k^{-1} * (M - dS_1)] \bmod (p-1)$$

(where k^{-1} is the multiplicative inverse of k modulo p)

Digital signature = (S_1, S_2)

Verifying: The receiver verifies the signature as follows.

He or she first checks whether $0 < S_1 < p$ and $0 < S_2 < p-1$, and then computes the two verification codes V_1 and V_2 as follows:

$$V_1 = e_1^M \bmod p$$
$$V_2 = [e_2^{S_1} * S_1^{S_2}] \bmod p$$

Now, the receiver tests whether $V_1 \equiv V_2$. If the condition is satisfied, the signature is accepted; else, it is rejected.

We can prove the verification as follows:

$$V_1 \equiv V_2 (\bmod p) \quad (1)$$

We have $V_1 = e_1^M \bmod p$ and $V_2 = [e_2^{S_1} * S_1^{S_2}] \bmod p$ (2)

Therefore, from (1) and (2), $e_1^M \equiv [e_2^{S_1} * S_1^{S_2}] (\bmod p)$

We know that $e_2 = e_1^d \bmod p$ and $S_1 = e_1^k \bmod p$

Therefore, we get:

$$e_1^M \equiv [(e_1^d)^{S_1} * (e_1^k)^{S_2}] (\bmod p)$$
$$e_1^M \equiv e_1^{[(d*S_1) + (k*S_2)]} (\bmod p)$$

The above congruence holds if and only if:

$M \equiv [(d * S_1) + (k * S_2)] \bmod (p-1)$ or,

$S_2 \equiv [(M - d*S_1) * k^{-1}] \bmod (p-1)$, which is same S_2 as in the signing process.

10. Explain DSS, its approaches and its algorithm with proof.

Ans.: The *Digital Signature Standard* (DSS) was published by the National Institute of Standards and Technology (NIST) as the *Federal Information Processing Standard* (FIPS 186). It was originally developed in 1991. However, it was then criticized by the public because of lack of security in the scheme. Thus, it was revised in 1993, and finally in 2000, an elaborated version of DSS came into existence, which was named *FIPS 186-2*. The DSS uses Secure Hash Algorithm (SHA) and presents a new digital signature scheme, *Digital Signature Algorithm* (DSA).

As in the ElGamal digital signature scheme, in the DSS scheme also two functions F_1 and F_2 are used to create two different digital signatures S_1 and S_2, respectively. However, in DSS scheme, the message digest (not the message) is used to create the digital signature S_2. The sender transmits S_1, S_2 and M to the receiver. On receiving the message and the two signatures, the receiver computes the message digest using the same hash function, and calculates the verification code V_c using another function F_3. Now, the receiver compares V_c with S_1; if both are congruent, the message is accepted; otherwise it is rejected. The DSS scheme is shown in Figure 8.4.

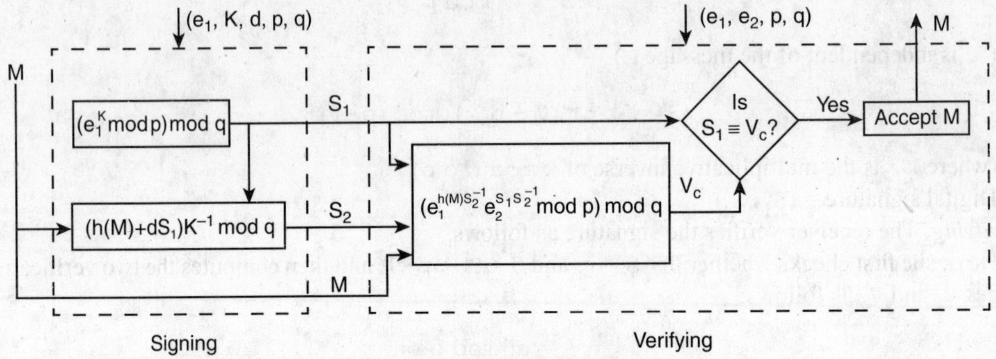

Figure 8.4 DSS Scheme

The key generation, signing and verifying algorithms for DSS scheme are described as follows. All the algorithms use the following global parameters:

L = length of the key in bits, where the number of bits are a multiple of 64; L lies between 512 and 1024 bits

p = prime number such that $2^{L-1} < p < 2^L$

q = a 160-bit prime factor of (p−1)

$e_1 = e_0^{(p-1)/q} \bmod p$, where e_0 is a primitive element in Z_p with $1 < e_0 < p-1$, such that $e_1 > 1$

M = message to be signed

h(M) = hash of message M using the SHA algorithm

Key generation: The sender generates his or her private and public keys as follows:

- *Private key:* The sender chooses a random integer d such that 0 < d < q; d becomes the private key of the sender
- *Public key:* The sender computes the following:

$$e_2 = e_1^d \bmod p$$

The public key of sender becomes (e_1, e_2, p, q)

Signing: To create the signature, the sender chooses a random number k, such that 0 < k < q, and then computes the value of S_1 and S_2 as follows:

$$S_1 = (e_1^k \bmod p) \bmod q$$

(S_1 is independent of the message M)

$$S_2 = [k^{-1} (h(M) + dS_1)] \bmod q$$

Digital signature = (S_1, S_2)

Verifying: The receiver verifies the signature as follows:

He or she first checks whether $0 < S_1 < p$ and $0 < S_2 < q$, and then computes the digest of the message using the same hash function h(M). The receiver finally computes the verification code V_c as follows:

$$V_c = [(e_1^y * e_2^z) \bmod p] \bmod q$$

where,

$$y = [h(M) * w] \bmod q$$
$$z = (S_1 * w) \bmod q$$

and

$$w = (S_2^{-1}) \bmod q$$

(w, y and z are intermediate variables)

Now, the receiver tests whether $S_1 \equiv V_c$. If the condition is satisfied, the signature is accepted; else, it is rejected.

Proof of the digital signature algorithm

To prove the algorithm, we have to show that $V_c = S_1$.

As we know that:

$$V_c = [(e_1^y * e_2^z) \bmod p] \bmod q$$
$$= [(e_1^{[h(M)w] \bmod q} * e_2^{(S_1 w) \bmod q}) \bmod p] \bmod q$$
$$= [(e_1^{[h(M)w] \bmod q} * e_1^{(dS_1 w) \bmod q}) \bmod p] \bmod q$$
$$= [(e_1^{[h(M)+dS_1]w \bmod q}) \bmod p] \bmod q$$
$$= [(e_1^{[h(M)+dS_1]k[1/(h(M)+dS_1)] \bmod q}) \bmod p] \bmod q$$

(Using $w = (S_2^{-1}) \bmod q$ and $S_2 = k[1/(h(M) + dS_1)] \bmod q$)

$$= [(e_1^{k \bmod q}) \bmod p] \bmod q$$
$$= (e_1^k \bmod p) \bmod q$$
$$= S_1$$

Hence, proved.

11. Why does each digital signature in the ElGamal and DSS schemes require a new value of k?

Ans.: In the ElGamal and DSS schemes, the sender chooses his or her private and public keys once and uses these keys to sign several documents. However, as we know, each time a message is sent, it should be signed with a unique digital signature; that is, no two documents can bear the same digital signature. Thus, to have a unique digital signature for every document, a new value of k (which is used in computing S_1 and S_2) is required.

12. How is DSS better than the RSA and ElGamal digital signature scheme?

Ans.: DSS is better than the RSA digital signature scheme because computing digital signatures in DSS requires lesser time than that in the RSA digital signature scheme for the same value of p.

DSS is also better than the ElGamal digital signature scheme because DSS scheme produces smaller digital signatures as compared to those produced by the ElGamal scheme, because $q < p$.

13. Explain the variations of digital signatures?

Ans.: The digital signature scheme has got many variations and additions to its main concept. Some of the variants of digital signature are discussed as follows:

- *Timestamped signature:* Some digital signatures include a timestamp value in order to prevent replay attacks. This is what we call *timestamped signatures*. In a replay attack, the documents can be replayed by a third party. For example, if A signs a request to the bank C to transfer a certain amount of money to B, B can intercept the document and replay it if there is no timestamp on the document. One way to handle such problems is to include the actual date and time. However, this may create a problem if the time zones are different or the clocks are not synchronized. Another solution is to use a *nonce* (which is a randomly generated number that can be used only once). The receiver makes a note that the particular nonce is used by the sender and cannot be used again. That is, a new nonce defines the present time and a used nonce defines the past time.
- *Blind signature:* The blind signature scheme was developed by David Chaum. The concept of blind signature is used when the sender does not want to reveal the contents of the message to the signer and just wishes get the message signed by the signer. Blind signatures are typically used in situations where the signer and the message author are completely different parties. Examples include electronic voting systems and electronic payment systems. The basic idea behind blind signatures is that the sender A first creates a message and blinds it. He then sends the blinded message to the signer B. B signs the blinded message and returns the signature on the blinded message to A. A unblinds the signature to obtain a signature on the original message.

  Blind signatures scheme can be implemented by using a number of public-key digital signature schemes such as RSA and DSS. Here, we will discuss the implementation using a variation of the RSA scheme. The steps are as follows:

  1. A selects a random number b, which is sometimes known as the *blinding factor*.
  2. A calculates the blinded message as follows:

     $$M_B = M * b^e \bmod n$$

     where, e = B's public key
     M = original message
     n = modulus defined in the RSA digital signature scheme
  3. A sends M_B to B.
  4. B signs M_B using the signing algorithm defined in the RSA digital signature scheme, as follows:

     $$S_{blind} = M_B^d \bmod n$$

     where,
     S_{blind} = signature on the blind version of message
     d = B's private key
  5. A removes the blind from the signature using the multiplicative inverse of b, as follows:

     $$S = S_{blind} * b^{-1} \bmod n$$

It can be easily proved that $S \equiv M^d \pmod{n}$; that is, the signature made on the original message M as defined in the RSA digital signature scheme. The proof is as follows:

$$\begin{aligned} S &\equiv S_{blind} * b^{-1} \pmod{n} \\ &\equiv M_B^d * b^{-1} \pmod{n} \\ &\equiv (M * b^e)^d * b^{-1} \pmod{n} \\ &\equiv M^d * b^{ed} * b^{-1} \pmod{n} \\ &\equiv M^d * b * b^{-1} \pmod{n} \\ &\equiv M^d \pmod{n} \end{aligned}$$

Hence, proved.

In the blind signature scheme, there are more chances of fraud. That is, it is possible that A gets a blind message signed by B that may later hurt him or her. For example, A may get a sign from B on a document that contains B's will. To deal with such type of situations, some laws have been passed that protect B in case he or she has signed a blind document that is against his or her interest.

- *Undeniable digital signature:* The digital signature schemes discussed so far consist of a signing algorithm and a verifying algorithm. That is, a signer can only create his or her signature using his or her private key, and anyone having the signer's public key can verify the signatures. Thus, the verification can be performed without the signer's consent or involvement. In some cases, a signer may not like it that anyone can verify his or her signatures. Thus, in order to increase the privacy of the signer, another scheme called *undeniable digital signature scheme* was proposed by David Chaum and Hans van Antwerpen in 1989. This scheme is a non-self-authenticating signature scheme in which no signatures can be verified without the signer's cooperation and notification.

  This scheme has three components, namely, *signing algorithm*, *verification protocol* and *disavowal protocol*.
  - *Signing algorithm:* This allows the signer (say, A) to sign a message.
  - *Verification (or confirmation) protocol:* This allows the signer to limit the users who can verify his or her signature. The verification process is interactive in nature and uses the *challenge/response mechanism* for verifying the signature, in which the verifier B sends a question (or challenge) to the signer A. A then sends a valid answer (response) to B, and B views the response to verify the signature.
  - *Disavowal (or denial) protocol:* Since the verification process requires the involvement of the signer, it is quite possible that the signer can freely decline the request of the verifier. This protocol prevents the signer from proving that a signature invalid when it is valid, and vice versa. To prove that the signature is a fake, A needs to take part in the denial protocol.

  The main advantage of this scheme is that if a signature is invalid, a fraud signer cannot prove it valid because he or she will not be able to successfully complete the verification protocol. In the same way, a fraud signer cannot deny a signature that is valid, as he or she will not be able to successfully complete the disavowal protocol.

14. Explain the mutual authentication protocol.

Ans.: The *mutual authentication protocol* enables the communicating parties to mutually satisfy themselves about their identities and exchange session keys between them. The main issues with authenticated key exchange are confidentiality and timeliness. *Confidentiality* can be achieved by communicating the essential identification and session key information in an encrypted form so that the compromise of session keys can be prevented. *Timeliness* is another important issue that must be considered for preventing message replay attacks. The authenticated key exchange can be managed either using the symmetric-key encryption technique or the public-key encryption technique.

Symmetric-key encryption technique

In this technique, a trusted key distribution centre (KDC) is involved who is responsible for generating a session key that is to be used for a short duration between the two communicating parties for a particular session, as well as for distributing that key to both the parties. Each party shares a master key with the KDC, and the KDC uses the master key for distributing the session key to ensure secure distribution of session keys.

Several protocols were proposed for secret key distribution using a KDC; however, each of them had some weaknesses. Finally, in the early 1990s, a protocol was presented for secure key distribution including authentication. The steps of this protocol are as follows:

- To initiate the authentication exchange, A generates a nonce N_A and sends it to B along with its identifier ID_A in plaintext. This nonce will be returned to A later in an encrypted message that includes the session key generated by KDC, to assure A of its timeliness.
- B sends a message to KDC that includes its identifier ID_B and a nonce N_B to request KDC for a session key. B's message also includes a block that instructs KDC to issue credentials to A. This block is encrypted with the secret (or master) key shared between the KDC and B, and includes A's identifier (ID_A), A's nonce (N_A) and the suggested expiration time for the credentials (T_E).
- KDC sends a message to A that includes the following:
  - Nonce received from B (N_B)
  - A block containing B's identifier (ID_B) to assure A that the second party is B itself, A's nonce (N_A) to assure A that this is a timely message and not a replay, a session key (K_S) generated by KDC, and the time of expiration of the key (T_E). This block is encrypted with the secret key shared between A and KDC, which is K_A.
  - A block containing A's identifier (ID_A), the session key (K_S), and the time of expiration of the key (T_E). This block is encrypted with the secret key shared between B and KDC (that is, K_B). It serves as a "ticket" for A for subsequent authentications.
- A transmits the ticket to B. A also sends B's nonce encrypted with the session key (K_S) to assure B that the message has come from A and not from a replay attack. B uses K_S to decrypt the nonce.

These steps are summarized as given below:

1. A→B $ID_A \| N_A$
2. B→KDC $ID_B \| N_B \| E_{K_B}[ID_A \| N_A \| T_E]$
3. KDC→A $E_{K_A}[ID_B \| N_A \| K_S \| T_E] \| E_{K_B}[ID_A \| K_S \| T_E] \| N_B$
4. A→B $E_{K_B}[ID_A \| K_S \| T_E] \| E_{K_S}[N_B]$

This protocol provides a secure and effective mechanism to establish a session with a secure session key. Suppose A establishes a session with B using this protocol, and then ends that session once the communication is over. Further, assume that within the same time limit T_E, A again wants to establish a new session with B. Now, A has the session key K_S that can be used for subsequent authentication to B but this time without the involvement of KDC. Thus, A can establish as many sessions he wants within the time limit provided by the protocol using the same session key. Once the time limit is over, a new session key must be requested from the KDC. The steps for establishing a new session without contacting KDC are as follows:

1. A→B $E_{K_B}[ID_A \| K_S \| T_E] \| N'_A$
2. B→A $N'_B \| E_{K_S}[N'_A]$
3. A→B $E_{K_S}[N'_B]$

Here, N'_A and N'_B are newly generated nonces that assure A and B that there is no replay attack. Note that T_E is the time relative to B's clock; thus, there is no need to synchronize clocks because B checks only self-generated timestamps.

Public-key encryption technique

In the public-key encryption technique, in addition to generating the session keys, KDC is also responsible for exchanging the public keys of A and B. In this technique, no master key is shared between the KDC and the communicating parties; rather, the public keys of KDC and the communicating parties are used for encryption. The steps of this protocol are as follows:

1. A sends a message to KDC informing that he or she wants to establish a secure connection with B. The message includes the identifiers of A (ID_A) and B (ID_B) in plaintext.
2. KDC returns a copy of the public-key certificate of B to A, which contains the identifier and public key of B (B_{PUB}), encrypted with the private key of KDC (KDC_{PRI}).
3. A generates a nonce N_A and sends it to B along with its identifier (ID_A) to inform B that he or she wants to communicate with B. A sends this information by encrypting it with B's public key (B_{PUB}).
4. On receiving this information from A, B sends a request to KDC for issuing the public-key certificate of A, and also for generating a session key (K_S). B's request includes the identifiers of A and B in plaintext, along with the nonce N_A encrypted with the public key of KDC (KDC_{PUB}).
5. KDC sends a copy of A's public-key certificate (A's identifier plus its public key) to B encrypted with KDC_{PRI}. KDC also sends the session key (K_S), nonce N_A and B's identifier (ID_B). This triplet informs A that K_S is bound to N_A in order to assure A that K_S is a newly generated session key and not an old one. The triplet is first encrypted with KDC_{PRI} to assure B that this information is from KDC itself, and then it is encrypted with B's public key to make sure that no other party can create a fraudulent connection with A.
6. B sends the triplet $\{N_A, K_S, ID_B\}$ still encrypted with KDC's private key along with the nonce N_B to A. This whole information is further encrypted with A's public key (A_{PUB}).
7. A decrypts the received information using the public key of KDC (KDC_{PUB}) to obtain the session key (K_S). Then, it sends the nonce N_B encrypted with the session key K_S to B to assure him or her that A has got the session key.

These steps are summarized as given below:

1. A→KDC $ID_A \| ID_B$
2. KDC→A $E_{KDC_{PRI}}[ID_B \| B_{PUB}]$
3. A→B $E_{B_{PUB}}[ID_A \| N_A]$
4. B→KDC $ID_B \| ID_A \| E_{KDC_{PUB}}[N_A]$
5. KDC→B $E_{KDC_{PRI}}[ID_A \| A_{PUB}] \| E_{B_{PUB}}[E_{KDC_{PRI}}[N_A \| K_S \| ID_B]]$
6. B→A $E_{A_{PUB}}[E_{KDC_{PRI}}[N_A \| K_S \| ID_B] \| N_B]$
7. A→B $E_{K_S}[N_B]$

Though this protocol provides protection against several attacks, the authors Woo and Lam themselves found an error and generated a revised version of the algorithm. In the new version of the protocol, the identifier of A (ID_A) is added to the information being encrypted with the private key of KDC in steps 5 and 6, as shown here:

5. KDC→B $E_{KDC_{PRI}}[ID_A || A_{PUB}] || E_{B_{PUB}}[E_{KDC_{PRI}}[N_A || ID_A || K_S || ID_B]]$
6. B→A $E_{A_{PUB}}[E_{KDC_{PRI}}[N_A || ID_A || K_S || ID_B] || N_B]$

The inclusion of ID_A binds the session key K_S to the identifiers of both A and B that are involved in the communication. ID_A is included because of the reason that the nonce N_A is considered unique among all the nonces generated by A only, and not among all nonces generated by all parties. Thus, the connection request of A is uniquely identified with the help of a pair $\{ID_A, N_A\}$ and not only by N_A as in prior protocols.

15. Explain one-way authentication protocol.

Ans.: In some applications, such as e-mail, it is not necessary for the sender and receiver to be online at the same time. The message sent by the sender is rather forwarded to the receiver's electronic mailbox, where it is stored until the receiver reads it. Thus, only one-way authentication is required.

Since the receiver may or may not be online at the time the sender sends an e-mail, a mail-handling mechanism is required that stores the e-mail when the sender sends it, and then forwards it to the receiver at some later time. As we know, an e-mail consists of a header and the message. The header of the e-mail must be clear so that it can be properly handled by the store-and-forward e-mail protocol such as SMTP.

There are two basic requirements for such applications. First, the plaintext form of the e-mail message must not be accessible to the mail-handling protocol. Thus, an e-mail message must be encrypted such that the decryption key is not known to the mail-handling system. Second, the recipient needs to be assured that the message has come from a supposed sender. One-way authentication can also be performed either using symmetric-key encryption technique or public-key encryption technique.

Symmetric-key encryption technique

While using the symmetric-key encryption technique in one-way authentication, the following steps are used.

1. The sender A sends the identifier of A and B, and a nonce N_1, to the KDC in plaintext.
2. The KDC then returns a message to A, which contains a newly generated session key K_S, B's identifier ID_B, the nonce N_1, and a block encrypted with the secret key shared between KDC and B (that is, K_B). This whole message is further encrypted with the secret key shared between KDC and A (that is, K_A). The inclusion of ID_B and N_1 in the message assures A that this is the original message and that it has not been altered by the KDC in any way. The nonce N_1 also helps A in verifying that it is not a replay of some previous message. The block encrypted with K_B contains K_S and ID_A and is intended for B. A will send this block to B as it is to establish the connection and prove A's identity.
3. A forwards to B the message originated from KDC for B, along with the e-mail encrypted with the session key K_S.

The protocol is summarized as follows:

1. A→KDC $ID_A || ID_B || N_1$
2. KDC→A $E_{K_A}[K_S || ID_B || N_1 || E_{K_B}[K_S || ID_A]]$
3. A→B $E_{K_B}[K_S || ID_A] || E_{K_S}[M]$

The main advantage of this protocol is that it guarantees that no user other than the intended recipient of the message will be able to read the message. Moreover, it provides a level of authentication that the message has come from an alleged sender. However, this protocol does not provide protection against replay attacks.

Public-key encryption technique

While using the public-key encryption technique for one-way authentication, one can achieve confidentiality, authentication or both. To achieve confidentiality, the sender needs to know the public key of the recipient. If A is the sender and B is the receiver, the following protocol may be used.

$$A \rightarrow B \quad E_{B_{PUB}}[K_S] \| E_{K_S}[M]$$

Here, A encrypts the message M with the session key K_S, and also encrypts the session key K_S with B's public key B_{PUB}, and sends it to B.

To achieve only authentication, B needs to know the public key of A. Thus, the following protocol may be used.

$$A \rightarrow B \quad M \| E_{A_{PRI}}[h(M) \| E_{AS_{PRI}}[T \| ID_A \| A_{PUB}]$$

In this protocol, A sends to B the message M, the digital signature encrypted with A's private key, and A's public-key certificate encrypted with the private key of the authentication server (AS_{PRI}). B first determines A's public key from the public-key certificate, and then verifies that it is authentic. B then uses the public key to verify the message itself.

To achieve both confidentiality and authentication, the message M can be encrypted with the session key K_S, which is also sent to B encrypting it with B's public key.

16. In the RSA scheme, let p = 3, q = 11 and d = 3. Calculate the public key. Now suppose A wants to send a message M = 107 to B. Sign and verify this message using the RSA digital signature scheme.

Ans.: Here, p = 3 and q = 11

Therefore,
$$n = p*q = 3*11 = 33$$

And,
$$\phi(n) = (p-1)*(q-1) = (3-1)*(11-1) = 2*10 = 20$$

Now,
$$d = 3$$

As we know,
$$e*d = 1 \bmod \phi(n)$$
$$e*3 = 1 \bmod 20$$
$$\Rightarrow e = 7$$

Therefore, the public key is (e, n), that is, (7, 33).

Signing:

Digital signature
$$S = M^d \bmod n = 107^3 \bmod 33 = 17$$

Verifying:

Copy of message $M' = S^e \bmod n$
$= 17^7 \bmod 33$
$= 8$

Now, we have to verify whether $M' \equiv M \pmod n$

$$8 \equiv 107 \bmod 33$$

$8 \equiv 8$, which is true.
Thus, the signature is verified.

17. In the ElGamal scheme, let p = 881, e_1 = 2 and d = 127. Calculate the value of e_2. Find the values of S_1, S_2, V_1 and V_2, if M = 400 and k = 17.

Ans.: Here, p = 881, e_1 = 2 and d = 127

Therefore,
$$e_2 = e_1^d \bmod p$$
$$= 2^{127} \bmod 881$$
$$= 684$$

Signing:

$$S_1 = e_1^k \bmod p$$
$$= 2^{17} \bmod 881$$
$$= 684$$
$$S_2 = [k^{-1} * (M - dS_1)] \bmod (p-1)$$
$$= [17^{-1} * (400-127*684)] \bmod (881-1) \quad (1)$$

The multiplicative inverse of 17 in Z_{880} is 673 (as 17*673 = 11441 mod 880 = 1). The multiplicative inverse can be obtained using the extended Euclidean algorithm discussed in Chapter 2 (Q12).

Therefore, Equation (1) can be written as follows:

$$S_2 = [673 * (400-86868)] \bmod 880$$

Since 86868 is not lying in Z_{880}, we need to take 86868 mod 880, which is 628. Thus, now the equation becomes:

$$S_2 = [673 * (400-628)] \bmod 880 \quad (2)$$

Since 400−628 comes out to be negative, we first take the additive inverse of 628, which can be computed as 880−628 = 252, and then add it to 400. Now, Equation (2) becomes

$$S_2 = [673 * (400+252)] \bmod 880$$
$$= [673 * 652] \bmod 880$$
$$= 438796 \bmod 880$$
$$= 556$$

Therefore, the digital signature = (S_1, S_2) = (684, 556)

Verifying: Since 0 < 684 < 881 and 0 < 556 < 880, we compute the two verification codes V_1 and V_2 as follows:

$$V_1 = e_1^M \bmod p$$
$$= 2^{400} \bmod 881$$
$$= 171$$

$$V_2 = [e_2^{S_1} * S_1^{S_2}] \bmod p$$
$$= [684^{684} * 684^{556}] \bmod 881$$
$$= 171$$

Since $V_1 \equiv V_2$, the digital signature is verified.

18. In the DSS scheme, let $q = 83$, $p = 997$, $e_0 = 3$ and $d = 23$. Calculate the values of e_1 and e_2. Find the values of S_1, S_2, V_1 and V_2, if $h(M) = 5000$ and $k = 31$.

Ans.: Here, $q = 83$, $p = 997$, $e_0 = 3$ and $d = 23$

Therefore,
$$e_1 = e_0^{(p-1)/q} \bmod p$$
$$= 3^{(997-1)/83} \bmod 997$$
$$= 3^{12} \bmod 997$$
$$= 40$$

Now,
$$e_2 = e_1^d \bmod p$$
$$= 40^{23} \bmod 997$$
$$= 668$$

Signing:

$$S_1 = (e_1^k \bmod p) \bmod q$$
$$= (40^{31} \bmod 997) \bmod 83$$
$$= 16$$
$$S_2 = [k^{-1} * (h(M) + dS_1)] \bmod q$$
$$= [31^{-1} * (5000+23*16)] \bmod 83 \quad (1)$$

The multiplicative inverse of 31 in Z_{83} is 75 (as $31*75 = 2325 \bmod 83 = 1$).
Therefore, Equation (1) can be written as follows:

$$S_2 = [75 * (5000+368)] \bmod 83$$
$$= [75 * 5368] \bmod 83$$
$$= 50 \quad (2)$$

Therefore, the digital signature = $(S_1, S_2) = (16, 50)$

Verifying: Since $0 < 16 < 83$ and $0 < 50 < 83$, we compute the verification code V_c as follows:
We first calculate the values of intermediate variables w, z and y.

$$w = (S_2^{-1}) \bmod q$$
$$= 50^{-1} \bmod 83$$
$$= 5 \bmod 83$$
$$= 5$$
$$y = [h(M) * w] \bmod q$$
$$= [5000 * 5] \bmod 83$$
$$= 17$$
$$z = (S_1 * w) \bmod q$$
$$= (16 * 5) \bmod 83$$
$$= 80$$
$$V_c = [(e_1^y * e_2^z) \bmod p] \bmod q$$
$$= [(40^{17} * 668^{80}) \bmod 997] \bmod 83$$
$$= 16$$

Since $S_1 \equiv V_c$, the digital signature is verified.

Multiple-choice Questions

1. Which of the following services is not provided by digital signatures directly?
(a) Message authenticity
(b) Message confidentiality
(c) Message integrity
(d) Nonrepudiation
2. Which of the following pair of keys is used to create and verify the digital signature, respectively?
(a) Signer's private key and verifier's public key
(b) Verifier's public key and verifier's private key
(c) Signer's private key and signer's public key
(d) Signer's public key and signer's private key
3. The sender encrypts the message with his or her private key to achieve __________.
(a) Authentication
(b) Confidentiality
(c) Both (a) and (b)
(d) None of these
4. RSA __________ be used for digital signatures.
(a) can
(b) cannot
(c) must
(d) must not
5. Which of the following is a property of a digital signature?
(a) It must be able to verify the author.
(b) It must be able to verify the date and time of the signature.
(c) It must be able to authenticate the contents of the message at the time of the signature.
(d) All of these
6. Which of these is a kind of attack possible on digital signatures?
(a) Ciphertext-only attack
(b) Known-message attack
(c) Key-only attack
(d) Both (b) and (c)
7. Which of these statements is not correct about DSS?
(a) It was published by the National Institute of Standards and Technology.
(b) It uses three functions to create a digital signature.
(c) An elaborated version of DSS was named as FIPS 186-2.
(d) It uses Secure Hash Algorithm (SHA).
8. Which of these is not a variation of a digital signature?
(a) Timestamped signature
(b) Blind signature
(c) Encrypted digital signature
(d) Undeniable digital signature

Answers

1. (b)	2. (c)	3. (a)	4. (a)	5. (d)	6. (d)
7. (b)	8. (c)				

9

Network Security

1. Explain the working principle of the Kerberos protocol.

Ans.: *Kerberos* is an authentication protocol that has been designed to be used in an open distributed environment, where the users at workstations request for the services on the servers distributed throughout the network. It basically provides a centralized authentication server that is responsible for authenticating users to servers and servers to users. Its name has been derived from Greek mythology after the name of a three-headed dog that guarded the gates of Hades. Kerberos has become very popular as it can also act as a KDC in addition to being an authentication protocol. It was originally developed as a part of Project Athena at the MIT. Several versions of Kerberos have evolved. However, the most commonly used version of Kerberos is version 4. The Kerberos protocol has four components, namely, *client workstation*, *authentication server* (AS), *ticket-granting server* (TGS) and *real server*.

- Client workstation is an entity that wants to access services from a server.
- Authentication server (AS) acts as a KDC in the Kerberos protocol. It is responsible for the verification of the identity of users during login. To get verified, the users first need to register themselves with the AS. Each registered user is assigned a unique ID and a password. All the IDs and their corresponding passwords are stored in a centralized database of AS. In addition to verifying the users, it also issues a session key to the requesting user, which is to be used between the user and the TGS, and sends a ticket for the TGS. AS also shares a unique secret key with each server, and hence, all the servers also need to register themselves with AS.
- Ticket-granting server (TGS) is responsible for issuing tickets for establishing connection with the real server. It also issues the session key, which is to be used between the user and the real server. Once a user has got verified by AS, he or she can contact TGS any number of times to obtain the tickets for different real servers.
- Real server provides the required services to the user. Here, the user uses its own process (client process) to access the server process using a client-server program (e.g. FTP).

The working of Kerberos is shown in Figure 9.1. To understand how the Kerberos protocol operates, consider a user A who wants to access the services of a real server B. The user A can access the processes running on B by performing the following steps.

1. The user A logs in to the workstation by entering his or her user ID (say, ID_A). The workstation then sends ID_A in plaintext to AS.

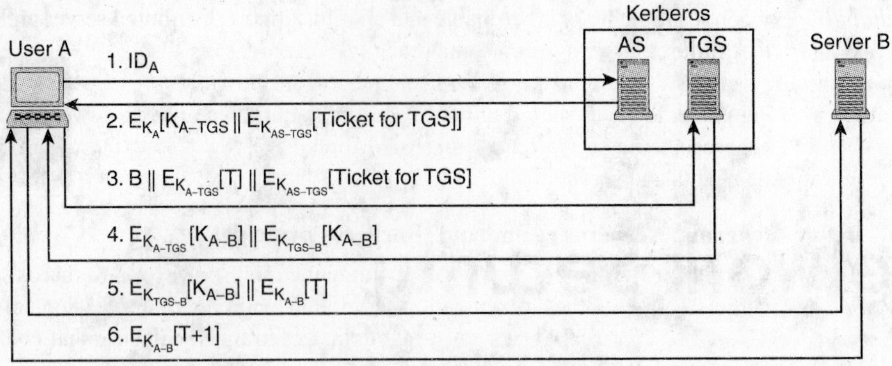

Figure 9.1 Kerberos Protocol

2. In response, the AS creates a message that includes two items: a randomly generated session key K_{A-TGS} and the ticket for TGS, which is encrypted with the secret key shared between the AS and TGS (K_{AS-TGS}). This whole message is encrypted with the symmetric key of A (K_A). The session key K_{A-TGS} is used by the user to contact the TGS. Now, this encrypted message is sent to A.
3. On receiving the message, A's workstation asks him or her for the password. When A enters the correct password, the workstation generates the symmetric key (K_A) by applying an appropriate algorithm (generally a hash function) on the password. The password is then immediately destroyed, so that it cannot be stolen by anyone. The symmetric key K_A is now used to decrypt the received message. Once the message is decrypted, the ticket for TGS and the session key K_{A-TGS} are extracted. Since the ticket is encrypted with the symmetric key of TGS, only TGS can open it. A now sends a message to TGS containing the ticket received from AS, the name of the real server (B) and a timestamp T encrypted with the session key K_{A-TGS}. This timestamp prevents replay attacks from any other user.
4. The TGS now sends two tickets each for A and B. Both these tickets contain the session key (K_{A-B}) to be used between A and B. A's ticket is encrypted with the secret key (K_{A-TGS}) shared between A and TGS, while the ticket for B is encrypted with the secret key (K_{TGS-B}) shared between TGS and B. This mechanism provides security for the whole process. No other user can extract K_{A-B}, as he or she does not know K_{A-TGS} or K_{TGS-B}. Moreover, step 3 cannot be replayed, since an unauthorized user cannot replace the timestamp with a new one (as he or she does not know K_{A-TGS}).
5. A now sends B's ticket with a timestamp encrypted with K_{A-B}.
6. B acknowledges the receipt of the ticket by adding 1 to the timestamp. It also encrypts the message with K_{AB} and sends it to A.

Now, suppose A wishes to receive services from different servers, then it only has to repeat steps 3 to 6. The first two steps involve the verification of A's identity, which remains same for all the servers. Thus, steps 1 and 2 need not be repeated.

2. Discuss the basic requirements for Kerberos.

Ans.: There are four basic requirements that have been defined for Kerberos. These requirements are as follows:

- *Security:* Kerberos should be secure enough to prevent eavesdroppers from obtaining any kind of information that is necessary to impersonate a user.

- *Reliability:* Kerberos should be highly reliable and should support distributed server architecture so that, in case of failure of one system, some other system can act as a backup.
- *Transparency:* Kerberos should be transparent, such that the user is not able to know that authentication is taking place; the user should only be required to enter his or her password.
- *Scalability:* Kerberos should support a modular, distributed architecture, so that it can support a large number of clients and servers.

3. Define the terms 'Kerberos realm' and 'Kerberos principal'.

Ans.: A typical Kerberos environment consists of an authentication server (or a Kerberos server), a number of clients all registered with the authentication server and a number of application servers that provide several services. The Kerberos server must maintain a centralized database that contains the user IDs and hashed passwords of all the users registered with the Kerberos server. It must also share a unique secret key with each application server. All servers need to get registered with the Kerberos server. Such an environment is called *Kerberos realm*. It is basically a single administrative domain.

The computer system where the Kerberos database is stored (referred to as *Kerberos master computer system*) should be kept in a physically secure room. The person having the Kerberos master password is only authorized to modify the contents of the Kerberos database. Though several read-only copies of this database can be kept on other Kerberos computer systems, changes can only be made on the master computer system. If there exist several Kerberos realms, then they must share secret keys and trust among themselves.

Kerberos principal is a unique identity to which Kerberos can assign tickets. In other words, all the services or the users known to a Kerberos system are referred to as *Kerberos principals*. Each Kerberos principal is identified by its principal name. A Kerberos principal has the following form:

```
primary[/instance]@REALM
```

Principal is divided into three parts: the *primary* (service or user name), the *instance*, and the *realm*.

- *Primary:* This is the first part of the principal. For a user, the primary is the `username` and, for a host, the primary is the word `host`.
- *Instance:* This is an optional string that qualifies the primary, and is separated from the primary by a slash (/). In case of a user, the instance is generally `NULL`; however, in some cases, it can have some value (e.g. `admin`).
- *Realm*: This is the last component of the principal, and is basically the Kerberos realm. It is generally separated from the rest of the principal by the '@' symbol. In most cases, it is your domain name and must be specified in upper-case letters.

For example, consider the following principals:

```
robert@ATHENA.MIT.EDU
robert/admin@ATHENA.MIT.EDU
```

In the first principal, `robert` is primary, instance is `NULL` and `ATHENA.MIT.EDU` is realm. In the second principal, `robert` is primary, `admin` is instance and `ATHENA.MIT.EDU` is realm.

4. Discuss the steps involved in inter-realm communication in Kerberos.

Ans.: In a system that crosses organizational boundaries, it is not feasible for all users to be registered with a single AS; rather, multiple ASs will exist with each AS responsible for the registration and authentication of the users and servers within a single realm. In case two users (say, `A` and `B`) of different realms want to communicate with each other, they need to obtain service tickets to access resources in foreign realms. In order to access such services, these steps are followed:

1. The user `A` contacts the AS of their realm asking for a ticket that will be used with the TGS of the foreign realm. If both the realms share keys and have established a trusted relationship between them, the corresponding AS of `A`'s realm delivers the requested ticket to `A`.
2. In case `A`'s realm does not share keys with the foreign realm, the AS of `A`'s realm will provide a ticket for an intermediary foreign realm that may be sharing the keys with the target realm.
3. The client can use this 'intermediary ticket' to communicate with the AS of the intermediary foreign realm, which will either follow step 2, or it will issue a ticket that can be used with the AS of the target realm (in case it shares keys with the target realm).
4. The client uses this ticket to obtain the service ticket from the TGS of the foreign realm.
5. The user can now use this service ticket to obtain the services of the desired server.

5. How is the encryption key generated from the password in Kerberos?

Ans.: In Kerberos, the user can enter a password of any length; however, the password is restricted to contain only those characters that can be represented in a 7-bit ASCII format. This password is used to generate the symmetric key of the user that is to be used for decrypting the messages received from AS. The steps involved in password-to-key transformation are as follows:

1. The user enters his or her password in the form of a character string (say, `s`).
2. The character string `s` is converted into a bit string (say, `b`) in such a way that the first character of `s` is stored in the first seven bits of `b`, the second character is stored in next seven bits and so on, as shown in Figure 9.2(a). That is:

   `b[0]` represents bit 0 of `s[0]`
   ...
   `b[6]` represents bit 6 of `s[0]`
   `b[7]` represents bit 0 of `s[1]`
   ...
   `b[13]` represents bit 6 of `s[1]`
   ...
   `b[7i+j]` represents bit `j` of `s[i]`   where, 0 <= `j` <= 6

3. The bits in the bit string `b` are aligned in a 'fanfold' manner, such that the bits 0 to 55 form the first row, then the bit 56 is placed below the bit 55, bit 57 is placed below 54, bit 58 is placed below 53 and so on, as shown in Figure 9.2(b).
4. A bitwise XOR operation is performed to compact the bit string to 56 bits. For example, if the bit string is of length 60, then

$$b[55] = b[55] \oplus b[56]$$
$$b[54] = b[54] \oplus b[57]$$
$$b[53] = b[53] \oplus b[58]$$
$$b[52] = b[52] \oplus b[59]$$

   This creates a 56-bit DES key [see Figure 9.2(b)]. Note that steps 3 and 4 are performed to compact the bit string.
5. The 56-bit string is then expanded to a 64-bit input key `K`. For this, the 56-bit key is divided into 7-bit blocks (total 8 blocks), and then each 7-bit block is mapped to a corresponding block of 8 bits, thus creating a 64-bit key.

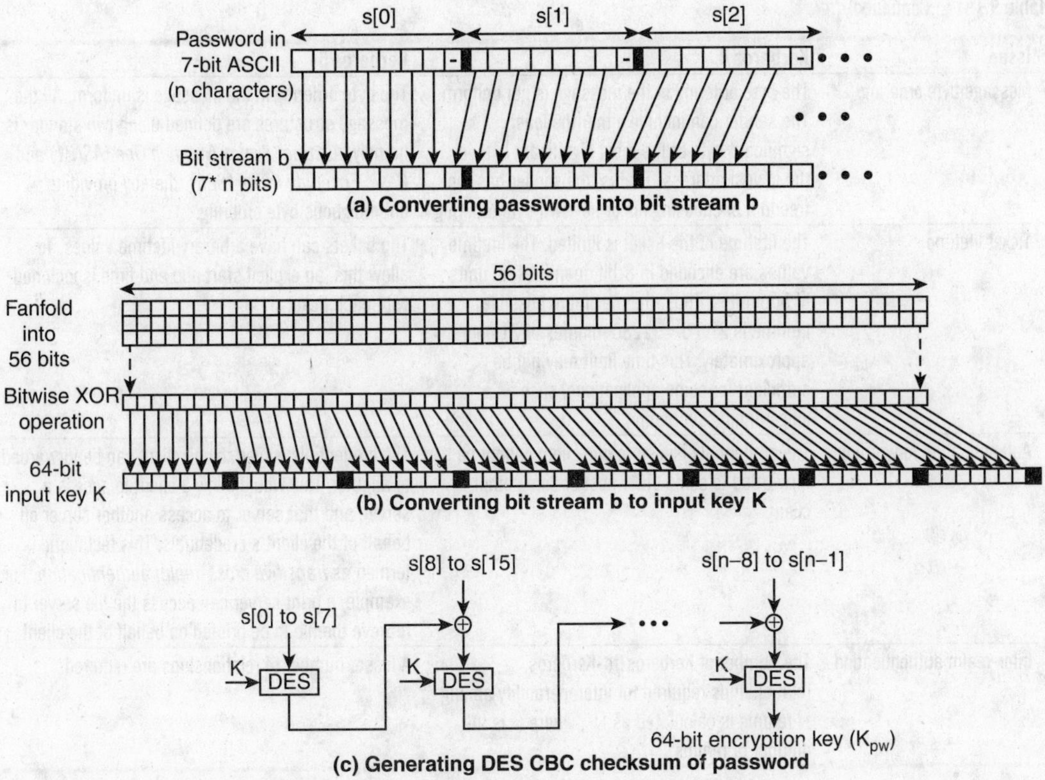

Figure 9.2 Password-to-key transformation in Kerberos

6. The password supplied by the user is encrypted with the key K using the cipher block chaining (CBC) mode of DES [see Figure 9.2(c)]. This process results in a 64-bit block, referred to as *CBC checksum*, which becomes the encryption key (say, K_{pw}) associated with the user's password.

6. Explain the differences between Kerberos version 4 and Kerberos version 5.

Ans.: Though Kerberos version 4 is most commonly used, it suffers from some environmental shortcomings and technical deficiencies. Kerberos version 5 attempts to overcome these problems. The differences between Kerberos versions 4 and 5 based on the environmental shortcomings are listed in Table 9.1.

Table 9.1 Difference between Kerberos 4 and Kerberos 5 based on Environmental Shortcomings

Issue	Kerberos 4	Kerberos 5
Encryption system dependence	Requires the use of DES algorithm.	Any encryption algorithm can be used. To make this possible, an encryption type identifier is attached with the ciphertext.
Internet protocol dependence	Uses only IP addresses, and no other address can be used in it.	Allows the use of any network address, such as the ISO network address. This is possible due to the reason that the network addresses are labelled with type and length.

(Continued...)

Table 9.1 (...Continued)

Issue	Kerberos 4	Kerberos 5
Message byte ordering	The byte ordering in the message is not uniform. The sender can include either the least significant byte or the most significant byte in the lowest address. That is, the sender has the freedom of choosing his or her own byte ordering.	The byte ordering in the message is uniform. All the message structures are defined using two standards, namely, *Abstract Syntax Notation One* (*ASN.1*) and *Basic Encoding Rules* (*BER*), thereby providing unambiguous byte ordering.
Ticket lifetime	The lifetime of the ticket is limited. The lifetime values are encoded in 8-bit quantities, in units of 5 minutes. Thus, the maximum possible lifetime is $2^8 * 5 = 1280$ minutes or 21 hours, approximately. This time limit may not be sufficient for some applications, such as a long-running simulation.	The tickets can have arbitrary lifetime values. To allow this, an explicit start and end time is included with each ticket.
Authentication forwarding	The credentials issued to one client cannot be forwarded to some other host or some other client.	The credentials issued to one client can be forwarded to another. This would allow a client to access a server, and that server to access another server on behalf of the client's credentials. This technique is termed as *transitive cross-realm authentication*. For example, a print server can access the file server to retrieve the file to be printed on behalf of the client.
Inter-realm authentication	The number of Kerberos-to-Kerberos relationships required for interoperability among N realms is calculated as N^2, where N is the number of realms.	A lesser number of relationships are required.

In addition to the environmental shortcomings mentioned in the preceding text, version 4 suffers from some technical deficiencies. Version 5 is intended to address these deficiencies. These deficiencies are listed in Table 9.2.

Table 9.2 Difference between Kerberos 4 and Kerberos 5 based on technical deficiencies

Issue	Kerberos 4	Kerberos 5
PCBC encryption	Uses a nonstandard mode of the DES algorithm known as *propagating cipher block chaining* (PCBC) for encryption. The PCBC was supposed to provide an integrity check as part of the encryption operation; however it is found to be prone to an attack that involves the interchange of ciphertext blocks.	Uses the standard cipher block chaining (CBC) mode for encryption. It provides explicit integrity mechanisms such as attaching hash code or checksum to the message before encryption using CBC.
Session keys	The session key included in each ticket serves two purposes. First, it is used by the client to encrypt the authenticator sent to the server associated with that ticket. Second, it can be used to encrypt the messages between a client and a server. Since the same ticket is used more than once for accessing a particular server, it leads to the possibility of a replay attack by a third party.	Allows a client and a server to negotiate a sub-session key, which is to be used only for the current session. Thus, if the client wishes to access the server again, he or she would require a new sub-session key.

(Continued...)

Table 9.2 (...Continued)

Issue	Kerberos 4	Kerberos 5
Password attacks	Does not provide a secured mechanism for preventing password attacks. Whenever AS sends a message to the client, it is encrypted with the key based on the client's password. This message can be captured by an opponent who may then attempt to decrypt it by trying various passwords. If the opponent chooses the right mechanism to acquire the password, then he or she can use it to acquire the authentication credentials from Kerberos.	Though version 5 does not completely prevent the password attacks, it provides a preauthentication mechanism that makes the password attacks more difficult.

7. Define the terms *forwardable, renewable* and *postdatable* tickets.

Ans.: Kerberos version 5 supports the use of forwardable, renewable and postdatable tickets.

- *Forwardable ticket:* This ticket can be used by the user to get a new ticket on behalf of the current credentials. This allows the user to get validated on other machines also. However, the user has to use a different IP address.
- *Renewable ticket:* As the name suggests, this ticket can be renewed by asking the KDC to issue a new ticket with an extended lifetime. Note that a ticket can only be renewed before the expiration of its time limit. It is similar to renewing an insurance policy or a credit card before the validity is expired.
- *Postdatable ticket:* This ticket is similar to a postdated cheque, which bears a starting time as some time in the future. Thus, the ticket is initially invalid. A postdatable ticket can only be used after getting it validated from the KDC during its valid lifetime.

8. Explain the X.509 authentication service and its certificates.

Ans.: X.509 was designed by ITU-T to describe the public-key certificates in a structured way. It is a part of the X.500 series of recommendations that define a directory service. A *directory* is basically a server or a set of servers distributed over a network that maintains a database of information about the users, such as mappings from user names to network addresses. X.509 provides authentication services to its users through the X.500 directory, which may act as the repository of public-key certificates associated with each user. Each certificate contains the public key of the user and is signed by the private key of the trusted certification authority (CA). It may be noted that only the CA can create the user certificates and place them in the directory. The directory server itself is not responsible for creating public keys or certificates; it simply acts as a warehouse of certificates for the users.

X.509 also defines a set of alternative authentication protocols based on the use of public-key certificates. The format of the certificate and the authentication protocols defined in X.509 are used in several contexts such as IP Security, S/MIME, SSL/TLS and SET, and hence it is considered to be an important standard.

The first version of X.509 was issued in 1988. Then, in 1993, its second version came out, to address some of the security concerns. A third version was released in 1995, which was revised in 2000. X.509 makes uses of the ASN.1 (Abstract Syntax Notation One) protocol, which defines the general format of the X.509 certificate with several fields, as shown in Figure 9.3. The description of these fields is as follows:

- *Version number:* This field differentiates among the various versions of the certificate format. That is, the version of X.509 is specified in this field. The first version number was 0, and the current version (third version) is 2.

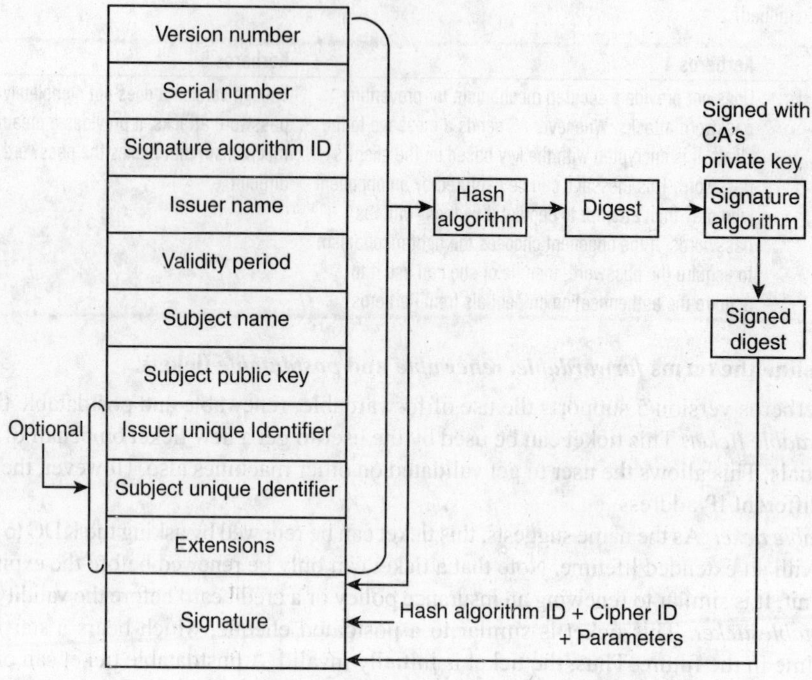

Figure 9.3 X.509 Certificate Format

- *Serial number:* This field contains an integer value assigned to each certificate. This value is unique within the issuing CA.
- *Signature algorithm ID:* This field specifies the algorithm used by CA to sign the certificate, together with any associated parameters.
- *Issuer name:* This field specifies the name of the CA that has created and signed the certificate. The name is usually specified as a hierarchy of strings that include the name of the country, state, organization, department and so on.
- *Validity period:* This field specifies the lifetime of the certificate. It includes the earliest time and latest time; the certificate is invalid before the earliest time and after the latest time.
- *Subject name:* This field specifies the entity to which this certificate refers. That is, this certificate certifies the public key of the user who is holding the corresponding private key. This field is also specified as a hierarchy of strings; one of the strings is called the *common name*, which is the actual name of the user.
- *Subject public key:* This field specifies the main content of the certificate, which is the public key. It also specifies the corresponding public-key algorithm and its associated parameters.
- *Issuer unique identifier:* This is an optional field that specifies the unique identifier of the authority issuing the certificate. This field allows having the same value in the *issuer name* field of two different certificates, provided they have different values in the *issuer unique identifier* field.
- *Subject unique identifier:* This is also an optional field, which specifies the unique identifier of the subject to which the certificate is issued. This field allows having the same value in the *subject name* field of two different certificates, provided they have different values in the *subject unique identifier* field.

- *Extensions:* This field is used by the issuers to add more private information to the certificate. The extensions were added in the third version of X.509. This is also an optional field.
- *Signature:* This field is divided into three sections as discussed in the following:
  - The first section includes all the other fields in the certificate.
  - The second section contains the digest of the first section, which is encrypted with the private key of CA.
  - The third section includes the algorithm identifier that has been used to create the second section.

9. Explain the terms *certificate renewable* and *certificate revocation* with respect to X.509. Also, discuss how the format of the X.509 certificate is different from that of the certificate revocation list?

Ans.: The X.509 certificates have a validity associated with them. If everything goes smoothly, then the certificates can be renewed by the CA. A new certificate is issued before the validity of the old one expires. This process is known as *certificate renewal*. However, sometimes, the certificate has to be revoked before the validity of the certificate expires. This is known as *certificate revocation*. The certificates can be revoked due to several reasons. Some of them are as follows:

- The private key of the user might have been compromised.
- The private key of the CA that can verify the certificates might have been compromised. In this case, the CA must revoke all unexpired certificates.
- The certificate authority is no longer willing to issue a certificate to the user.

The certificate revocation is implemented by periodically issuing a *Certificate Revocation List* (CRL), which contains all the revoked certificates that have not expired till the issue date of the CRL. A typical format of CRL is shown in Figure 9.4. It contains many fields, some of which are the same

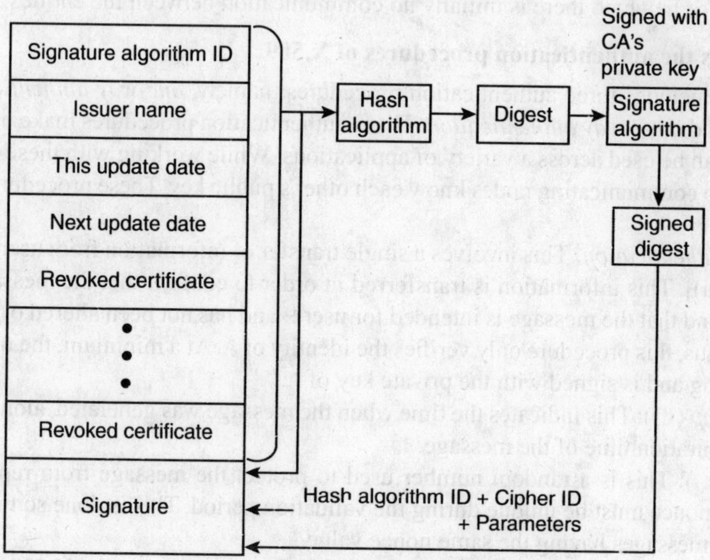

Figure 9.4 Certificate Revocation List Format

as in the X.509 certificate. The fields common to both X.509 certificates and CRL are *signature algorithm ID*, *issuer name* and *signature*. The fields that are new in CRL are as follows:

- *This update date:* This field defines the issue date of CRL.
- *Next update date:* This field specifies the date when the list will be issued next.
- *Revoked certificate:* This is a repeated list of all the certificates that are not expired and have been revoked. Each list is divided into two sections, namely, *user certificate serial number* and *revocation date*.

10. What do you understand by directory authentication service?

Ans.: The directory authentication service is used when two entities wish to communicate with each other, and each of them needs to authenticate the other. That is, both the sender and receiver need to ensure that the other communicating party is the one that it claims to be. There are two types of directory authentication services, namely, *peer entity authentication* and *data origin authentication*.

- *Peer entity authentication:* This authentication service enables the user to verify the identity of a peer entity involved in the communication process. It prevents an entity from masquerading as another entity or an unauthorized replay of a previously established connection. The peer entity service can be used during the establishment phase or occasionally during the data transfer phase of a connection. Note that there must be an association between the two parties for peer entity authentication.
- *Data origin authentication:* This authentication service enables the recipient to verify that the message has not been tampered with in transit (data integrity) and that it has originated from the expected sender (authenticity). That is, it is used to verify the original source of a received message. The data origin authentication services allow the receiver to verify the identity of the message as belonging to the original message creator even if the message has passed through one or more intermediaries before arriving at the receiver. Note that unlike peer entity authentication, no association between the sender and receiver is required. Thus, this type of service is suitable for e-mail service in which there is initially no communication between the entities.

11. Discuss the authentication procedures of X.509.

Ans.: X.509 includes three authentication procedures, namely, *one-way authentication*, *two-way authentication* and *three-way authentication*. These authentication procedures make use of public-key signatures and can be used across a variety of applications. While working with these procedures, it is assumed that two communicating nodes know each other's public key. These procedures are discussed in the following.

- *One-way authentication:* This involves a single transfer of information from user A to user B [see Figure 9.5(a)]. This information is transferred in order to confirm that the message is generated by user A, and that the message is intended for user B and has not been altered or replayed by any intruder. Thus, this procedure only verifies the identity of A. At a minimum, the message includes the following and is signed with the private key of A.
  - *Timestamp* (t_A): This indicates the time when the message was generated, along with the validity or expiration time of the message.
  - *Nonce* (r_A): This is a random number used to protect the message from replay attacks. The value of nonce must be unique during the validation period. This is done so that B can discard any new messages having the same nonce value.
  - *Identity of* B (ID_B): This is included so that the user B can access the X.509 directory and be sure that the message is intended for him or her only.

- *Signed data* (`sgnData`): This is the information that is actually conveyed between the two users. This information is included within the scope of the signature, thus ensuring its authenticity and integrity.
- *Encrypted data* ($E_{B_{PUB}}[K_{AB}]$): This includes the session key K_{AB}, encrypted with B's public key (B_{PUB}). This key is used after the authentication process gets over.

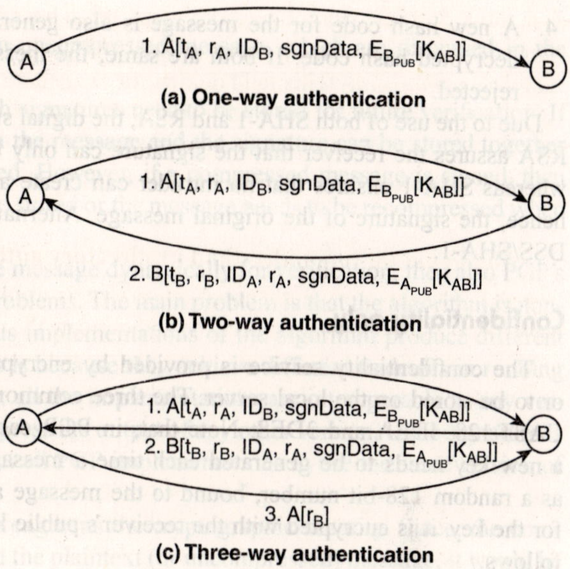

Figure 9.5 Authentication Procedures

- *Two-way authentication:* This involves a two-way transfer of information; first from user A to B, and then from user B to A. This two-way transfer allows both users to verify each other's identity. First, A sends a message containing the same fields as described in one-way authentication to B. Then, B replies to A with a message including t_B, r_B, ID_A, r_A, `sgnData` and optionally $E_{A_{PUB}}[K_{AB}]$, and the message is signed by B [see Figure 9.5(b)]. The inclusion of nonce r_A in the reply message ensures that the reply is valid and has come from B, whereas r_B protects the information being transferred by B from replay attacks.
- *Three-way authentication:* This involves the three-way transfer of information from A to B. In this procedure, a third message from A to B is included, in addition to two messages that are the same as described in two-way authentication. The third message contains a signed copy of the nonce r_B signed by A [see Figure 9.5(c)]. Since both the nonces are echoed back by the other side, each user can check the returned nonce to detect replay attacks. This approach is useful when synchronized clocks are not available.

12. Explain the services of PGP.

Ans.: *PGP* (stands for *pretty good privacy*) is a simple protocol that was invented by Phil Zimmermann to provide confidentiality, authentication and integrity services for electronic mail and other file storage applications. PGP offers various services, which are discussed as follows:

Authentication only

PGP provides digital signature service for authentication. Suppose user A wants to send a message to B, then, to achieve authentication, these steps are followed.

1. A creates a message, and applies the SHA-1 algorithm to find the 160-bit hash code of the message.
2. The generated hash code is encrypted with RSA using A's private key. The resultant encrypted code is then added to the beginning of the message.
3. On receiving the message, B decrypts the message with RSA using A's public key and extracts the hash code.

AH Tunnel Mode

In the tunnel mode AH, a new outer IP header is inserted into the packet, and the AH is inserted in between the original IP header and the new outer IP header. The addresses of the original source and destination are included in the inner IP header, while the addresses of firewalls or other security gateways are included in the new outer IP header. AH protects the entire inner IP packet, including the inner IP header. The new outer IP header is also protected, except for the mutable and unpredictable fields. The AH tunnel mode for both IPv4 and IPv6 packets is shown in Figure 9.11.

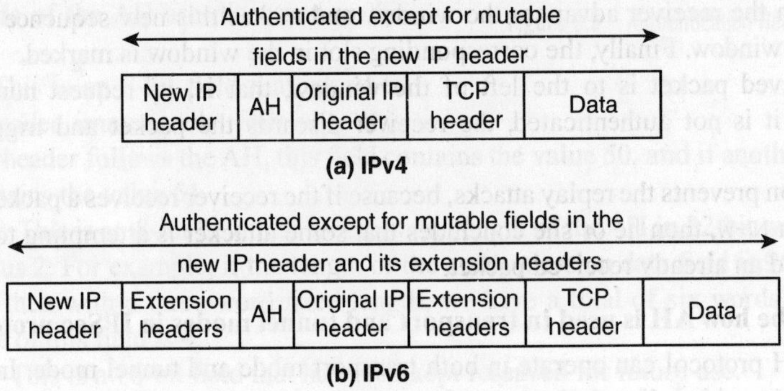

Figure 9.11 Tunnel mode AH

28. Explain the ESP protocol.

Ans.: The ESP protocol provides confidentiality and integrity of the messages. Optionally, this protocol can also provide an authentication service. The ESP packet format (containing a header and a trailer) is made up of seven fields (see Figure 9.12). These fields are discussed in the following text:

- *Security parameters index (SPI):* This is a 32-bit field that uniquely identifies the security associations for traffic to which the datagram belongs. It is used in combination with the source and destination IP addresses, as well as the security protocol used (AH or ESP). The SPI value ranges from 1 to 255, and these values have been reserved by the Internet Assigned Numbers Authority (IANA) for future use.
- *Sequence number:* This is a 32-bit field that contains a number that increases monotonically. Initially, counter of both the sender and receiver is set to zero. This field prevents the replay

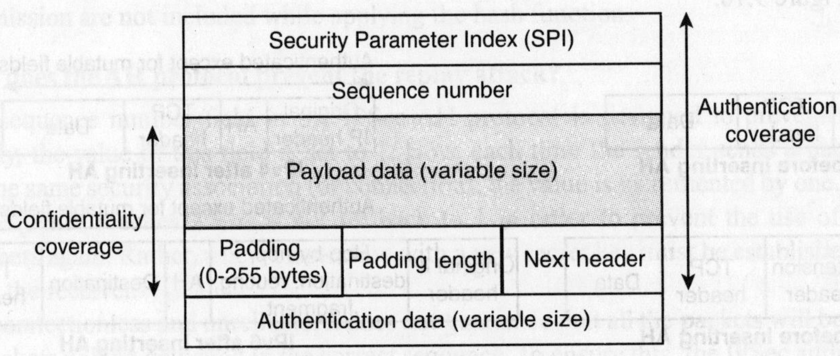

Figure 9.12 IPSec ESP format

- It provides complete privacy as the parties involved in the communication can access the information only when and where necessary.

To understand the working of SET, it is important to know the participants of the SET system. The main participants of SET system are:

- *Cardholder:* The person who owns the card (such as MasterCard, Visa) and does the purchasing on the Internet.
- *Merchant:* The organization or the individual who sells goods or offers services to the cardholder. Usually, these goods and services are offered via a website.
- *Issuer:* The financial institutions (such as banks) that issue the credit cards and are responsible for the payment of purchases made by the cardholder.
- *Acquirer:* This is also a financial institution that is responsible for establishing an account with the merchant and processing payment card authorizations and payments. Generally, a merchant accepts many credit cards issued by different banks. Since the merchant cannot deal with all the banks, or it cannot have account in all the banks, therefore, it needs an acquirer who provides authorization to the merchant that the card account is valid and active. The acquirer also transfers the payments electronically to the merchant's account. The issuer subsequently reimburses the acquirer over some kind of payment network for electronic funds transfer.
- *Acquirer payment gateway:* This is an interface between SET and the computer networks of banks for authorization and payment functions.
- *Certification authority (CA):* This is an organization that offers different classes of certificates for cardholders, merchants and payment gateways.

Working of SET

Before using SET, both the cardholder and the merchant must register with the CA. After the registration process, the working of SET involves many steps, which are as follows:

1. The customer browses the merchant's website to evaluate the products offered by the merchant. He or she then selects the products to be purchased and adds them to the shopping cart.
2. The customer then uses a single message to communicate with the merchant and payment gateway. The message has two parts, namely, *purchase order*, which is used by the merchant, and *card information*, which is used by the merchant's bank (acquirer).
3. The card information is then forwarded to the acquirer.
4. The acquirer contacts the issuer and checks about payment authorization.
5. If the purchase is authorized, the issuer sends the authorization to the acquirer.
6. A copy of the authorization is also forwarded to the merchant.
7. The merchant completes the order and informs the customer about it.
8. Merchant captures the transaction from its bank.
9. Finally, the credit card invoice is printed by the issuer and provided to the customer.

Dual Signatures

As stated in step 2 of SET, the customer uses a single message to communicate with the merchant and the payment gateway. Therefore, the customer has to ensure that the merchant will not be able to view the payment instruction, and that the acquirer will not be able to view the order instruction. Also, the order and payment has to be linked together, so that the customer can prove that the payment is for the particular order. This whole process is implemented using a concept known as dual signature. The creation of dual signature involves five steps, which are as follows:

1. The customer creates the Payment Information Message Digest (PIMD) by taking the hash (using SHA-1) of the Payment Information (PI).
2. The customer creates another digest, that is, the Order Information Message Digest (OIMD) by taking the hash (again using SHA-1) of the Order Information (OI).
3. Both the PIMD and OIMD are combined together.
4. The combined result is again passed through the hash algorithm SHA-1, and a new digest, Payment Order Message Digest (POMD), is created.
5. Finally, the customer encrypts the POMD with his or her private key using the RSA algorithm, thereby creating the dual signature (DS). This POMD is available to both the merchant and the payment gateway.

Now, the cardholder sends OI, DS and PIMD to the merchant. The merchant verifies that the order information has come from the cardholder, and not from any imposter, by following these steps:

1. The merchant computes its own OIMD by taking hash of OI.
2. The PIMD received from the customer and the computed OIMD are then combined to form a new POMD (say, POMD1).
3. The merchant decrypts the received DS to recover the original POMD.
4. The merchant then compares POMD and POMD1. If both are equal, the message is accepted; otherwise, it is rejected.

Similarly, the payment gateway receives PI, DS and OIMD from the cardholder. Then, it verifies that the payment information has come from the cardholder and not from anyone else. For this, it uses a similar process as used by the merchant to verify the order information. To protect the payment information from the merchant, the cardholder encrypts PI, DS and OIMD with one-time session key K. The key K is also encrypted with the private key of the payment gateway. These two together form a digital envelope, which is sent to the merchant. The merchant is supposed to send this envelope to the payment gateway. Since the merchant does not know the public key of the payment gateway, it cannot decrypt the envelope to obtain the payment details. The payment gateway verifies the authenticity of the cardholder by following these steps.

1. The payment gateway computes its own PIMD by taking hash of PI.
2. The OIMD received from the customer and the computed PIMD are then combined to form a new POMD (say, POMD1).
3. The payment gateway decrypts the received DS to recover the original POMD.
4. The payment gateway then compares the POMD and POMD1. If both are equal, it is verified that the message has come from the cardholder, and not from any imposter.

38. Differentiate between SSL and SET.

Ans.: SSL and SET are both Internet security protocols. However, they differ in some aspects as SET is more secured than SSL. The authentication mechanism used in SET is very complex, which makes it almost impossible for both the sender and receiver to commit any kind of fraud. In a nutshell, SET has been specifically designed for secured e-commerce transactions involving online payments, while SSL has been designed only for exchanging messages over the Internet. The main differences between SSL and SET are listed in the Table 9.8.

Table 9.8 SSL versus SET

Issue	SSL	SET
Main objective	To allow exchange of data in an encrypted form	To support e-commerce-related payment mechanisms
Certification	The certificates are exchanged between the two parties.	A trusted third party certifies all the parties involved in the communication process.
Authentication	The authentication mechanism is not very strong.	The authentication mechanism is very strong.
Risk of merchant fraud	It is prone to merchant fraud as financial data is provided to the merchant.	It is free from this fraud as financial data is given to the payment gateway only.
Risk of customer fraud	It is prone to this kind of fraud as the customer can refuse to pay later; there is no mechanism that can prevent such kind of fraud.	The payment instructions are digitally signed by the customer. Thus, there is less chance of such fraud.
Action in case of customer fraud	Merchant is responsible if a customer later refuses to pay.	Payment gateway is responsible in case of customer fraud.
Practical usage	High	Less

Multiple-choice Questions

1. Which server acts as KDC in the Kerberos protocol?
   (a) TGS (b) AS
   (c) Real server (d) None of these
2. Which encryption algorithm is used in the Kerberos 4 protocol?
   (a) AES (b) Block cipher
   (c) DES (d) Triple DES
3. In which year was X.509 first issued?
   (a) 1988 (b) 1978
   (c) 1982 (d) 1994
4. Who issues the PGP certificates?
   (a) ITU-T (b) IEEE
   (c) IETF (d) The users themselves
5. What are the two modes that IPSec protocol works on?
   (a) On and Off (b) Transport and Tunnel
   (c) Forward and Backward (d) Linked and Unlinked
6. Which of the following are IPSec protocols?
   (a) PGP and S/MIME (b) Kerberos 4, Kerberos 5
   (c) AH and ESP (d) SSL and SET
7. Which algorithm solves the man-in-the-middle attack problem?
   (a) Diffie-Hellman (b) RSA
   (c) Oakley (d) ISAKMP

8. Which of the following Internet security protocols is used for secure credit card payments?
   (a) SET (b) PGP
   (c) SSL (d) TLS
9. The _______ protocol uses the Fortezza algorithm.
   (a) TLS (b) SET
   (c) ESP (d) SSL
10. In which protocol is the payment gateway used?
   (a) SET (b) PGP
   (c) TLS (d) SSL

Answers

1. (b)	2. (c)	3. (a)	4. (d)	5. (b)	6. (c)
7. (c)	8. (a)	9. (d)	10. (a)		

10

System Security

1. What do you mean by the term intruders? Explain intrusion techniques in brief.

Ans.: *Intruders* are the attackers who attempt to breach the security of a network. They attack the network in order to get unauthorized access. Intruders are of three types, namely, *masquerader*, *misfeasor* and *clandestine user*.

- *Masquerader* is an external user who is not authorized to use a computer, and yet tries to gain privileges to access a legitimate user's account. Masquerading is generally done either using stolen IDs and passwords, or through bypassing authentication mechanisms.
- *Misfeasor* is a legitimate user who either accesses some applications or data without sufficient privileges to access them, or has privilege to access them, but misuses these privileges. A misfeasor is generally an internal user.
- *Clandestine user* is either an internal or external user who gains administrative control of the system and tries to avoid access control and auditing information.

Intrusion Techniques

The intruders always indulge in finding some way to gain access to the system or to increase the number of privileges assigned to them. To do this, the intruders need access to information that should have been protected, such as some legitimate user's password. After learning the password of an authorized user, intruders can use it to log on to the system and misuse the privileges assigned to the authorized user. Some techniques that the intruders can use to learn others' passwords are as listed here:

- They can try the passwords that are by default assigned to standard accounts such as administrator, as it is possible that the administrators may not change their passwords.
- They can thoroughly test all the short passwords made up of one, two or three characters.
- They can intercept the communication between the host system and a remote user.
- They can use a malicious program, such as a Trojan horse, to get around the restrictions imposed on access.
- They can try the words that are available in the system's online dictionary or that are expected to be used.
- They can try the users' personal information such as their IDs, phone numbers, room numbers, names of their spouses and children, birthdates, etc.

Besides learning passwords, the intruders can go for other ways to gain access to the system or to gain further privileges. For example, they can exploit attacks such as buffer overflows on a program that executes with certain privileges.

2. Discuss password protection approaches.

Ans.: Generally, passwords are stored by the system in a password file along with the user IDs. Thus, to protect passwords from being captured by the intruders, it is necessary to protect the password file. There are two ways to protect the password file, as listed here:

- *One-way function:* The system does not store the passwords in a clear form in the password file; rather, it applies a function on the user's password and stores the resulting value in the password file. Whenever a user attempts to log on to the system with the help of his or her user ID and password, the system applies the same function on the supplied password. Then it checks whether the newly computed value matches with the stored value. If so, the user is authenticated and allowed access; otherwise, access is denied. The advantage of using this method of protecting the password file is that even if an intruder gets access to the password file, he or she will not be able to get the passwords.
- *Access control:* Another means of protecting the password file is by restricting access to the password file. Only a few users such as the system administrator must be allowed to access the password file.

3. Explain any two approaches for intrusion detection.

Ans.: To prevent intruders from getting unauthorized access to the system, *intrusion prevention* and *intrusion detection* can be used. *Intrusion prevention* is a process that involves detecting the signs of intrusion and attempting to stop the intrusion efforts. On the other hand, *intrusion detection* is a process that involves monitoring the actions occurring on the network or in the computer systems. In intrusion detection, analysis is done to detect the sign of violations of computer security policies, standard security policies or acceptable use of policies.

It is not possible to completely prevent the efforts of intruders as they constantly try to find their way into the secured system. Hence, we mainly focus on intrusion detection, as it helps collect more information about intrusions. There are generally two approaches for intrusion detection, as listed here:

- *Statistical anomaly detection:* In this category, the behaviour of legitimate users is evaluated over some time interval. That is, their actions are captured as statistical data and then, by applying certain rules on the collected data, their behaviour is checked to determine the legitimacy of the users. This can be achieved by two ways, namely, *threshold detection* and *profile-based detection*.
  - *Threshold detection:* In threshold detection, thresholds are defined for all users as a group, and the total number of events that are attributed to the user are measured against these threshold values. The number of events is assumed to round up to a number that is most likely to occur, and if the event count exceeds this number, then intrusion is said to have occurred.
  - *Profile-based detection:* In profile-based detection, profiles for all users are created, and then matched with available statistical data to find out if any unwanted action has been performed. A user profile contains several parameters; therefore, change in a single parameter is not a sign of alert.
- *Rule-based detection:* In this category, certain rules are applied on the actions performed by the users. These rules can determine whether an action performed by any user is suspicious enough to be classified as an intrusion attempt. Rule-based detection is classified into two types, namely, *anomaly detection* and *penetration identification*.

- *Anomaly-based detection:* In anomaly-based detection, the usage patterns of users are collected, and certain rules are applied to check any deviation from the previous usage pasterns. The collected patterns are defined by the set of rules that includes past behaviour patterns of users, programs, privileges, time-slots, terminals, etc. The current behaviour patterns of the user are matched with the defined set of rules to check whether there is any deviation in the patterns. In this approach, a large database of rules is needed.
- *Penetration identification:* In penetration identification, an expert system is maintained that looks for any unwanted attempts. This system also contains rules that are used to identify the suspicious behaviour and penetrations that can exploit known weaknesses. Here, the rules are generated by interviewing experts such as system administrators and security analysts. The data collected in the interview process consist of known penetration scenarios and events that may threaten the security of the system. Thus, the rules are confined to the system and the operating system that is being used.

4. Explain audit records.

Ans.: An *audit record* (also known as *audit log*) is a very important tool used in intrusion detection. Audit records are used to track the actions performed by users. If any user tries to get unauthorized access in a network, then traces of such actions can be detected in these records, so that appropriate measures can be taken. Audit records can be categorized into two types, namely, *native audit records* and *detection-specific audit records*.

- *Native audit records:* Almost all multiuser operating systems come with in-built accounting software that collects information about the actions of each user. The advantage of using this approach is that there is no need for additional collection software. However, the disadvantage is that some of the needed information may not be available in the native audit record or may be in a form that is not convenient to use.
- *Detection-specific audit records:* These records record only specific information that is related to the detection of unauthorized access in a network. These types of records contain more focused information, but duplication of information may happen. The advantage of using this approach is that it could be made vendor-independent and can be ported onto different systems. However, the disadvantage of this approach is the extra overhead, as two accounting packages need to remain on a single machine.

Irrespective of the type, each audit record contains some fields, as listed here:

- *Subject:* This field gives the information of the user or process or terminal who has started an action.
- *Action:* This field defines the operation performed by the user (subject) on an object. For example, read/write, login, execute, print, I/O activity, etc.
- *Object:* This field provides the information of the receiver who has received the action. For example, database record, a disk file or an application program.
- *Exception-condition:* This field stores the result of any exception condition, if any occurs because of the actions performed by the subject on the object.
- *Resource-usage:* This field records the information regarding the usage of resources in performing an action. For example, the disk space, or CPU time used by an action, number of lines printed or displayed, or number of I/O units used.
- *Time-stamp:* This field indicates the unique date and time stamp that indicates when an action was executed.

5. Why is distributed intrusion detection needed? Explain its architecture.

Ans.: A typical organization consists of a large collection of hosts distributed over a LAN or supported by an internetwork. One way to detect intrusion in such an organization is to use stand-alone intrusion detection systems on individual hosts. Though this type of defence is possible, it has not proved to be much effective. Thus, a better and more effective defence is required, which is achieved through coordination and cooperation among the intrusion detection systems across the network.

Figure 10.1 shows the architecture of a distributed intrusion detection system that was developed at the University of California. It consists of the following three components:

- *Host agent module:* This is an audit collection module that runs as a background process on the system being monitored. It is responsible for collecting information related to security on the host and reporting this to the central manager.
- *LAN manager agent module:* This module works in a similar manner as that of a host agent module. However, the difference is that it examines the LAN traffic, as its name implies, rather than security-related events. It also reports the results of analysis to the central manager.
- *Central manager module:* This is the main module that is responsible for processing and correlating the reports received from the host agent module and LAN manager agent module in order to detect the intrusion.

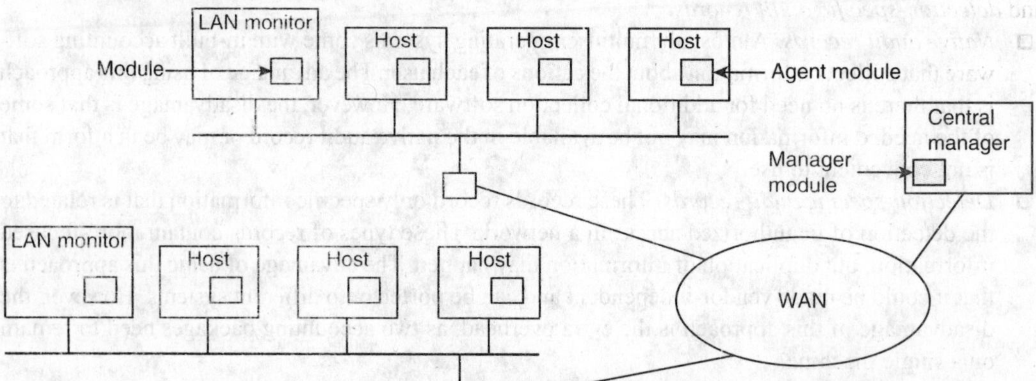

Figure 10.1 Architecture of Distributed Intrusion Detection System

6. List some issues in the design of distributed intrusion detection systems.

Ans.: Although distributed intrusion detection systems are an effective way to prevent intrusion across the network, there are still some issues in its design. These issues are discussed as follows:

- In case different hosts in a network are not similar (that is, heterogeneous environment), the native audit collection system used by each host may differ. Further, if intrusion detection is used, different hosts may have their own format for security-related audit records. This necessitates a distributed intrusion detection system to deal with different audit formats.
- The intrusion detection system can be implemented using either centralized or decentralized architecture. If centralized architecture is used, the entire audit data is collected and analyzed at

a single central location. Though centralizing the data makes the task of correlating the reports easier, it results in a serious bottleneck in case of failure of the central location. On the other hand, if decentralized architecture is used, we have more than one location to collect and analyze the data. To work effectively, the coordination and exchange of information among these locations is required, which results in an extra overhead. Therefore, the choice of which architecture is to be employed is a matter of concern.

- As many nodes in the network are responsible for collecting and analyzing the audit data, either the raw audit data or summary data needs to be transmitted across the network. This necessitates ensuring the integrity and confidentiality of data being transmitted. Integrity refers to ensuring that the data is not altered by the intruder, and confidentiality is about maintaining the secrecy of the data.

7. What are honeypots?

Ans.: *Honeypots* are a recent innovation in intrusion detection technology. They are the traps that are designed to attract the potential intruders and, thus, track their activities. The main aim of such systems is to collect the information about the intruder's activities, deviate them from accessing the critical systems and boost them to stay on the system for more time so that the network administrator can take actions accordingly.

Honeypots are fabricated to look like real systems by putting real-looking information into them, so that they appear valuable to the potential intruders. However, legitimate users are not allowed to know about or access these systems. Thus, if anyone accesses the honeypots, he or she is a potential attacker. Honeypots are equipped with sensors and loggers to detect accesses and to track the intruder's activities.

8. How are passwords stored in a password file in the UNIX operating system? How are users authenticated?

Ans.: Earlier, in the UNIX operating system, passwords of all users were stored in plaintext in the password file, and the password file was protected by allowing it to be accessed only by the system administrator and privileged users. However, this practice may prove dangerous because any mistake in programming or any other error can make the password file vulnerable to attack. Thus, a new scheme is now used in the UNIX operating system, where the passwords are not stored in plaintext in the password file; instead, a hash of the password is computed and stored in the password file.

Each user in UNIX is allowed to choose a password of maximum eight printable characters, which are converted using 7-bit ASCII to form a 56-bit value. This 56-bit value is used as the encryption key in the encryption function, `crypt(3)`. The `crypt(3)` function is based on the Data Encryption Standard (DES) algorithm. In UNIX, DES algorithm is modified with the help of 12-bit *salt*—a value indicating the time a password was assigned to a user. To store a password in the password file, the modified DES algorithm takes a 64-bit block consisting of 0s and encrypts it using the 56-bit encryption key. The resulting 64-bit ciphertext block serves as input for the next encryption. A total of 25 encryptions are performed, and the final obtained 64-bit ciphertext is converted to 11 printable characters. This hashed password is then stored in the password file along with the user ID and the salt.

At the time a user attempts to log on to the system, he or she presents his or her user ID and password to the system. The UNIX operating system uses the supplied user ID as index to find the corresponding entry in the password file. After finding the entry, it extracts the plaintext salt and hashed password. The salt along with the password supplied by the user are given as input to the `crypt(3)` function, which then repeats the same process as described earlier to compute the hash of the password. If the newly computed value matches with the stored value in the password file, the user is authenticated; otherwise, the access is denied.

9. Discuss some password selection strategies.

Ans.: Generally, users choose passwords that are short and easy to remember. However, such passwords may be easily guessed, making it simple for intruders to hack into the corresponding user's accounts. On the other hand, if passwords given to the users are long and are randomly generated, it is not effectively possible to crack the passwords. However, such passwords are hard to remember for the users. Thus, some password-selection strategies have been introduced with the aim of building a password that cannot be easily guessed and can be easily remembered. These strategies are listed here:

- *User education:* This strategy is based on educating the users about the importance of using strong passwords that are difficult to guess. The users can also be provided with certain guidelines that help them in choosing hard-to-guess passwords. Though this strategy is simple, it generally fails, especially when there are a large number of users. This is because many users simply ignore the guidelines of selecting strong passwords, while others are unable to judge what a strong password is.
- *Computer-generated passwords:* In this strategy, the system randomly generates passwords for the users. Being random, these passwords may or may not be correctly pronounceable. Thus, it becomes difficult for the users to remember the passwords. The situation becomes even worse in case the password is not pronounceable because, in that case, the user does not have any choice except to write down the password somewhere, which makes it subject to be stolen by an intruder. Therefore, this technique is not so popular among the users.
- *Reactive password checking:* In this strategy, the system executes its own password cracker at regular intervals of time to identify passwords that can be guessed easily. The idea is to determine easy-to-guess passwords and to reject them, thus, improving password security. The system also notifies the corresponding users about the cancellation of their passwords. The disadvantage of this strategy is that any easy-to-guess password in the system remains vulnerable to attack as long as it is not found by the password cracker of the system.
- *Proactive password checker:* This strategy allows users to select their passwords on their own. However, it provides sufficient guidance to the users at the time of password selection so that they can select passwords that are strong as well as easy to remember. To achieve this, the system may employ certain rules that must be followed by each user while selecting the password. For example, the system may enforce a rule that the password must be minimum eight characters long and must be the combination of lower case letters, upper case letters and numeric digits. Now, at the time of password selection, if all rules are followed by the user, the system allows the password, else rejects it.

  The proactive password checker strategy is based on creating a balance between the strength of the password and user acceptability. This is essential because, if the system chooses a complex algorithm for determining whether a selected password is acceptable, then too many password rejections may occur and, as a result, the user may not find the system user-friendly. In contrast, if the system uses a simple algorithm, then it may enable a password cracker to understand the basis of password selection and, thus, help them to guess the passwords easily.

10. What do you understand by malicious software?

Ans.: *Malicious software* (shortened form *malware*) are programs that generate threats to the computer system and stored data. They could be in the form of viruses, worms, Trojan horses, logic bombs and zombie programs. All malicious programs fall under two categories: one that require a host program such as an application program or a system program in order to be executed by the operating system, and another that can be executed by the operating system independently. Some examples of malicious programs belonging to first category include viruses and logic bombs, while worms and zombie programs are examples of the second category.

11. What is a virus? Explain different types of viruses.

Ans.: *Virus* (stands for *Vital Information Resources Under Seize*) is a program or small code segment that is designed to replicate, attach to other programs and perform unsolicited and malicious actions. It enters into the computer system from external sources such as CD, pen drive or e-mail and executes when the infected program is executed. Further, as an infected computer gets in contact with an uninfected computer (for example, through computer networks), the virus may pass on to the uninfected system and destroy data.

Just as flowers are attractive to the bees that pollinate them, virus host programs are deliberately made attractive to victimize the user. They become destructive as soon as they enter a system or are programmed to lie dormant until activated by a trigger. The different types of virus are discussed as follows:

- *Boot sector virus:* This virus infects the master boot record of a computer system. This virus moves the boot record to another sector on the disk, or replaces it with the infected one. It then marks that sector as a bad sector on the disk. This type of virus is very difficult to detect since the boot sector is the first program that is loaded when a computer starts. In effect, the boot sector virus takes full control of the infected computer.
- *File-infecting virus:* This virus infects files with the extensions *.com* and *.exe*. This type of virus usually resides inside the memory and infects most of the executable files on a system. The virus replicates by attaching a copy of itself to an uninfected executable program. It then modifies the host programs and, subsequently, when the program is executed, it executes along with it. File-infecting virus can only gain control of the computer if the user or the operating system executes a file infected with the virus.
- *Polymorphic virus:* This virus changes its code as it propagates from one file to another. Therefore, each copy of virus appears different from others; however, they are functionally similar. This makes the polymorphic virus difficult to detect, like the stealth virus. The variation in copies is achieved by placing superfluous instructions in the virus code or by interchanging the order of instructions that are not dependent. Another more effective means to achieve variation is by using encryption. A part of the virus, called the *mutation engine*, generates a random key that is used to encrypt the rest of the virus. The random key is kept stored with the virus, while the mutation engine changes by itself. At the time the infected program is executed, the stored key is used by the virus to decrypt itself. Each time the virus replicates, the random key changes.
- *Stealth virus:* This virus attempts to conceal its presence from the user. It makes use of compression such that the length of infected program is exactly same as that of the uninfected version. For example, it may keep intercept logic in some I/O routines so that when some other program requests for information from the suspicious portions of the disk using these routines, it will present the original uninfected version to the program. The Stoned Monkey virus is an example

of stealth virus. This virus uses 'read stealth' capability, and if a user executes a disk-editing or anti-virus program to examine the main boot record, the user would not find any evidence of infection.

- *Multipartite virus:* This virus infects both boot sectors and executable files, and uses both mechanisms to spread. It is the worst virus of all because it can combine some or all of the stealth techniques along with polymorphism to prevent detection. For example, if a user runs an application infected with a multipartite virus, the virus activates and infects the hard disk's master boot record. Moreover, the next time the computer starts; the virus gets activated again and starts infecting every program that the user runs. One-half virus is an example of a multipartite virus, which exhibits both stealth and polymorphic behaviour.

12. What are the typical phases of operation of a virus?

Ans.: Virus is a destructive program that attaches to other programs, replicates itself and performs malicious actions when the host program is executed. The whole operation of a virus involves the following four phases.

- *Dormant phase:* This is the initial phase in the lifetime of a virus. During this phase, the virus remains idle; however, later, it is activated due to occurrence of some events including the date, time, capacity of disk beyond limit or the presence of some other program or file. It may be noted that this phase exists only in case of some viruses and not all.
- *Propagation phase:* During this phase, the virus replicates itself and infects other programs as well as some disk areas by putting its identical copies (referred to as *clones*) into them. All the infected programs now contain the same virus, which has already entered into the propagation phase.
- *Triggering phase:* In this phase, the virus is activated to enter the execution phase, so that it can perform its intended action. The activation of the virus may occur due to the events as specified in dormant phase. In addition, it also takes into account the number of times a single copy of virus replicates itself.
- *Execution phase:* This is the last phase of the virus's operation where it performs the function for which it was designed. The functions performed by viruses range from simple harmless functions such as displaying a message on the screen to serious malicious functions such as destroying programs and data files.

13. Write a short note on the following:

(a) Worms
(b) Trojan horses
(c) Logic bomb
(d) Spyware

Ans.: (a) *Worms:* Worms are programs constructed to infiltrate into legitimate data processing programs and alter or destroy the data. They often use network connections to spread from one computer system to another; thus, worms attack systems that are linked through communication lines. Once active within a system, worms behave like a virus and perform a number of disruptive actions. To reproduce themselves, worms make use of network medium such as: network mail facility, in which a worm can mail a copy of itself to other systems, remote execution capability, in which a worm can execute a copy of itself on another system and remote log in capability, whereby a worm can log into a remote system as a user and then use commands to copy itself from one system to another.

Both worms and viruses tend to fill computer memory with useless data thereby preventing users from using memory space for the intended applications or programs. In addition, they can destroy or modify data and programs to produce erroneous results, as well as halt the operation of a computer system or network. Similar to a virus, the operation of a network worm also involves dormant, propagation, triggering and execution phases.

(b) *Trojan horse:* A Trojan horse is a malicious program that appears to be legal and useful but concurrently does something unexpected, such as destroying existing programs and files. It does not replicate itself in the computer system and, hence, it is not a virus. However, it usually opens the way for other malicious programs such as viruses to enter into the computer system. In addition, it may also allow unauthorized users to access the information stored in the computer.

Trojan horses spread when users are convinced to open or download a program because they think it has come from a legitimate source. They can also be included in software that is freely downloadable. They are usually subtler, especially in the cases where they are used for espionage. They can be programmed to self-destruct, without leaving any evidence other than the damage they have caused. The most famous Trojan horse is a program called back orifice, which is an unsubtle play of words on Microsoft's Back Office suite of programs for NT server. This program allows anybody to have the complete control over the computer or server it occupies.

(c) *Logic bomb:* A logic bomb is a program or portion of a program that lies dormant until a specific part of program logic is activated. The most common activator for a logic bomb is date. The logic bomb periodically checks the computer system date and does nothing until a pre-programmed date and time is reached. It could also be programmed to wait for a certain message from the programmer. When logic bomb sees the message, it gets activated and executes the code. A logic bomb can also be programmed to activate on a wide variety of other variables such as when a database grows past a certain size or a user's home directory is deleted. For example, the well-known logic bomb is a Michelangelo, which has a trigger set for Michelangelo's birthday. On the given birth date, it causes system crash or data loss or other unexpected interactions with existing code.

(d) *Spyware:* Spyware are the small programs that install themselves on computers to gather data secretly about the computer user without his or her consent and report the collected data to interested users or parties. The information gathered by the spyware may include e-mail addresses and passwords, net surfing activities, credit card information, etc. Spyware often gets automatically installed on your computer when you download a program from the Internet or click any option from pop-up windows in the browser.

14. What is an antivirus? What are its approaches?

Ans.: An *antivirus* is an application software that is used for providing protection against malicious software. It is a software utility that (upon installing on a computer) detects viruses and, if found, tries to remove them. The built-in scanner of antivirus software scans all the files on the computer's hard disk to look for particular types of code within programs. Most antivirus programs include an auto-update feature that enables the program to download profiles of new viruses so that it can check for the new viruses as soon as they are discovered. The most popular available antivirus software includes Norton antivirus, McAfee antivirus and Quick Heal antivirus.

Antivirus Approaches

A simple and ideal approach against threat of viruses is to prevent them from entering into the system. Practically, it is not possible to achieve total prevention; however, the frequency of successful virus attacks can be reduced. Thus, an alternative approach is used that is based on the *detection*, *identification* and *removal* of viruses from the infected programs.

- *Detection:* In case the system has been infected by viruses, the first step is to identify that the infection has occurred and where it has occurred, that is, the location of the virus.
- *Identification:* After the infection has been detected and the virus located, the next step is to determine the specific type of virus that has infected the file.
- *Removal:* After identifying the specific virus in a file, the final step is to remove it completely from the infected file and to bring the file back to its original state. The virus must be removed from all the systems in the network in order to prevent it from spreading further.

15. List and brief the different generations of antivirus software.

Ans.: Earlier, viruses were simple code fragments; thus, antivirus software packages used for those viruses were also simpler. However, with the evolution in virus as well as antivirus technology, the attackers have generated more complex viruses that are not easily detectable. To protect against such viruses, antivirus software have also grown complex. The growth of antivirus software has been divided into four generations which are as follows:

- *First generation:* The antivirus software of this generation used simple scanners that rely on virus signatures to detect viruses. It detects viruses that have basically the same structure and the same bit pattern in all copies. However, these types of scanners can detect only the known viruses. Another type of scanner used in the first generation maintains a record of the program length, and monitors the change in length for detecting the viruses.
- *Second generation:* The antivirus software of this generation used heuristic scanners that rely on some heuristic rules to detect virus infections. One approach to detect virus infection is to scan the files and look for code fragments that are usually related to viruses. For example, in case of a polymorphic virus, the scanner may determine the starting of the encryption loop and then find the encryption key. Once the scanner has found the key, it cleans the virus infection from the infected program by decrypting the code fragment with the key and then returns the virus-free program back to service.

  Another approach for detecting virus infection is integrity checking. In this approach, a checksum is added at the end of each program. If any program gets infected by a virus, however, with no change in the checksum, the change in program can be detected by performing an integrity check. On the other hand, if a virus is so complex that it changes the checksum in addition to the program, then an encrypted hash function can be used to deal with the virus. By storing the encryption key at a different location from that of the program, we can prevent a virus from generating a new hash code and then encrypting it. Moreover, the use of the hash function instead of checksum prevents the virus from adapting the program to generate the same hash code as previously.
- *Third generation:* The antivirus software of this generation are the memory-resident programs that do not take into account the structure of viruses or heuristic rules to identify them. Rather, they scan the program to look for a small set of actions that indicate the infection and then deal with the viruses. An advantage is that it is not required to maintain any signatures or rules for a wide range of viruses in order to detect an infection.
- *Fourth generation:* The antivirus software of this generation are the packages that use scanning and activity trapping components in conjunction. These packages also comprise the access control capability, which restricts the viruses from entering into the system and updating the files for spreading the infection. All these features collectively strengthen the ability of the antivirus software.

16. What is digital immune system? Explain how it works.

Ans.: With the increased use of Internet-based capabilities such as integrated mail systems (Lotus Notes and Microsoft Outlook) and mobile-program systems (Java and ActiveX), the threat of

Internet-based virus propagation has also risen. Therefore, IBM has developed the digital immune system in response to these Internet-based virus threats. The goal of this system is to offer a very fast response time so that the viruses can be removed instantly as they enter into the system. Whenever a new virus is introduced into an organization, it is automatically captured by the digital immune system, which then examines it, adds detection and shielding for it and removes it from the system. The immune system also passes the information related to that virus to the other systems that are running the IBM antivirus, so that those systems can detect this virus before it begins to run.

The operation of the digital immune system involves the following steps (see Figure 10.2):

1. The monitoring program installed on each client machine in the organization detects the presence of a virus using various heuristic rules based on system behaviour, virus signatures or unexpected changes in the programs. In case any program on a client machine is found infected by a virus, the monitoring program sends a copy of that program to the administrative machine within the organization.
2. The administrative machine encrypts the copy of infected program received from monitoring program and forwards it to a central virus analysis machine.
3. The virus analysis machine is responsible for analyzing the infected program to detect new viruses. It creates an environment in which the infected program can be executed and analyzed. During execution, the structure and behaviour of the virus is analyzed and, based on this analysis, a virus signature is extracted. Now, the virus analysis machine examines the infected program for the extracted signature and produces a prescription for identifying and removing that virus.
4. The prescription produced by the virus analysis machine is then sent back to the administrative machine from where the infected program came.
5. The administrative machine sends the prescription to the infected client machine as well as to other client machines in the organization.
6. The prescription is also forwarded to all the subscribers and the individual user who are outside the organization network, so that they too can protect their systems from the new virus.

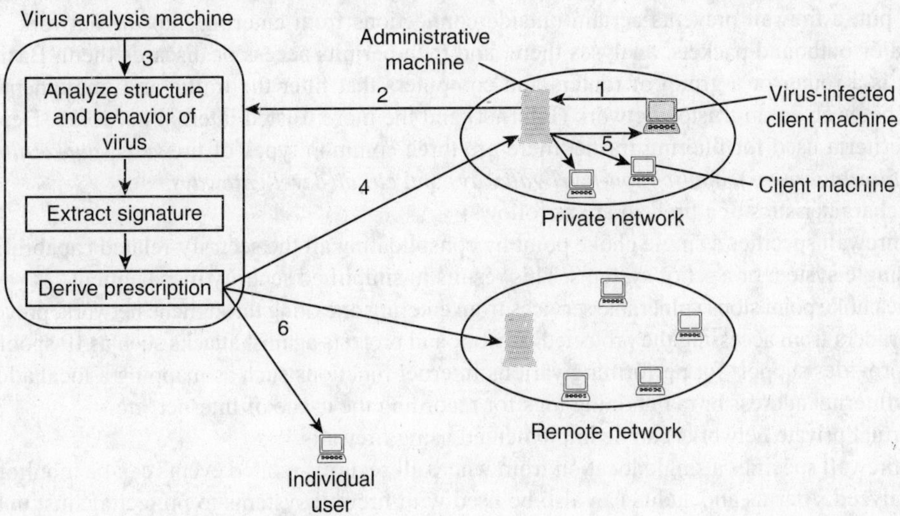

Figure 10.2 Operation of Digital Immune System

17. Discuss on behaviour-blocking software?

Ans.: *Behaviour-blocking software* is an approach to countering viruses that, unlike other approaches, is integrated with the operating system of a host computer. To detect a program for viral infections, it monitors the behaviour of a program in real time to determine any malicious actions. In case any attempt for a malicious action is detected, the behaviour-blocking software blocks the malicious action before it can affect the system. Certain malicious actions for which a program is analyzed are as follows:

- Attempts for viewing, opening, deleting and modifying files
- Attempts for formatting disk drives
- Starting network communications
- Changes in important system settings
- Changes in the logic of executable files.

Behaviour-blocking software can block the malicious behaviours of a program in real time and/or terminate the entire program if it detects that the program may cause threat as it executes. The advantage of this software over other antivirus approaches is that it is able to detect and then block the malicious actions even if the instructions of a malicious code are modified or rearranged in order to evade detection. However, the disadvantage is that the as behaviours of a malicious code can be identified only after actually executing it on the machine, the malicious code may cause severe destruction to the system before its behaviours have been detected and blocked by the behaviour-blocking software.

18. What do you mean by firewall? Describe its characteristics.

Ans.: The progressive use of the Internet in organizations has opened up possibilities for the outside world to interact with internal networks, creating a great threat to the organization. Usually, organizations have huge amount of confidential data, leaking of which may prove to be a serious setback. Moreover, it is also necessary to protect the internal network against malicious programs such as virus and worms. Therefore, some mechanism is needed to ensure that the valuable data within the organization remains inside, as well as that outside attackers cannot break the security of the internal network.

A *firewall* is a mechanism that protects and isolates the internal network from the outside world. Simply put, a firewall prevents certain outside connections from entering into the network. It traps inbound or outbound packets, analyses them, and then permits access or discards them. Basically, a firewall is a router or a group of routers and computers that filter the traffic and implement access control between an un-trusted network (Internet) and the more trusted internal networks. Depending on the criteria used for filtering traffic, there are three common types of firewalls: *packet filters* (or *packet-filtering router*), *application-level gateways* and *circuit-level gateways*.

The characteristics of a firewall are as follows:

- A firewall specifies a single choke point by consolidating all the security-related capabilities into a single system or a set of systems. This results in simplified security management.
- The choke point stops vulnerable services from entering or exiting through the network, prevents the intruders from accessing the protected network and protects against attacks such as IP spoofing.
- It provides support for performing various Internet functions such as mapping a local address to an Internet address or maintaining logs for recording the usage of Internet, etc.
- Virtual private networks can be implemented using firewalls.
- A firewall specifies a single location from where all security-related events can be monitored and analyzed. Alarms and audits can also be used with firewall systems to protect against unauthorized events.

19. List some limitations of firewalls.

Ans.: Though the firewall is an effective means of providing security to an organization, it has certain limitaions, which are as follows:

- A firewall provides effective security to the internal network if it is configured as the only entry-exit point in the organization. However, if there are multiple entry-exit points in the organization and firewall is implemented at just one of them, then the incoming or outgoing traffic may bypass the firewall. This makes the internal network susceptible to attack through the points where the firewall has not been implemented.
- A firewall is designed to protect against outside attacks. However, it does not have any mechanism to protect against internal threats such as an employee of a company who unknowingly helps an external attacker.
- The firewall does not provide protection against any virus-infected program or files being transferred through the internal network. This is because it is almost impossible to scan all the files entering in the network for viruses. To protect the internal network against virus threats, a separate virus detection and removal strategy should be used.

20. Discuss the packet-filtering router firewall.

Ans.: A *packet-filtering router*, also known as *screening router* or *screening filter*, is the one of the oldest firewall technologies that operates at the network layer. It examines the incoming and outgoing packets by applying a fixed set of rules on them and, thus, determines whether to forward the packets or to reject them. The rules used for filtering the packets are defined based on the following information contained in a network (IP) packet.

- The IP address of the system from where the packet has come
- The IP address of the system for which the packet is destined
- The transport layer protocol used such as TCP or UDP
- Transport-level address (that is, port number) of source and destination, which identifies the application such as Telnet or SNMP
- The interface of the router where the packet came from or is destined to.

The filtering rules specify which packets are allowed to pass through and in which direction they should flow, that is, from external to internal network or vice versa. Each rule has a specified action associated with it, either to allow or to deny a packet. Thus, there are two sets of filtering rules: *allow*, which permits the traffic, and *deny*, which discards the traffic. While examining a packet, if a match is found with any of the *allow* set of rules, then the packet is forwarded to the desired destination. On the other hand, if a match is found with any of the *deny* set of rules, the packet is discarded. In case no match is found, the default action is taken. The default policy can be either to *forward* or *discard* the packet. The former default policy provides more ease of use to the end users; however, it offers a reduced level of security. In contrast, the latter default policy is more conservative; however, it provides more security. Therefore, generally, the implementation of a firewall is initiated with default *discard* policy and, later, packet filtering is enforced by applying the rules one by one.

Advantages

Some advantages of packet filters are as follows:

- They are simple, since a single rule is enough to indicate whether to allow or deny the packet.
- They are transparent to the users; the users need not know the existence of packet filters.

- They operate at a fast speed as compared to other techniques.
- The client computers need not be configured specially while implementing packet-filtering firewalls.
- They protect the IP addresses of internal hosts from the outside network.

Disadvantages

Some disadvantages of packet filters are as follows:

- They are unable to inspect the application layer data in the packets and thus, cannot restrict access to ftp services.
- It is a difficult task to set up the packet-filtering rules correctly.
- They lack support for authentication and have no alert mechanisms.
- Being stateless in nature, they are not well suited to application layer protocols.

21. What kind of attacks is possible on packet-filtering firewalls. Suggest appropriate countermeasures.

Ans.: Though packet-filtering firewalls operate at a fast speed and do not require users to be aware of packet filters, they are still prone to some attacks, which are as follows:

- *IP address spoofing:* In this attack, an intruder external to the organization's network sends a packet towards the network. The IP address of this packet is the same as that of one of the hosts in the network. The attacker thinks that he or she can penetrate into the internal network by spoofing IP address and, therefore, can attack on the systems easily. To prevent such attacks, packet-filtering firewalls should discard all the packets coming to the organization's network, which contains the IP address of any internal host.
- *Source routing attack:* In this attack, an intruder specifies the pre-defined route that a packet should take to reach its destination by selecting a particular option in the IP packet header. By choosing such an option, the intruder hopes that the packet-filtering firewall will bypass the security measures of checking the source routing information. The countermeasure for this attack is that packet-filtering firewalls should discard all the packets that are using this option.
- *Tiny fragment attack:* In this attack, an intruder takes advantage of the IP packet fragmentation option and intentionally divides the original IP packet into small fragments. This is done to force the TCP header information to go into a separate packet fragment. The intruder hopes that the filtering rules that are based on the TCP header information can be circumvented this way, and that the packet-filtering firewall can be fooled such that it will examine only the first fragment of the packet and the rest will bypass through it without any checks. This attack can be prevented by discarding all the fragmented packets that are using TCP as the upper-layer protocol type.

22. Write a short note on application-level gateways.

Ans.: An application-level gateway operates at the application layer of the OSI model. It is also termed as a *proxy server* (or simply called *proxy*), which handles the flow of application-level traffic. The operation of application-level gateways is as follows:

1. A user contacts the application gateway with the help of a TCP/IP application such as Telnet, FTP or HTTP.
2. In response, the application gateway asks the user for the name, IP address and other information about the remote host that is to be accessed. It also asks the user to present its user ID and password to access the gateway.

3. The user supplies a valid user ID, password and other desired information to the gateway.
4. After verifying the user, the application gateway contacts the application running on the remote host on behalf of the user. The TCP segments comprising the application data are exchanged between the two end points.
5. Now, the application gateway serves as a proxy of the original user and delivers application data in both directions, from remote host to the user and vice versa.

Advantages

Application-level gateways are considered the most secure type of firewalls since they provide a number of advantages, which are as follows:

- The entire communication between the internal and external network happens only through the application gateways. This protects the internal IP addresses from the external network.
- The use of application gateways provides transparency between the users and the external network.
- They understand and implement high-level protocols such as HTTP and FTP.
- They support functions such as user authentication, caching, auditing and logging.
- They can process and manipulate the packet data.
- Strong user authentication can be enforced with application gateways.
- They can disallow access to certain network services and allow others at the same time.

Disadvantages

Some disadvantages of application-level gateways are as follows:

- Each new network service requires a number of proxy services to be added. Thus, application-level gateways are not scalable.
- The addition of proxy services causes client applications to be modified.
- Application gateways operate at a slower speed and, as a result, network performance degrades.
- As they rely on the support provided by the underlying operating system, they are vulnerable to the bugs in the system.

23. When the system administrator trusts the internal users, what type of firewall is to be used? What are its advantages and disadvantages?

Ans.: For a situation where the system administrator trusts the internal users, circuit-level gateways are the best suited. Circuit-level firewalls operate in a similar manner as that of packet-filtering firewalls, except that they operate at the session and transport layers of the OSI model. Whenever a session is to be established between a host in the internal network and a host outside the internal network, two TCP connections are to be established, one between the TCP user in the internal network and the circuit-level gateway, and another between the circuit-level gateway and the TCP user in the external network. After both the connections have been established, the circuit-level gateway forwards the packet from one connection to another without inspecting their contents. This is because, in circuit-level gateways, the session is validated before opening the connections. Thus, there is no need to examine the packet contents once the session has been established.

Circuit-level gateways maintain a virtual table to store session-related information of all the valid connections. This information includes the session date, a unique session identifier, connection state, IP addresses of source and destination, the sequencing information and the physical network interface through which the packet has come and has to go. Rather than allowing all packets that meet the rule set requirements to pass, it allows only those packets that are part of a valid, established connection.

Advantages

Some advantages of circuit-level gateways are as follows:

- They operate at a faster speed as compared to application-level gateways.
- They offer more security than packet filters.
- They are not subject to IP address spoofing attacks.
- They perform network address translation (NAT) by changing source node IP address to its own and, thus, protecting internal host IP addresses from the external network.

Disadvantages

Some disadvantages of circuit-level gateways are as follows:

- They are unable to perform security checks on higher-level protocols.
- They can restrict access only to TCP protocol subsets.
- They have only a confined audit event generation capability.

24. What is the role of bastion host?

Ans.: A *bastion host* is a system in an organization's internal network that acts as a vital point in the security of the network. This system is distinguished from other systems by the firewall administrator and serves as a platform for an application-level or circuit-level gateway. The hardware platform of the bastion host executes a secured version of the operating system and, therefore, behaves like a trusted system. Moreover, only limited proxy applications that are considered necessary by the network administrator, such as Telnet, DNS and SMTP, are installed on the bastion host. It requires additional authentication if any user wants access to these proxy services, and each proxy service needs its own authentication. Thus, the role of bastion host is to enhance the security of the network, so that it becomes more difficult for intruders to gain access to the internal network.

25. Describe the common types of firewall configurations.

Ans.: Firewalls may be implemented as a single system, such as a single packet filter or a single application gateway, or it may be implemented as a combination of packet filters and application gateways. There are three possible firewall configurations, which are as follows:

- *Screened host firewall, single-homed bastion:* In this firewall configuration, a packet filter and an application gateway (bastion host) are used in combination. The packet filter checks the traffic from the Internet to the internal corporate network and from the internal corporate network to the Internet, based on the specific rule. It allows packets from outside the network to enter the internal network if it is destined for the application gateway. Similarly, it allows packets from the internal network to move to the outside network only if the packet has originated from the application gateway. The application gateway is responsible for performing authentication and proxy functions.

  This firewall configuration enhances the security of the network by implementing both packet-level and application-level filtering. The intruder now has to penetrate two separate firewalls in order to breach the security of the network. Moreover, it allows the network administrator more freedom in defining security policy. However, the demerit of this configuration is that internal hosts are connected to the packet filter as well as the application gateway. Therefore, if the security of the packet filter router is compromised, then an intruder can gain access to the whole internal network.

- *Screened host firewall, dual-homed bastion:* In this firewall configuration, the internal hosts of the network are not directly connected to the packet filter. Rather, the packet filter is directly connected only to the application gateway, which has separate connections with the internal hosts. This arrangement overcomes the problem of a screened host, single-homed bastion configuration. Thus, even if the packet filter is successfully attacked by an intruder, he or she gains access only to the application gateway and not to the whole network.
- *Screened subnet firewall:* In this firewall configuration, two packet filters and one application gateway are used. One of the packet filters connects the outside network with the application gateway and other packet filter connects the internal hosts with the application gateway. It is the most secured type of configuration as an intruder has to attack three levels before gaining an access to the internal network.

26. What do you understand by a trusted system?

Ans.: A computer and operating system that can be relied upon to a determined level to implement a given security policy is referred to as a *trusted system*. In other words, a trusted system is defined as the one system whose failure may cause a specified security policy to be compromised. Trusted systems are of prime importance in areas where it is required to protect the system resources or the information on the basis of levels of security defined; that is, where multilevel security is needed. For example, in military, the information is classified into various levels such as unclassified (U), confidential (C), secret (S) and top secret (TS), and each user is allowed to access only certain levels of information. In addition to military, the trusted systems are also being prominently used nowadays in banking and financial areas.

Central to the trusted systems is the *reference monitor*, which is an entity residing in the operating system of a computer and entrusted the responsibility of making all the access-control-related decisions on the basis of the defined security levels. The reference monitor is expected to be tamperproof, always invoked and subject to independent testing.

Multiple-choice Questions

1. Which of the following is a type of intruder?
   (a) Masquerader (b) Misfeasor
   (c) Clandestine user (d) All of these
2. The __________ strategy aware all the users about the importance of non-guessable or strong passwords.
   (a) User education (b) Reactive password checking
   (c) Proactive password checker (d) None of these
3. A virus is a computer __________.
   (a) File (b) Network
   (c) Program (d) Database
4. A __________ replicates itself by creating its own copies, in order to bring the network to a halt.
   (a) Worm (b) Virus
   (c) Trojan horse (d) Logic bomb

5. The __________ generation of antivirus software uses heuristic scanners.
   (a) First (b) Second
   (c) Third (d) Fourth
6. The digital immune system was developed by __________.
   (a) HCL (b) IEEE
   (c) ANSI (d) IBM
7. The firewall should be situated __________.
   (a) Outside a network (b) Inside a network
   (c) Between a network and the outside world (d) None of these
8. __________ firewall is mostly used in small businesses.
   (a) Packet-filtering (b) Circuit-level gateway
   (c) Application-level gateway (d) None of these
9. Circuit-level gateways are __________ as compared to packet filters.
   (a) Less secure (b) More secure
   (c) Slower (d) None of these
10. The trap set to attract the potential intruders is known as __________.
   (a) Honeypot (b) Trapdoor
   (c) Proxy (d) All of these

Answers

1. (d)	2. (a)	3. (c)	4. (a)	5. (b)	6. (d)
7. (c)	8. (a)	9. (b)	10. (a)		

Index

V

W

X